Student's Book

Pathway to Science 5

Glue your picture here.

Name

Richmond

What happens to food after I eat it?

One way to answer this question is to learn how to use:

Scientific Research Skills

These skills will help you explain events that happen in our surroundings.

The development of these skills does not require you to follow one method step by step. Instead, they can be adapted to each question you wish to answer.

Let's learn about scientific skills! These skills will be applied in the experiments in your book. Soon you will be able to answer your own questions about the mysteries of the world around you.

We will show you a new and fun way to learn about science!

Richmond
t Aldates
rd
1ST
ed Kingdom

way to Science Student's Book Level 5

: Edition: 2014
eteenth Reprint: March 2022
N: 978-607-06-0908-4

way to Science 5 is a collaborative work, created and designed by
Department of Educational Research of Santillana.
ichmond Publishing, S.A. de C.V. 2014
Río Mixcoac No. 274, Col. Acacias,
ito Juárez, C.P. 03240, Ciudad de México

lisher: Justine Piekarowicz
tor: Dominic Wright
and Design Coordinator: Marisela Pérez
-Press Coordinator: Daniel Santillán

strations: Juan Esteban del Pino Briceño, Sergio Quijada Valdés,
andro Rojas Contreras

tographs: César Vargas Ulloa
EPOSITORIO: Grupo Santillana; ©THINKSTOCK: Hemera p. 120
ett Mulcahy); iStock pp. 62 (Jacek Chabraszewski), 74 (Elena
panova), 75 (Blaj Gabriel), 77 (Natalia Klenova), 89 (Jeff_Hu), (Elena
weitzer); PhotoObjects.net p. 61 (PhotoObjects.net); p. 177 (Fuse)
Ⓘ 2005 Volker Brinkmann p. 11, *Salmonella typhimurium*
Ⓘ 2009 Louise Docker p. 13, *Xylocopa aeratus*
Ⓘ 2011 Oxfam East Africa p. 74, Collecting water
Ⓘ ⓞ 2011 Deuterostome p. 13, *Euglena viridis*
2005 Rocky Mountain Laboratories/NIAID/NIH p. 13, *Escherichia coli*
2012 NASA/NOAA/GSFC/Suomi NPP/VIIRS/Norman Kuring p. 126, Earth
ver Design: Erika Martínez
ver Photograph: iStock, Octopus eye

rst published by Santillana del Pacífico S.A. de Ediciones

nted in Brazil by Forma Certa Gráfica Digital
te: 808137
digo: 292709084 / 2025

Introduction

Welcome to **Pathway to Science.** Follow this pathway to a very special place. This is an educational space for you to develop the skills necessary for your personal and social growth.

- It welcomes everyone to explore. You will find information, texts, pictures and activities presented in a simple and friendly manner. You will discover that learning here is fun!
- This is a place where we can all learn to share and live together through activities that help us reflect on our values and learn to respect others.
- It is open to people from all over the world, a place where you can continue to learn more and interactively with the help of the latest technology.
- It is filled with adventures and challenges where you will find different experiences to help you understand the world around you, take care of yourself and respect the environment.

We will be walking with you every step of the way!
All you need is curiosity and the desire to learn.

How is your textbook organized?

Pathway to Science 5 is organized into four units. In each unit, you will find:

Initial Pages

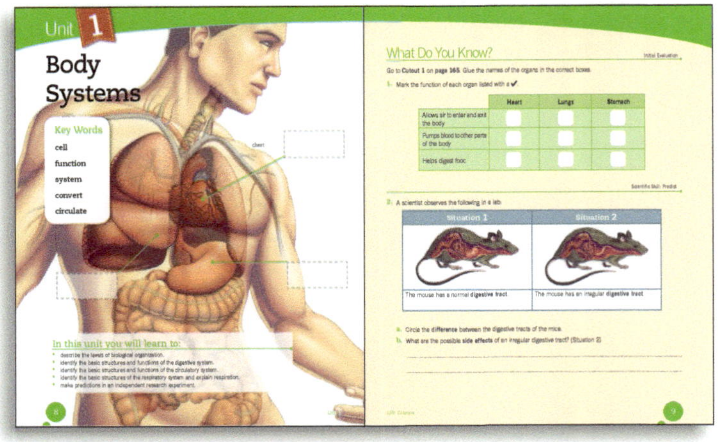

- Number and title of the unit
- Learning objectives
- Initial evaluation

Organized into Sections

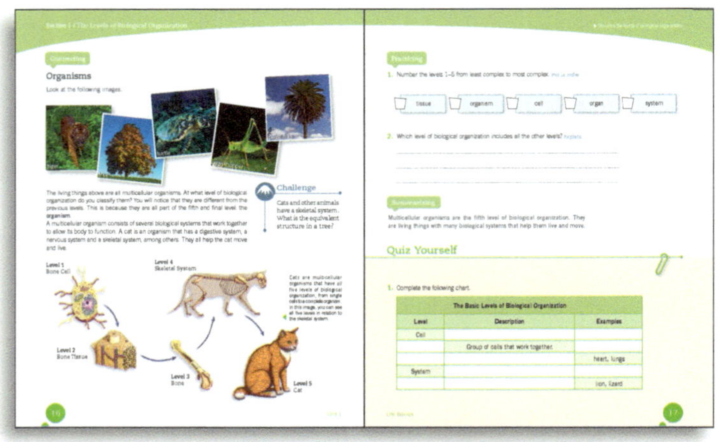

- Connecting
  Observe, read and answer
- Exploring
- Practicing
- Summarizing
- Quiz Yourself

Fun Features

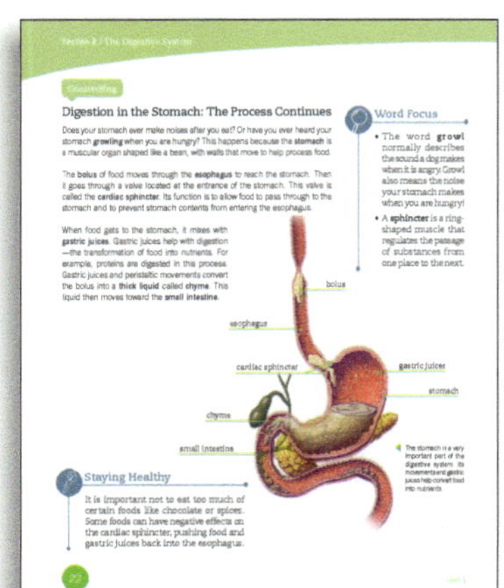

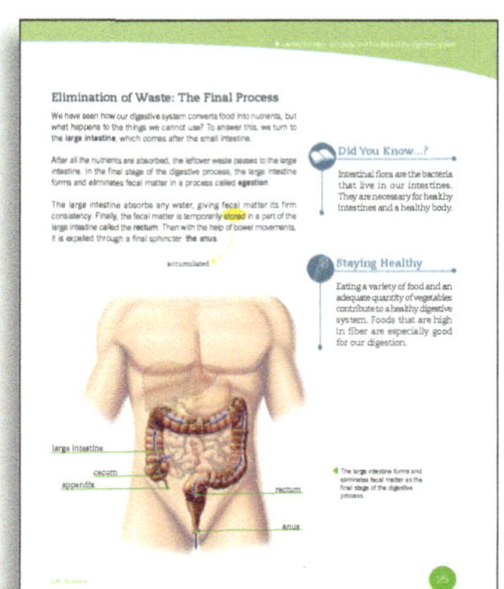

- Education through Values
- Staying Healthy
- Did You Know...?
- Remember!
- Tip
- Word Focus
- Fun Fact!
- Challenge

Evaluation Pages

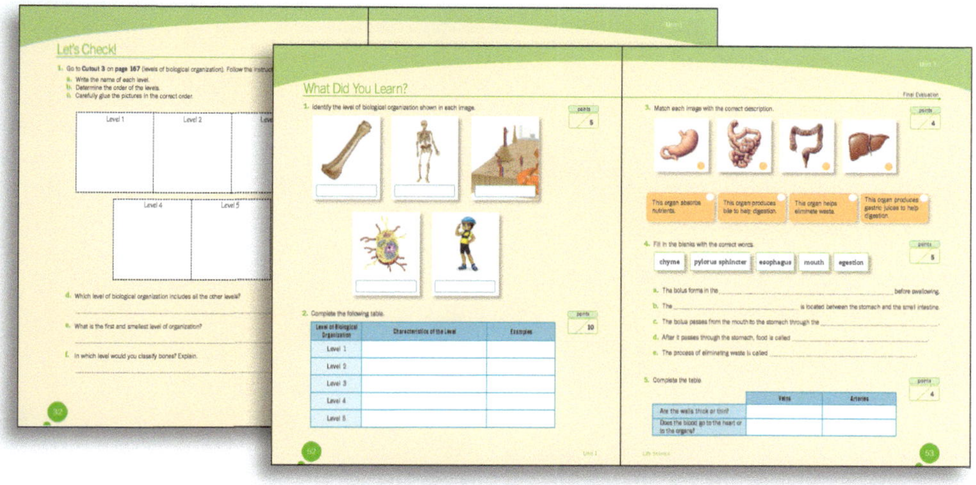

- What Do You Know?
  Initial Evaluation
- Let's Check!
  Intermediate Evaluation
- What Did You Learn?
  Final Evaluation

Special Pages

- Science Lab
- Test Study Pages
  Summary and Review

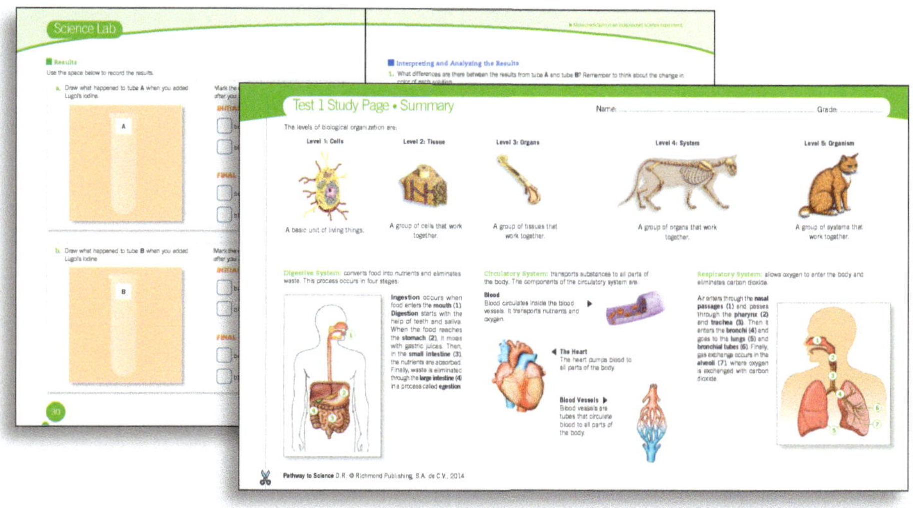

Support Pages

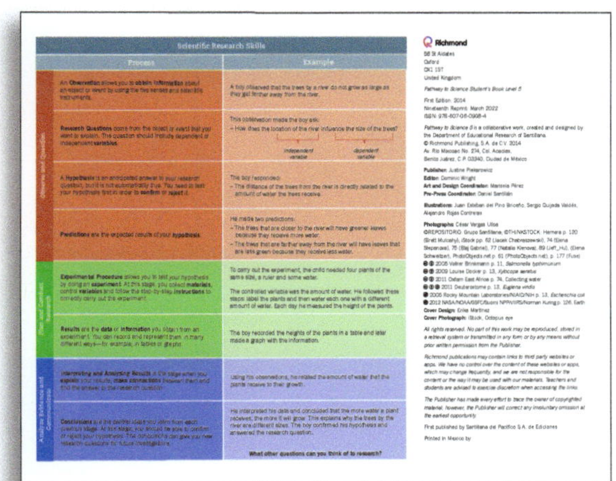

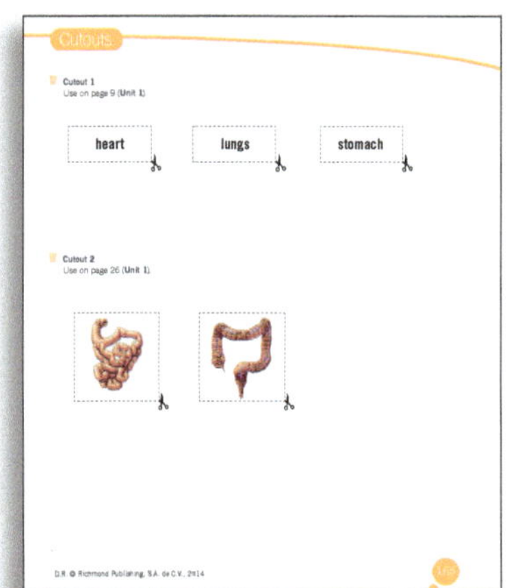

- Scientific Research Skills Foldout
- Cutouts
- Activity Cards

Table of Contents

Unit 1

Body Systems

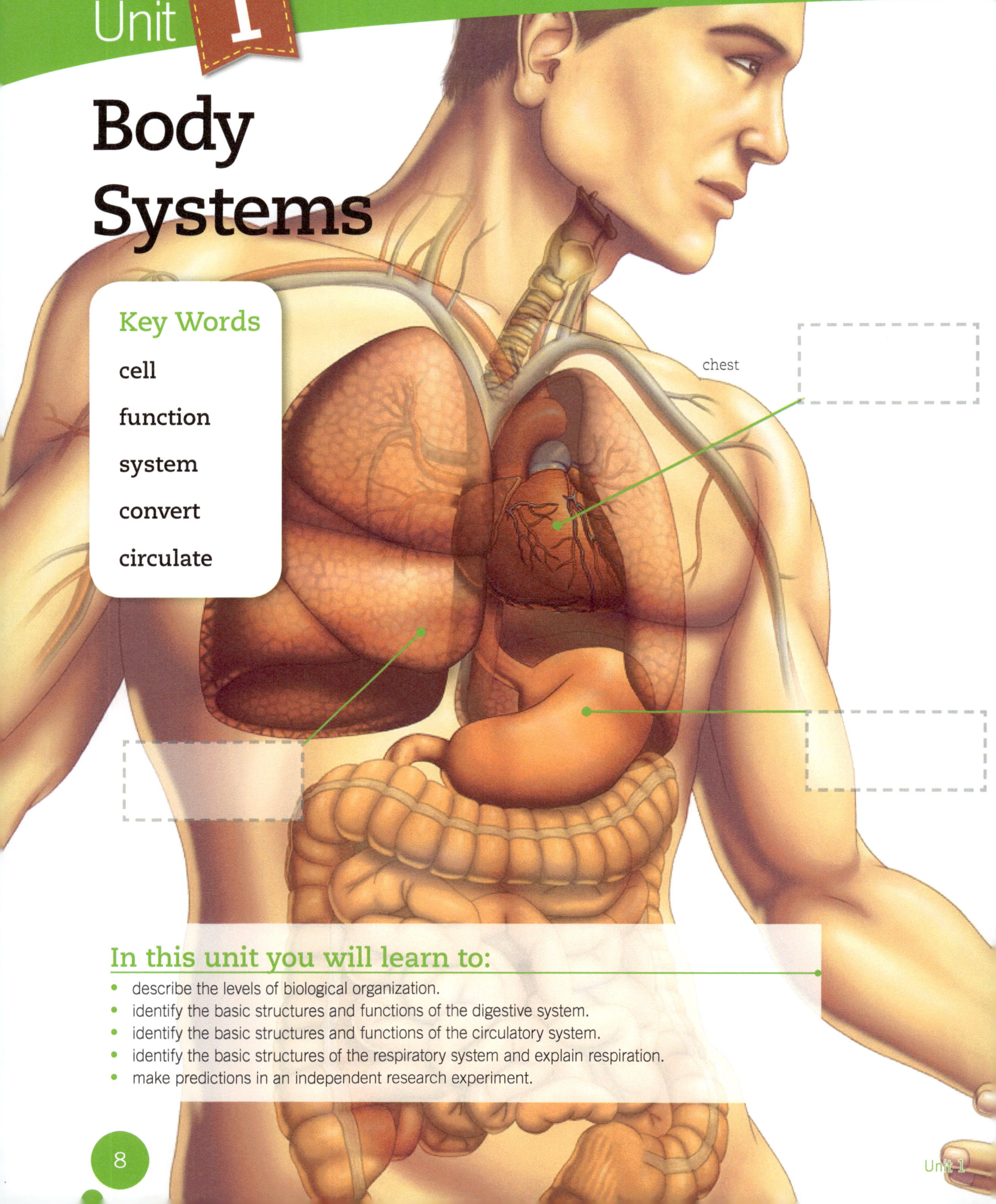

Key Words

cell

function

system

convert

circulate

In this unit you will learn to:

- describe the levels of biological organization.
- identify the basic structures and functions of the digestive system.
- identify the basic structures and functions of the circulatory system.
- identify the basic structures of the respiratory system and explain respiration.
- make predictions in an independent research experiment.

What Do You Know?

Initial Evaluation

Go to **Cutout 1** on **page 165**. Glue the names of the organs in the correct boxes.

1. Mark the function of each organ listed with a ✔.

	Heart	Lungs	Stomach
Allow air to enter and exit the body			
Pumps blood to other parts of the body			
Helps digest food			

Scientific Skill: Predict

2. A scientist observes the following in a lab:

Situation 1	Situation 2

The mouse has a normal **digestive tract**.	The mouse has an irregular **digestive tract**.

a. Circle the **difference** between the digestive tracts of the mice.

b. What are the possible **side effects** of an irregular digestive tract? (Situation 2)

____

____

Section 1

The Levels of Biological Organization

Connecting

The Discovery of Cells

Think about the smallest object visible to the naked eye. Thanks to the microscope, we can now see objects that we could not see before. Robert Hooke, an English scientist, invented the **microscope** in the 17th century. He used his invention to look closely at thin slices of cork.

cork → spongy bark of a tree

Based on his observations, Hooke drew the pieces of cork he saw. He showed they consisted of smaller parts that he named **cells**. After many years, it was proven that cells are present in all living things.

proven → demonstrated

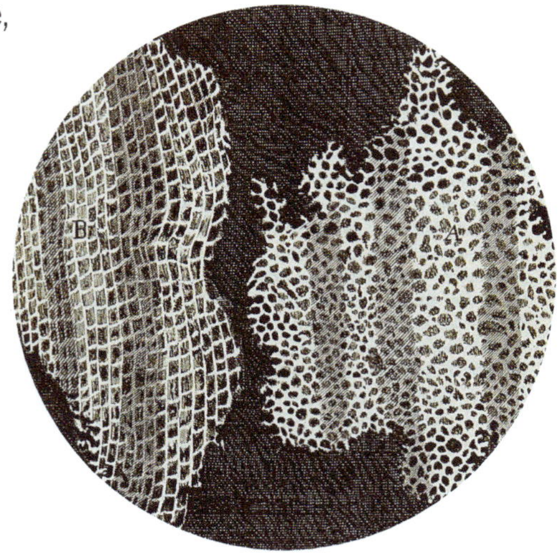

Drawing of Hooke's observations.

Classifying Living Things

Look at the images and identify similarities between the two organisms.

Do they have anything in common? It does not look like it, but they are actually very similar. Even if we cannot see it, organized cells form both organisms. Cells group together and create more complex parts. For example, cells form the bones and muscles of animals, and the leaves and stems of plants.

We can see that living things are created in a specific way: from small to big and from simple to complex. In other words, living things have levels of **organization** that go from the cell to the entire organism.

Did You Know...?

The levels of biological organization are studied by different areas:

- **chemistry:** atoms to macromolecules.
- **biology:** cells to organisms.
- **ecology:** organisms and the environment.

The Cell

Every living thing on the planet is different, and there is a great variety of plants and animals. However, they all have one thing in common: they consist of cells. **The cell is the first and smallest level of biological organization**. Although it is a small structure, it is complex. The existence of life depends on the components of the cell working together. In the following image, you can see a cell from the nervous system.

Did You Know...?

It is estimated that a human has 75,000,000,000,000 (75 trillion) cells.

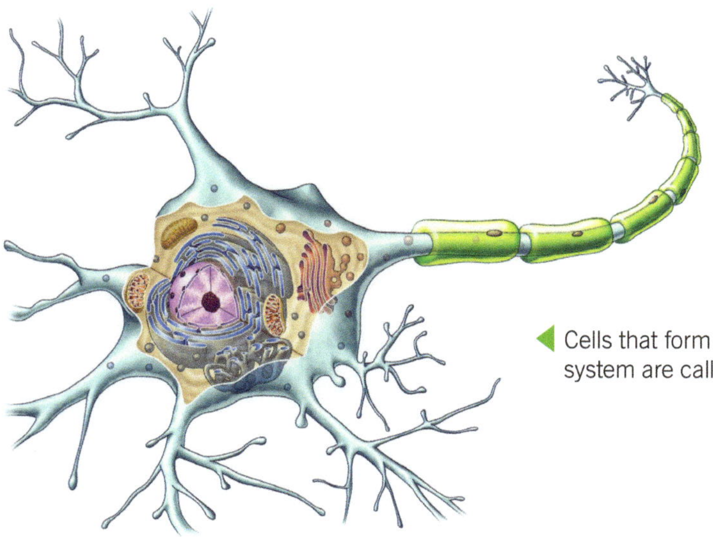

Cells that form part of the nervous system are called neurons.

Single-celled Organisms

Living things come in different shapes and sizes and have a different number of cells. Some organisms consist of many cells (**multicellular**) and are easily visible. Others consist of one cell (**unicellular**). Without a microscope, most unicellular organisms are invisible. We call them microorganisms. In microorganisms, life processes like feeding, growth and reproduction all occur in one cell.

feeding: the act of eating food

Challenge

Microscope and microorganism both start with **micro**. What do you think **micro** means?

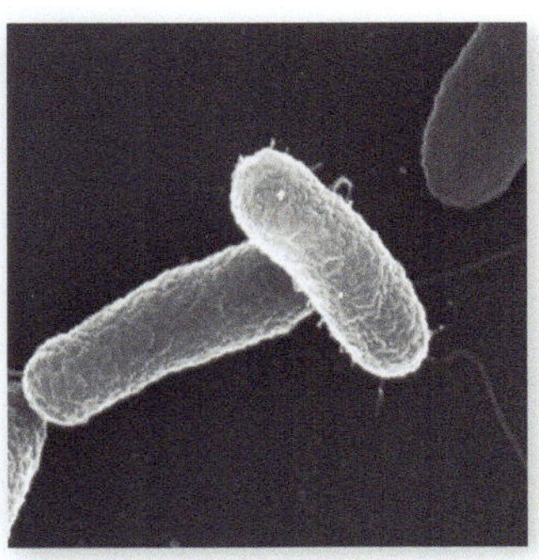

bacteria

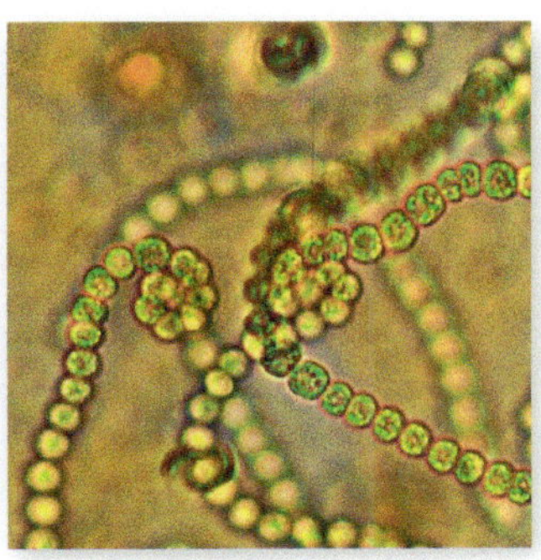

bacteria

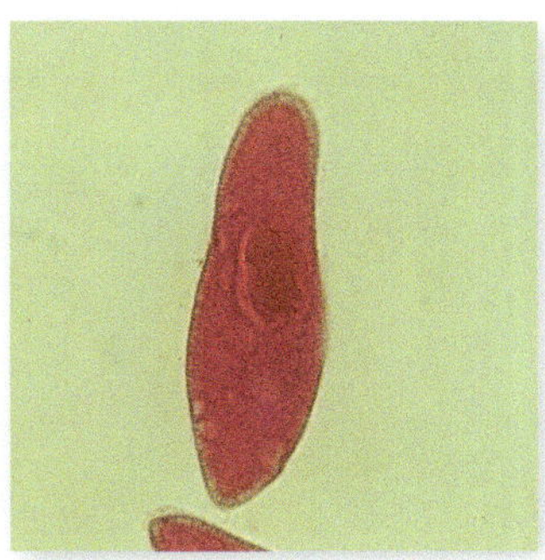

protozoa

Here you can see some unicellular organisms. They are part of the first level of the biological system.

The Organization of Multicellular Organisms

The cell is the first level of biological organization. Unicellular organisms consist of just one cell and never grow more than that. Think about your body. How many cells do you think you have? **Multicellular** beings, like humans, have millions of cells that unite and organize to form tissues, organs and systems. These join to form a whole organism. Below you can see the different levels of biological organization.

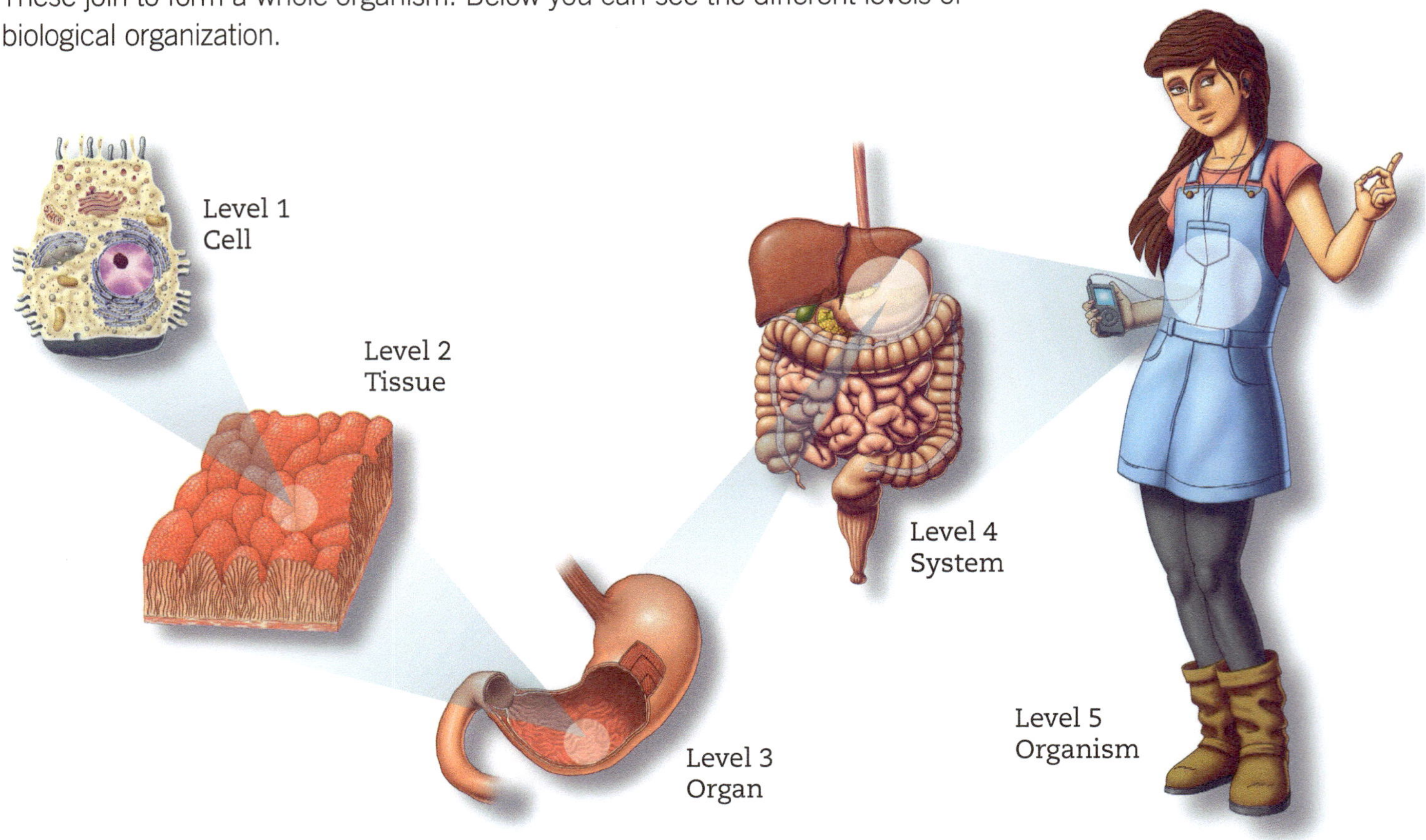

Tissue

continue to exist

Your body has millions of cells, but they cannot survive alone, so they form **tissue**. Tissue is the **second level of biological organization**. It consists of a group of cells that are similar in shape and size. They communicate to **complete a certain function**. Each type of cell forms different tissue and has unique functions.

In the image, you can see an example of human tissue. Muscle tissue, consisting of muscle cells, contracts and relaxes to move different parts of the body.

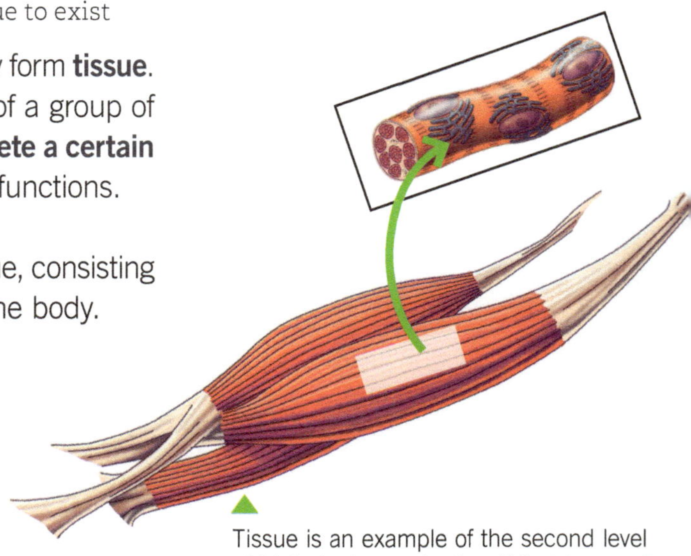

Tissue is an example of the second level of biological organization. What types of organisms have tissue?

Challenge

Human beings are organized from small, simple cells to complex systems. Is it possible to find organs in unicellular beings?

Practicing

1. Write a **U** in the boxes next to unicellular organisms and an **M** next to the multicellular ones. Identify

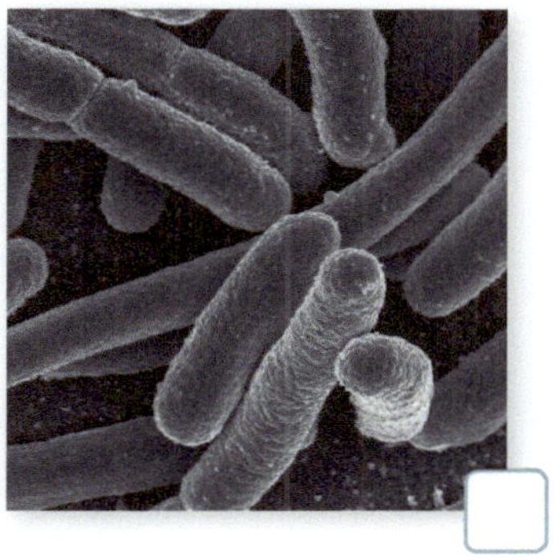

2. Jonathan looks at this sample in his laboratory and confirms that it is tissue.

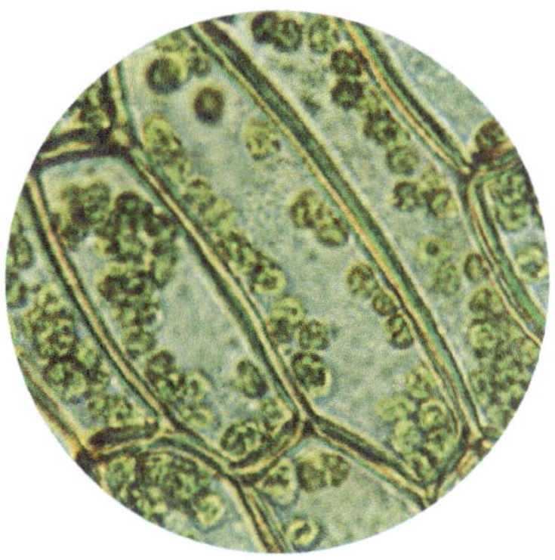

a. Why does Jonathan classify this as tissue? Explain

____

____

Summarizing

In nature, some living things consist of one cell (unicellular organisms), and others consist of many cells (multicellular organisms).
Multicellular organisms possess millions of cells. Cells come together to form increasingly complex structures: tissues, organs, systems and finally organisms.
Tissue is the second level of biological organization and consists of groups of cells that have the same function. Examples are muscle tissue and nerve tissue.

Connecting

Organs

organs that clean the blood

Have you ever heard of the lungs, kidneys or the heart? These are all examples of **organs**: **the third level of biological organization**. An organ consists of various groups of tissues working together to complete the same function. For example, in plants, leaves are the organs responsible for photosynthesis. Leaves consist of two types of tissues: the epidermis and the mesophyll.

Word Focus

Photosynthesis is the process by which plants produce food using carbon dioxide, water and sunlight.

Groups of tissues work together to perform the same function. They form organs, like this leaf.

execute

everything around you

Animal organs are more complex than plant organs. For example, think of our eyes. They allow us to see light and our surroundings. To perform this function, the eye has many types of tissues and structures that work together to allow us to see. The following image shows the structure of the eye. Pay attention to the different tissues.

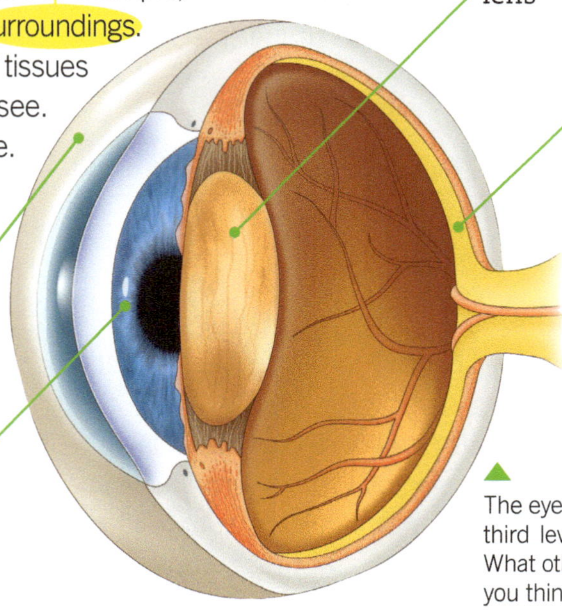

The eye is an organ. It represents the third level of biological organization. What other examples of this level can you think of?

Systems

The fourth level of biological organization is a **system**. A system is a group of organs that work together to perform the same function.

For example, the nervous system consists of two principal organs: the brain and the spinal cord. The two organs work together to control other organs and to adjust to the environment.

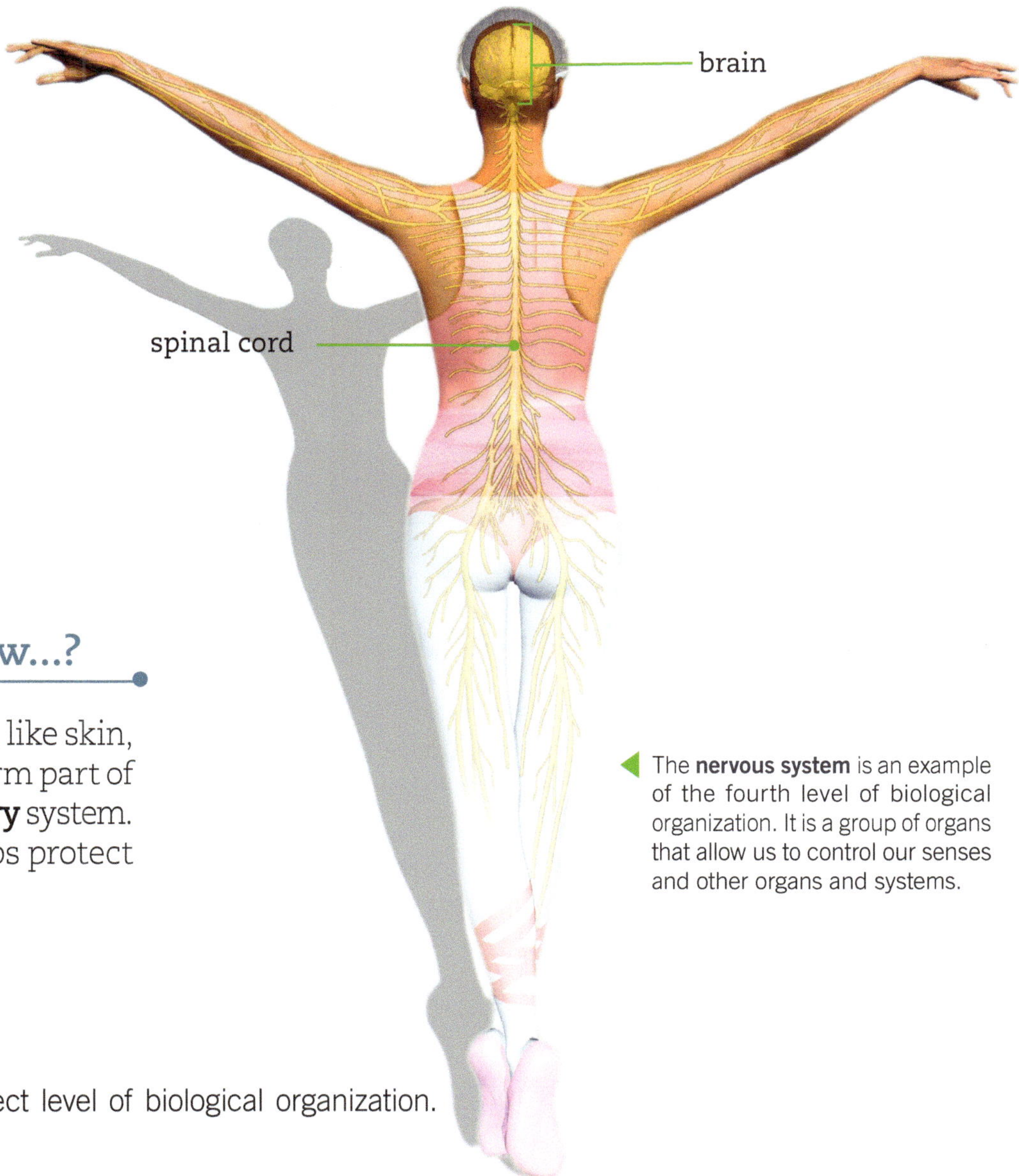

The **nervous system** is an example of the fourth level of biological organization. It is a group of organs that allow us to control our senses and other organs and systems.

Did You Know...?

Some structures, like skin, hair and nails, form part of the **integumentary** system. This system helps protect our bodies.

Practicing

1. Complete the table with the correct level of biological organization.
Compare and Contrast

Structure	Neuron	Muscle	Brain	Nervous System	Leaves
Level					

Summarizing

Organs are the third level of biological organization. They are groups of tissues that work together.
Systems are the fourth level of biological organization. They are groups of organs that work together.

Connecting

Organisms

Look at the following images.

The living things above are all multicellular organisms. At what level of biological organization do you classify them? You will notice that they are different from the previous levels. This is because they are all part of the fifth and final level: the **organism**.

A multicellular organism consists of several biological systems that work together to allow its body to function. A cat is an organism that has a digestive system, a nervous system and a skeletal system, among others. They all help the cat move and live.

Challenge

Cats and other animals have a skeletal system. What is the equivalent structure in a tree?

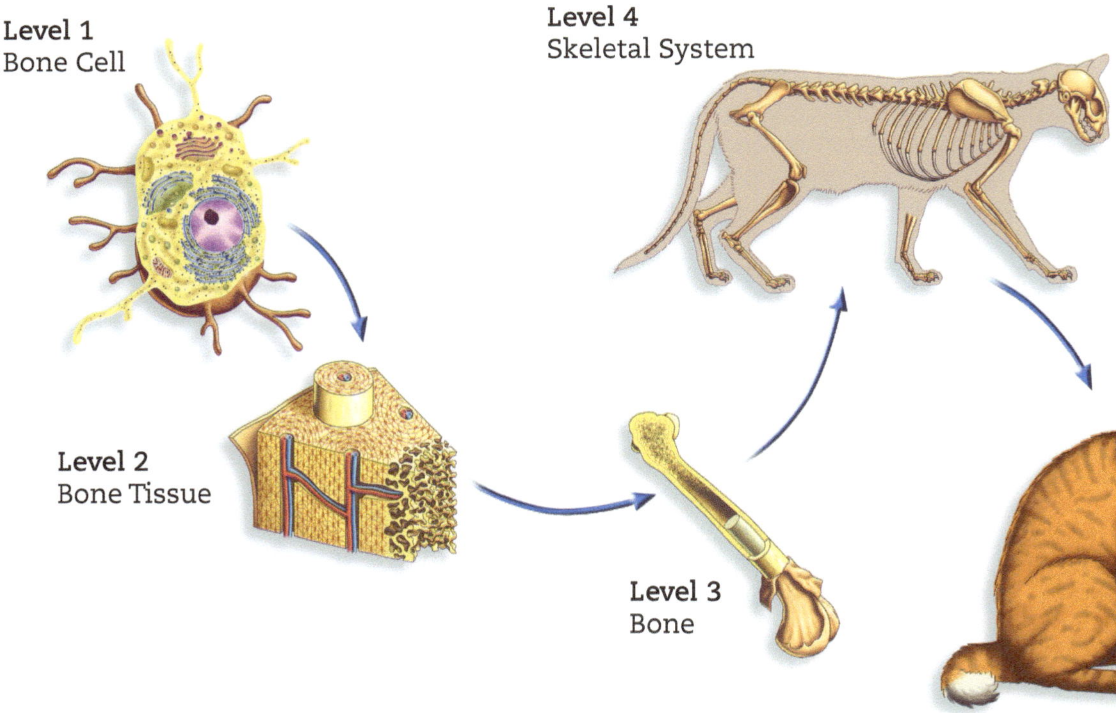

Cats are multicellular organisms that have all five levels of biological organization, from single cells to a complete organism. In this image, you can see all five levels in relation to the skeletal system.

Practicing

1. Number the levels 1–5 from least complex to most complex. Put in order

☐ tissue ☐ organism ☐ cell ☐ organ ☐ system

2. Which level of biological organization includes all the other levels? Explain

____

____

____

Summarizing

Multicellular organisms are the fifth level of biological organization. They are living things with many biological systems that help them live and move.

Quiz Yourself

1. Complete the following chart.

The Basic Levels of Biological Organization		
Level	**Description**	**Examples**
Cell		
	Group of cells that work together.	
		heart, lungs
System		
		lion, lizard

Section 2

The Digestive System

Connecting

The Organs of the Digestive System

Have you ever wondered what happens to food after you swallow it? Where does it go? How is it used? The answers to these questions are related to one of the systems in our bodies: the **digestive system**. This system consists of a group of organs that **convert** food into **nutrients** and eliminate what we do not need.

swallow: pass from the mouth to the stomach

The digestive organs surround the digestive tract, which starts at the **mouth** and ends at the **anus**. This system also includes a group of **digestive glands**. The glands secrete various substances that convert food into **nutrients**. Nutrients give our bodies the energy we need to live.

secrete: produce and emit

Look at the following image of the digestive system. Pay attention to all the organs.

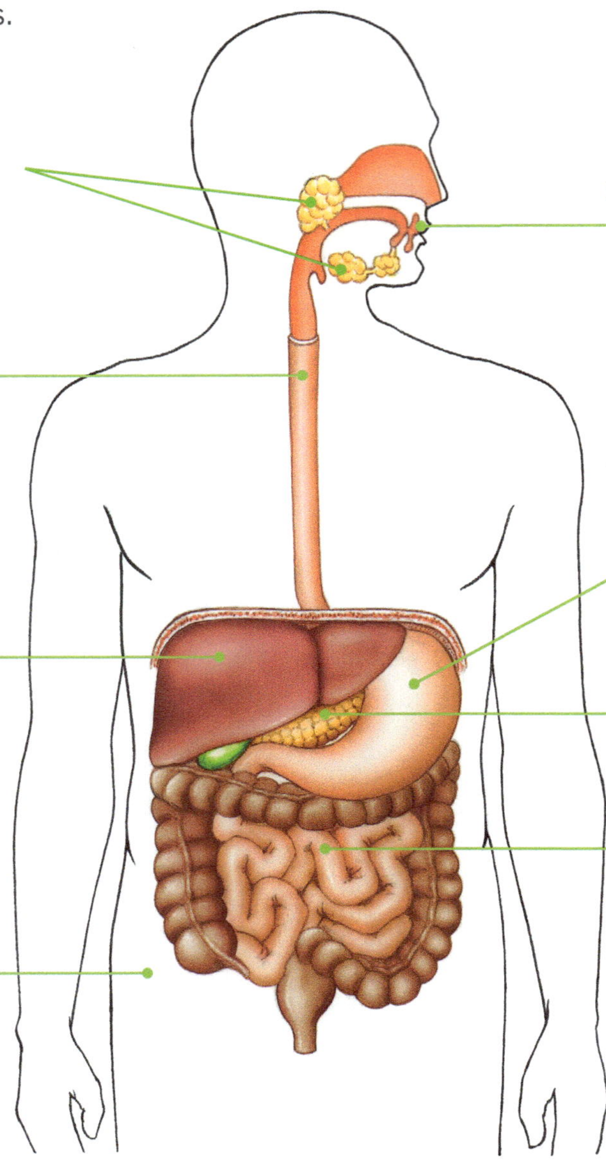

The digestive system consists of the **digestive tract** and **digestive glands**. Its purpose is to convert food into nutrients, which give us energy.

The Digestive Process

Our digestive system converts food into simpler substances called **nutrients**, which enter our cells and give us the energy we need to live. This process, called the **digestive process**, consists of four stages, which occur in the following order:

- **ingestion:** when food enters the mouth
- **digestion:** the transformation of food in the digestive tract
- **absorption:** when nutrients enter the blood
- **egestion:** the elimination of waste through the anus

Did You Know...?

Nutrients are components of food that give energy to an organism. They also help regulate and repair the body. Nutrients are classified as: **carbohydrates**, found in foods like bread; **proteins**, found in foods like eggs; **lipids and fat**, found in oils; and **vitamins and minerals**, found in fruits and vegetables.

Practicing

1. Label each organ of the digestive system. Identify

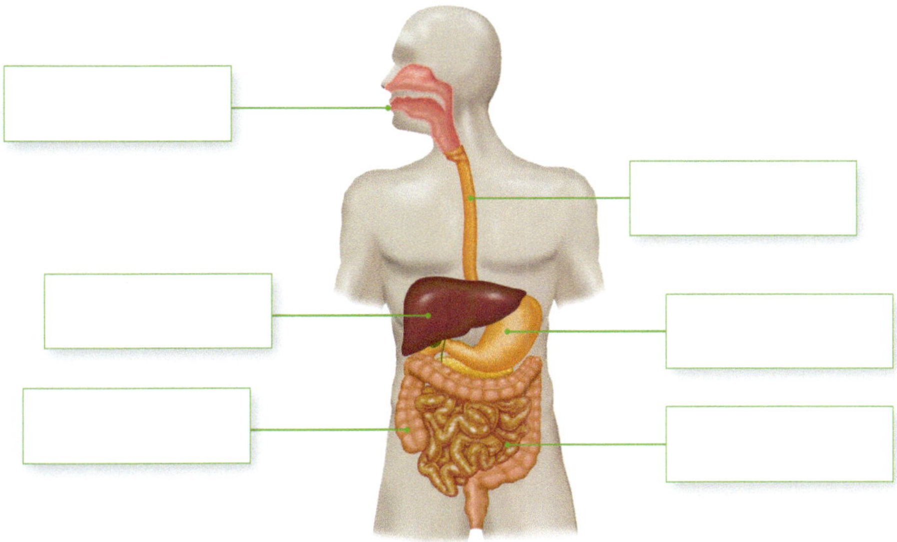

2. Put the stages of the digestion process in order. Sequence

egestion – digestion – ingestion – absorption

☐ → ☐ → ☐ → ☐

Summarizing

The digestive system allows the body to absorb nutrients and eliminate waste. The stages of the digestive process are: ingestion, digestion, absorption and egestion.

Connecting

The Beginning of the Digestive Process

As you already know, the digestive process consists of four stages: ingestion, digestion, absorption and egestion.

Ingestion is the first stage, and it begins the moment you start to eat.

Put a piece of bread in your mouth, but do not chew. Wait one minute, and then chew and **swallow** it. Did you notice any change in the food? This is because **digestion** begins in the mouth. **Teeth** are used to chew food and break it down into smaller pieces. Salivary glands in the mouth produce saliva. The tongue moves and mixes the food with the saliva. All these processes make a **bolus**, a ball of food ready to be swallowed and to continue down the digestive tract.

chew: bite repeatedly with the teeth

Remember!

Each animal's teeth are adapted to the type of food it eats. A carnivore has long, sharp teeth to rip meat, while herbivores have large, flat teeth to chew plants.

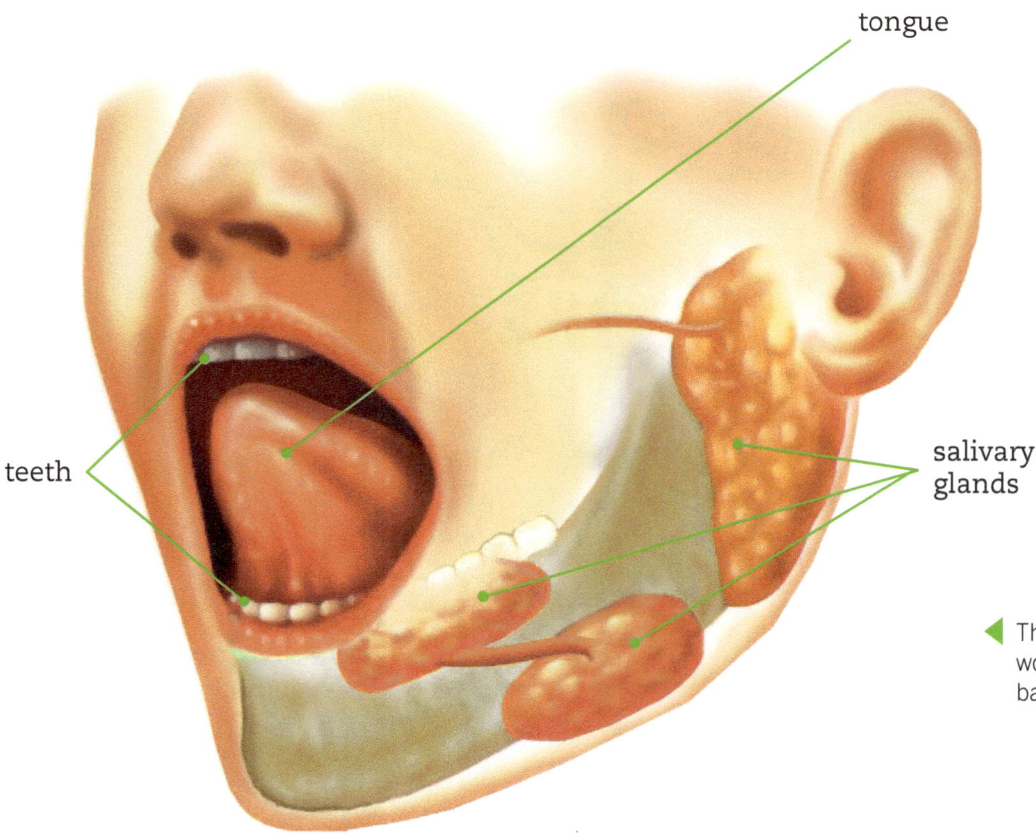

The mouth, teeth, tongue and saliva all work together to convert food. Why can't babies eat solid food?

Swallowing

Take a sip of water. Did you notice what happens in the back of your mouth? The process of moving liquid from the mouth to the stomach is called **swallowing**. Swallowing consists of two stages. The first stage is voluntary and occurs when we push food to the back of the mouth. The second stage is involuntary and occurs when the food enters the digestive tract and moves down the esophagus to the stomach.

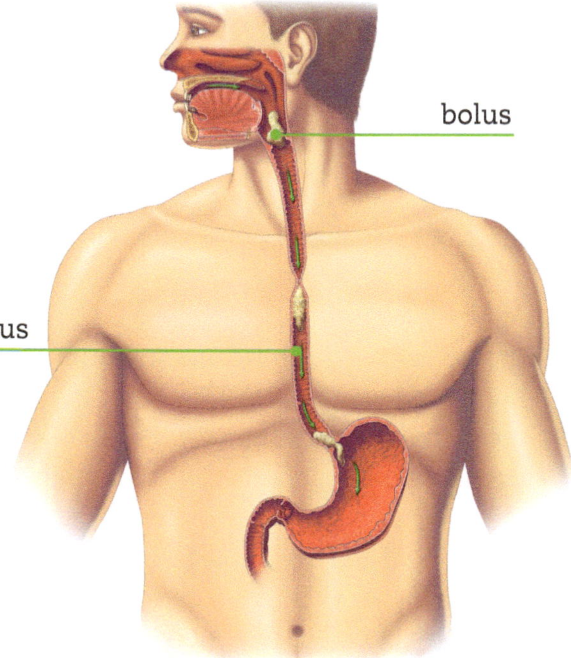

Swallowing is a mechanism that allows food to enter our bodies. After the food is swallowed, peristaltic movements help push the food through the digestive tract.

Peristaltic Movements

We have talked about food moving through the digestive tract. How does this happen? The esophagus expands and contracts to push the bolus down to the stomach. These movements are called **peristaltic movements**.

contracts: becomes smaller

Practicing

1. Put a small ball inside a tube that has the same **diameter** as the ball. Use your fingers to squeeze the tube and push the ball to the other side. If the ball represents the bolus, what does the tube represent? What movement are you demonstrating with your hands? Explain. Interpret

____

____

____

____

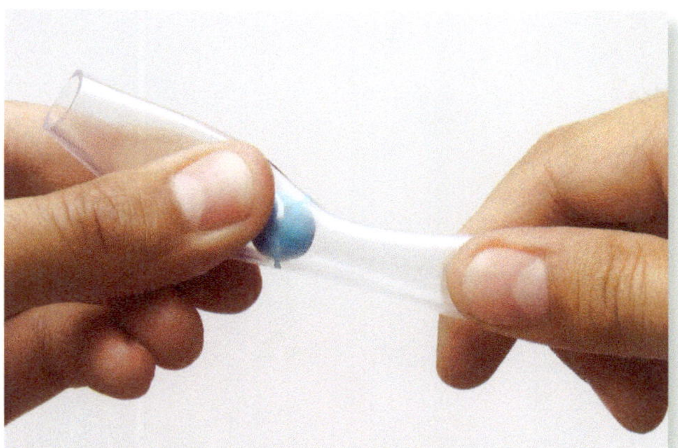

Summarizing

Ingestion is the first step of the digestive process. Digestion begins in the mouth when food is converted into a bolus and pushed down the esophagus. Peristaltic movements move the food through the different organs of the digestive system.

Word Focus

Diameter is the length of a straight line passing through the center of something from one side to the other. In this case, it is the thickness of the tube.

straight: without curves

Connecting

Digestion in the Stomach: The Process Continues

Does your stomach ever make noises after you eat? Or have you ever heard your stomach **growling** when you are hungry? This happens because the **stomach** is a muscular organ shaped like a bean, with walls that move to help process food.

The **bolus** of food moves through the **esophagus** to reach the stomach. Then it goes through a valve located at the entrance of the stomach. This valve is called the **cardiac sphincter**. Its function is to allow food to pass through to the stomach and to prevent stomach contents from entering the esophagus.

When food gets to the stomach, it mixes with **gastric juices**. Gastric juices help with digestion —the transformation of food into nutrients. For example, proteins are digested in this process. Gastric juices and peristaltic movements convert the bolus into a **thick liquid** called **chyme**. This liquid then moves toward the **small intestine**.

Word Focus

- The word **growl** normally describes the sound a dog makes when it is angry. Growl also means the noise your stomach makes when you are hungry!
- A **sphincter** is a ring-shaped muscle that regulates the passage of substances from one place to the next.

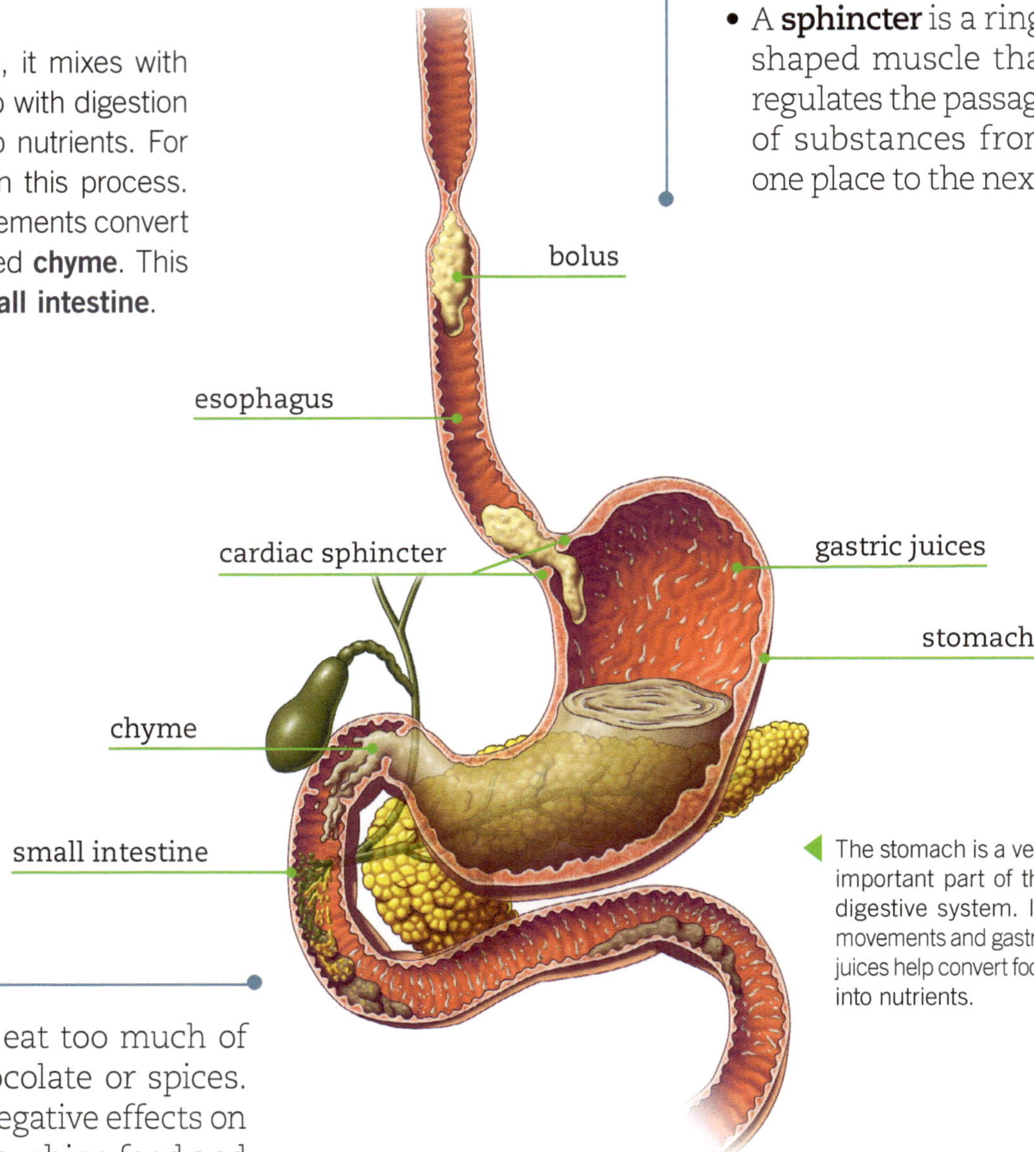

The stomach is a very important part of the digestive system. Its movements and gastric juices help convert food into nutrients.

Staying Healthy

It is important not to eat too much of certain foods like chocolate or spices. Some foods can have negative effects on the cardiac sphincter, pushing food and gastric juices back into the esophagus.

The End of the Digestive Process

We have already seen that, with the help of the stomach, the bolus is converted into a thick liquid called chyme. The digestive process continues as this liquid leaves the stomach through a valve called the **pylorus sphincter** and enters the **small intestine**.

The most important part of digestion happens in the small intestine with the help of different fluids. They are: **bile**, produced by the liver; **pancreatic juice**, produced by the pancreas; and **intestinal juice**, produced by the small intestine. Through the action of these juices, the chyme becomes a **thinner liquid** called **chyle**. This is the last transformation of nutrients before the third stage of the digestive process: **absorption**.

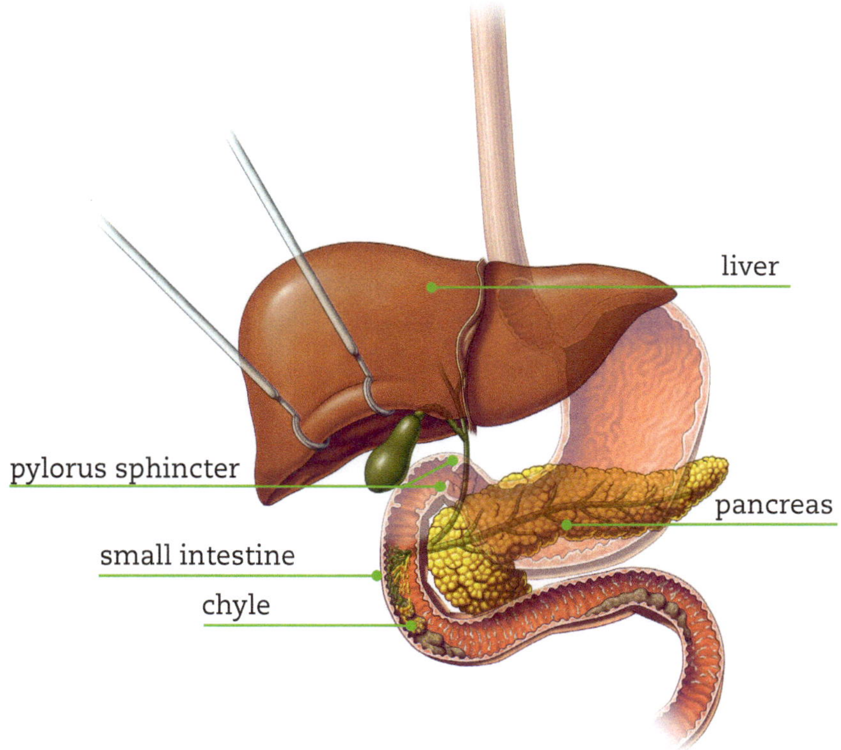

Practicing

1. Complete the diagram by writing how food changes in each stage. Identify

mouth → [ ] stomach → [ ] small intestine → [ ]

2. Explain the functions of the stomach and the small intestine during digestion. Explain

____

____

Tip

In these terms, "ph" is pronounced as "f", and "ch" is pronounced as "k."

Summarizing

The stomach has walls made of muscle to move and digest the food. It also produces gastric juices that help make chyme.

The small intestine produces intestinal juices, which combine with bile (from the liver) and pancreatic juice (from the pancreas) to help make chyle.

Connecting

Absorption

After the chyle is formed, it continues through the small intestine and the next stage of the digestive process starts: **absorption**. During this process, most of the nutrients and water go through the **small intestinal wall**. Small hairs called villi allow the nutrients to reach the blood, which carries them to all the cells of the organism.

The **intestinal villi** on the walls of the intestine increase the efficiency of absorption. In fact, if we could extend all the villi of a human being, they would cover an area of 300 square meters, about the area of a tennis court. The following image shows the structures involved in absorption.

associated with

Did You Know...?

A human's small intestine can be seven meters long, the same as the width of a professional soccer goal.

Tip

Villi is pronounced "vil-lie." The singular form is villus.

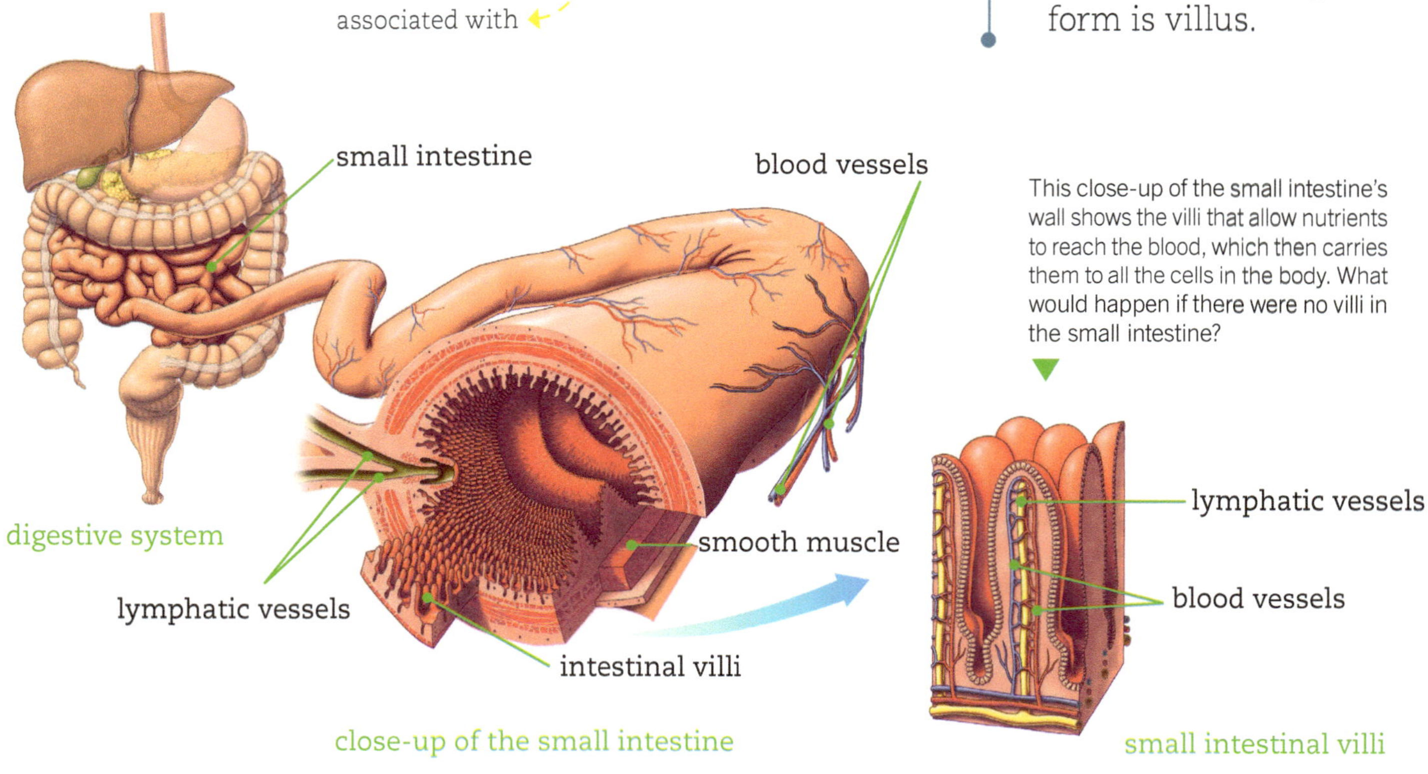

This close-up of the small intestine's wall shows the villi that allow nutrients to reach the blood, which then carries them to all the cells in the body. What would happen if there were no villi in the small intestine?

The villi are very important in the absorption process. For example, every day our small intestine receives six liters of chyle, which is reduced to one liter after absorption. Do you know what happens to the rest? It passes through the bloodstream to reach all the cells, providing the organism with basic materials and energy.

Elimination of Waste: The Final Process

We have seen how our digestive system converts food into nutrients, but what happens to the things we cannot use? To answer this, we turn to the **large intestine**, which comes after the small intestine.

After all the nutrients are absorbed, the leftover waste passes to the large intestine. In the final stage of the digestive process, the large intestine forms and eliminates fecal matter in a process called **egestion**.

The large intestine absorbs any water, giving fecal matter its firm consistency. Finally, the fecal matter is temporarily stored in a part of the large intestine called the **rectum**. Then with the help of bowel movements, it is expelled through a final sphincter: **the anus**.

accumulated

Did You Know...?

Intestinal flora is the bacteria that live in our intestines. They are necessary for healthy intestines and a healthy body.

Staying Healthy

Eating a variety of food and an adequate quantity of vegetables contribute to a healthy digestive system. Foods that are high in fiber are especially good for our digestion.

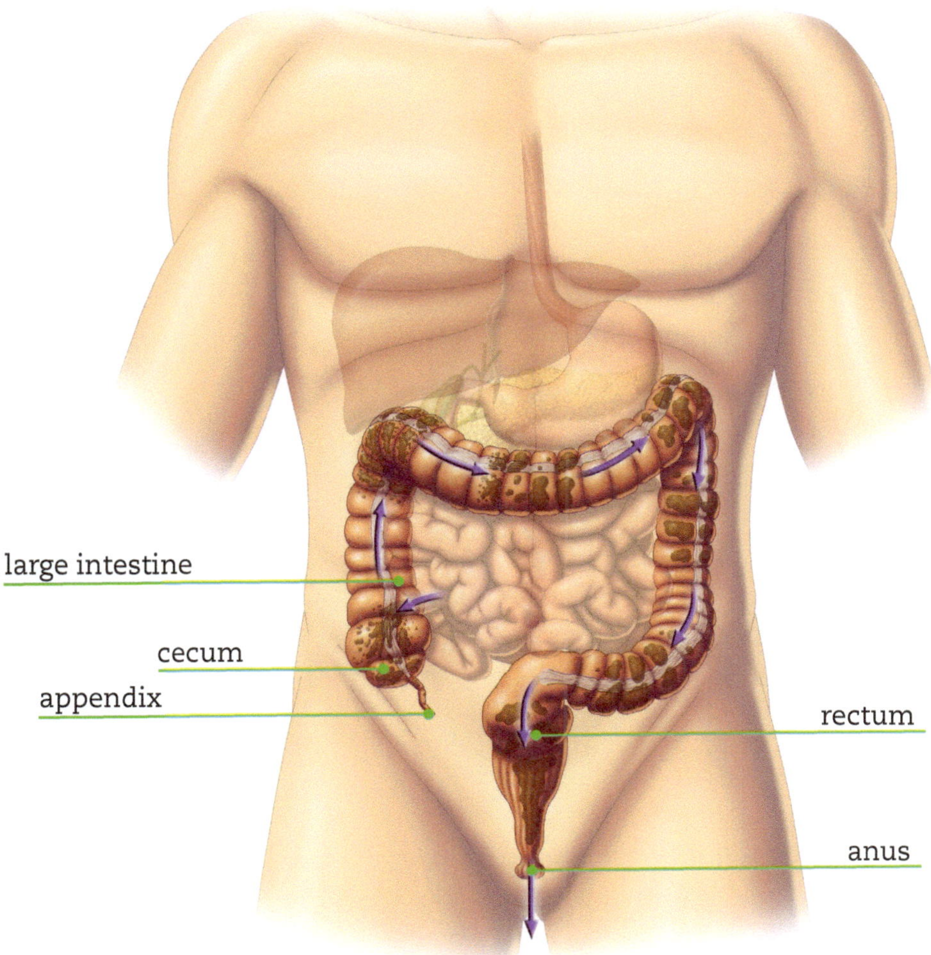

The large intestine forms and eliminates fecal matter as the final stage of the digestive process.

Practicing

1. A study measured the amount of food circulating in different areas of the digestive tract from **ingestion** to **egestion**. Look at the table and answer the following questions.

Digestive Tract Content of an Animal				
Part of the Tract	Mouth	Stomach	Small Intestine	Large Intestine
Amount of Food (grams)	490	490	80	70

a. What happened to the amount of food as it circulated through the digestive system? Interpret

____

b. According to the table, where does the most absorption occur? Interpret

____

2. Go to **Cutout 2** on **page 165**. Glue each organ according to its function. Identify

Helps with the absorption of nutrients.		Absorbs water and eliminates fecal matter.	

Summarizing

Absorption is when nutrients pass from the digestive tract to the bloodstream. Absorption occurs through the villi in the small intestine. The large intestine absorbs water and forms fecal matter.

Quiz Yourself

1. Look at the diagram and do the activities.

a. Match each part of the digestive system with the correct word. Then describe its function.

b. On the diagram, draw arrows to show the path of food through the digestive system.

Mouth: ______________________

Esophagus: ______________________

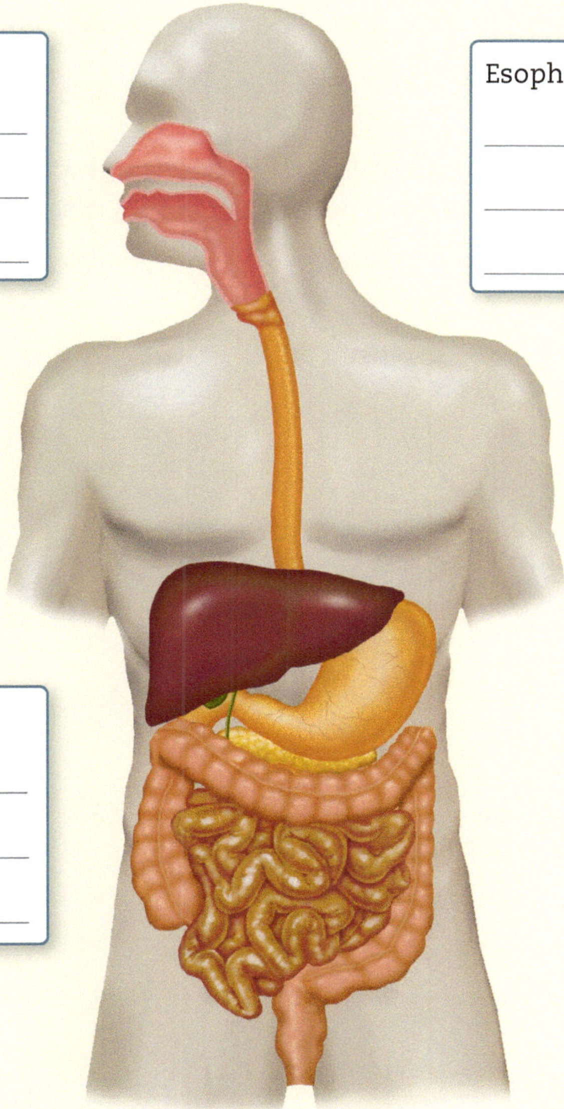

Stomach: ______________________

Large Intestine: ______________________

Small Intestine: ______________________

2. What would happen if food passed directly from the stomach to the large intestine?

____

____

Scientific Skill: Predict

The Function of Saliva

Basic Framework

The digestive system converts food into more simple substances called nutrients. These nutrients give us the energy we need to live. To be able to convert food into **energy**, the digestive system consists of several organs, each with a specific function. The digestive process starts in the mouth, with the help of teeth and saliva. Saliva is a secretion containing amylase, which breaks down food starches. Starch is a nutrient found in potatoes, corn and dough.

secretion: liquid produced by an organ

Observation

A group of students conducted an experiment in a laboratory. They observed two samples: one of potato and saliva and another of potato and water. One changed color when **povidone** or Lugol's iodine (antiseptic solutions) was added. Why do you think the colors are different?

antiseptic: destroying bacteria

Research Question

What is the effect of saliva on food?

Hypothesis

Mark the correct hypothesis for the research question.

☐ Amylase breaks down food starch into simpler substances.

☐ Amylase does not have any effect on food starch.

Predictions

Based on the situation described in the observation stage, answer:

a. What will the saliva do to the potato?

____

How do you formulate predictions?

- Based on a situation, answer the questions.
- To answer, use your hypothesis and any previous knowledge you might have.

The questions guide you in formulating a prediction. Your prediction helps you answer the questions.

Experimental Procedure

1. In groups of four students, collect the following supplies:
   - 1 grated potato (reduced to small strips)
   - Lugol's iodine (or povidone)
   - water
   - 2 syringes (without the needles)
   - 2 test tubes
   - 1 marker
   - 1 teaspoon
   - 1 dropper
2. Gather (collect) some saliva in your mouth and extract it with a syringe.
   Be careful: The syringe should not have a needle.
3. Mark the test tubes **A** and **B** with the marker.
4. Follow the steps for each tube as indicated in the diagram:

Evidence of amylase's activity appears because Lugol's iodine, a special coloring, recognizes food starches. If the food has starches, the color will change from brown to blue.

Use one of the syringes to extract saliva and the other to add water to the test tubes.

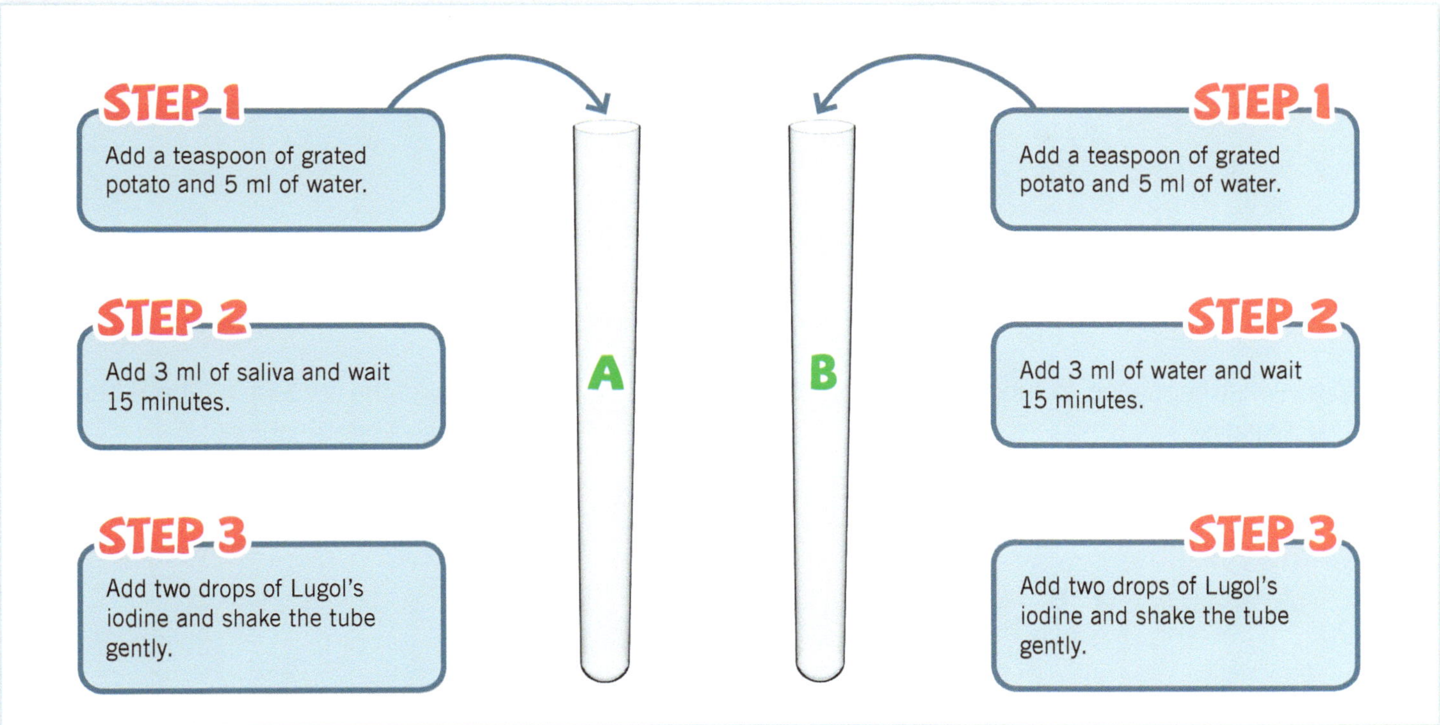

5. Observe the initial color of each tube and mark it in the **Results** section.
6. Wait 15 minutes and observe any changes in color.
7. In this experiment, why did you add three more milliliters of water to tube **B**?

____

____

Results

Use the space below to record the results.

a. Draw what happened to tube **A** when you added Lugol's iodine.

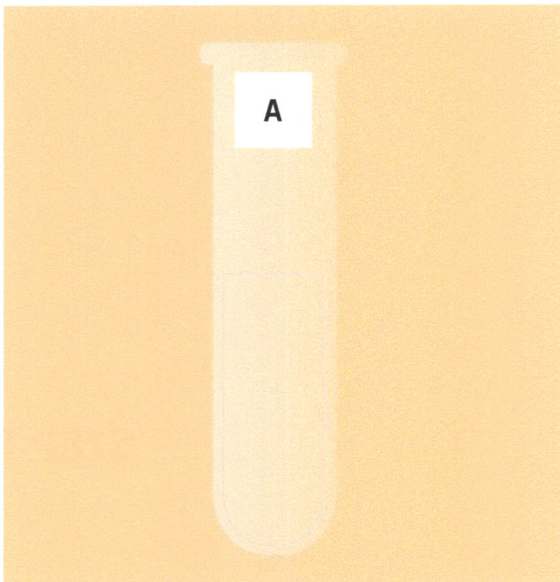

Mark the color of the content in tube **A** before and after you added Lugol's iodine.

INITIAL COLOR

☐ brown

☐ blue

FINAL COLOR

☐ brown

☐ blue

b. Draw what happened to tube **B** when you added Lugol's iodine

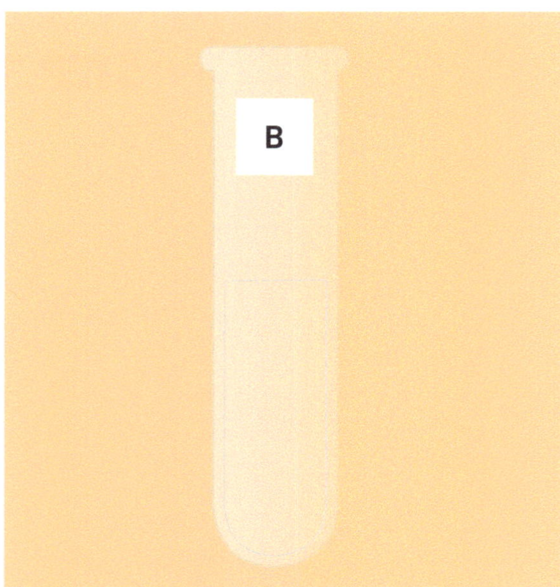

Mark the color of the content in tube **B** before and after you added Lugol's iodine.

INITIAL COLOR

☐ brown

☐ blue

FINAL COLOR

☐ brown

☐ blue

Interpreting and Analyzing the Results

1. What differences are there between the results from tube **A** and tube **B**? Remember to think about the change in color of each solution.

____

____

2. What do you think caused the difference in color between tube **A** and tube **B** after adding Lugol's iodine?

In tube A: ____

In tube B: ____

3. Which observation proves that saliva breaks down starch?

____

____

Conclusions

1. Did the experiment prove the hypothesis? Explain.

____

____

2. What function does amylase serve in the digestion of food like potatoes?

____

3. Why is it important to break down the starch in foods? Look at the **Basic Framework** to help you answer.

____

____

4. What other foods can you use in this experiment? Explain. Use the **Basic Framework** to help you answer.

____

____

Let's Check!

1. Go to **Cutout 3** on **page 167** (levels of biological organization). Follow the instructions.

points
/ 8

a. Write the name of each level.
b. Determine the order of the levels.
c. Carefully glue the pictures in the correct order.

Level 1	Level 2	Level 3

Level 4	Level 5

d. Which level of biological organization includes all the other levels?

____

e. What is the first and smallest level of organization?

____

f. In which level would you classify bones? Explain.

____

2. Determine which stage of the digestive process is represented in each photograph and in which organ the stage occurs.

points
/ 8

Situation	Stage	Organ

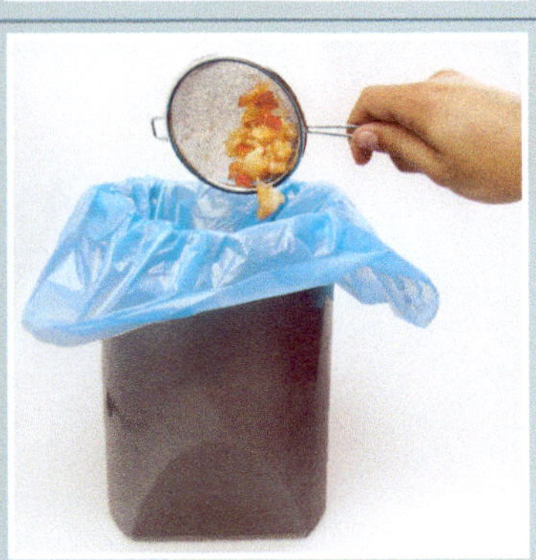		

Section

3 The Circulatory System

Connecting

Understanding the Circulatory System

Have you ever felt your heart beat? Put your hand on your chest and try to feel it. We are not always conscious of our heart beating, but it is always working. It is part of the **circulatory system**. In the previous section, you learned that the digestive system converts food into nutrients and that these nutrients pass into the bloodstream, which carries them to all parts of the body. The circulatory system is a very efficient transportation system.

pulsate

After absorption in the small intestine, nutrients travel through blood vessels (part of the circulatory system) to reach all the cells of an organism.

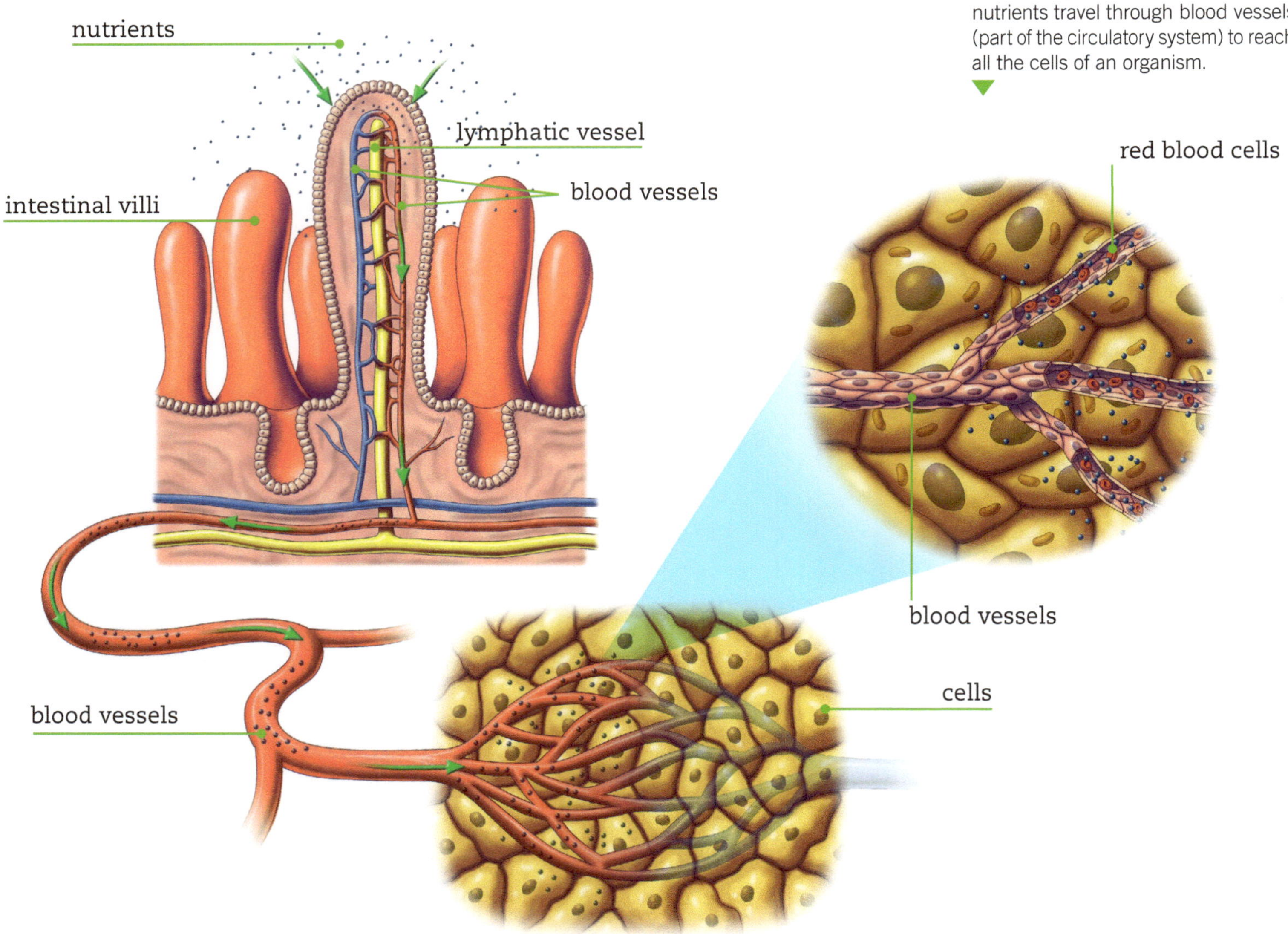

The circulatory system transports substances like water, nutrients and cell waste through the organism. It keeps every part of the body supplied with the necessary elements to function.

provided with or stocked

Circulatory System Components

The circulatory system consists of three large components that work together to transport substances such as nutrients and waste through the body. The three components are: the **heart**, **blood** and **blood vessels**, as seen in the diagram below.

Did You Know...?

In the 15th century, an English doctor named William Harvey was the first to correctly describe the relationship between the heart, blood and blood vessels. He said that blood goes to all parts of the body through the blood vessels with the help of the heart.

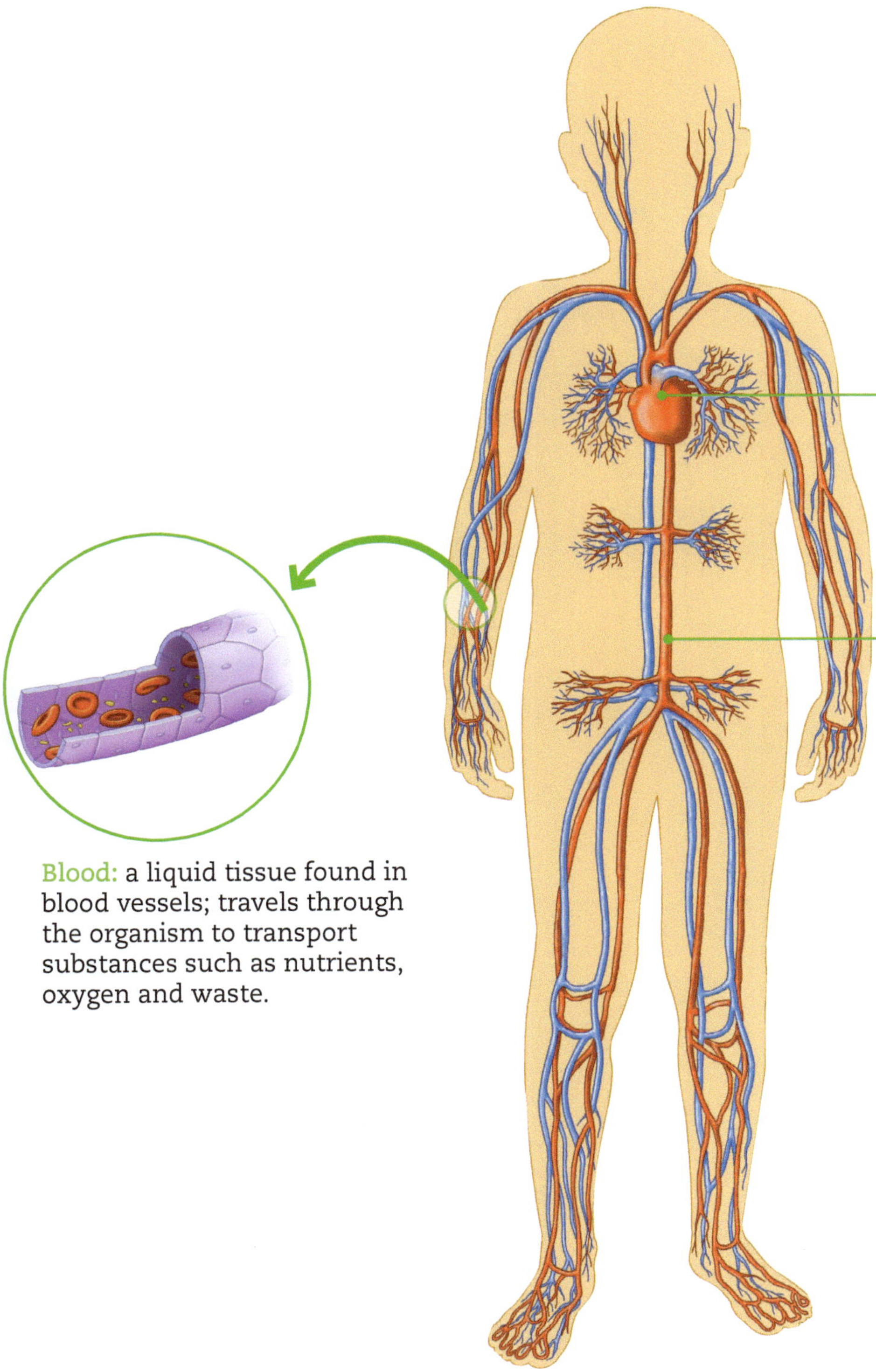

Heart: muscular organ that contracts to pump blood through the organism.

contract and force to move

Blood Vessels: tubes that transport blood to all parts of the body.

Blood: a liquid tissue found in blood vessels; travels through the organism to transport substances such as nutrients, oxygen and waste.

Challenge

The circulatory system moves a liquid (blood) through the body. Name two different systems in machinery or other areas that have a similar system. Compare and contrast the systems.

◀ The heart, blood and blood vessels are parts of the circulatory system.

Our Blood

Now that you know that blood travels to all parts of the body, have you ever wondered what blood looks like? To the naked eye, it just looks like a red liquid, but it is actually a liquid tissue consisting of cells. If you extract blood from a person and examine it under a microscope, you can see the cells. Remember that cells are very small.

unassisted vision

When you extract a sample of blood, it is possible to study all its components.

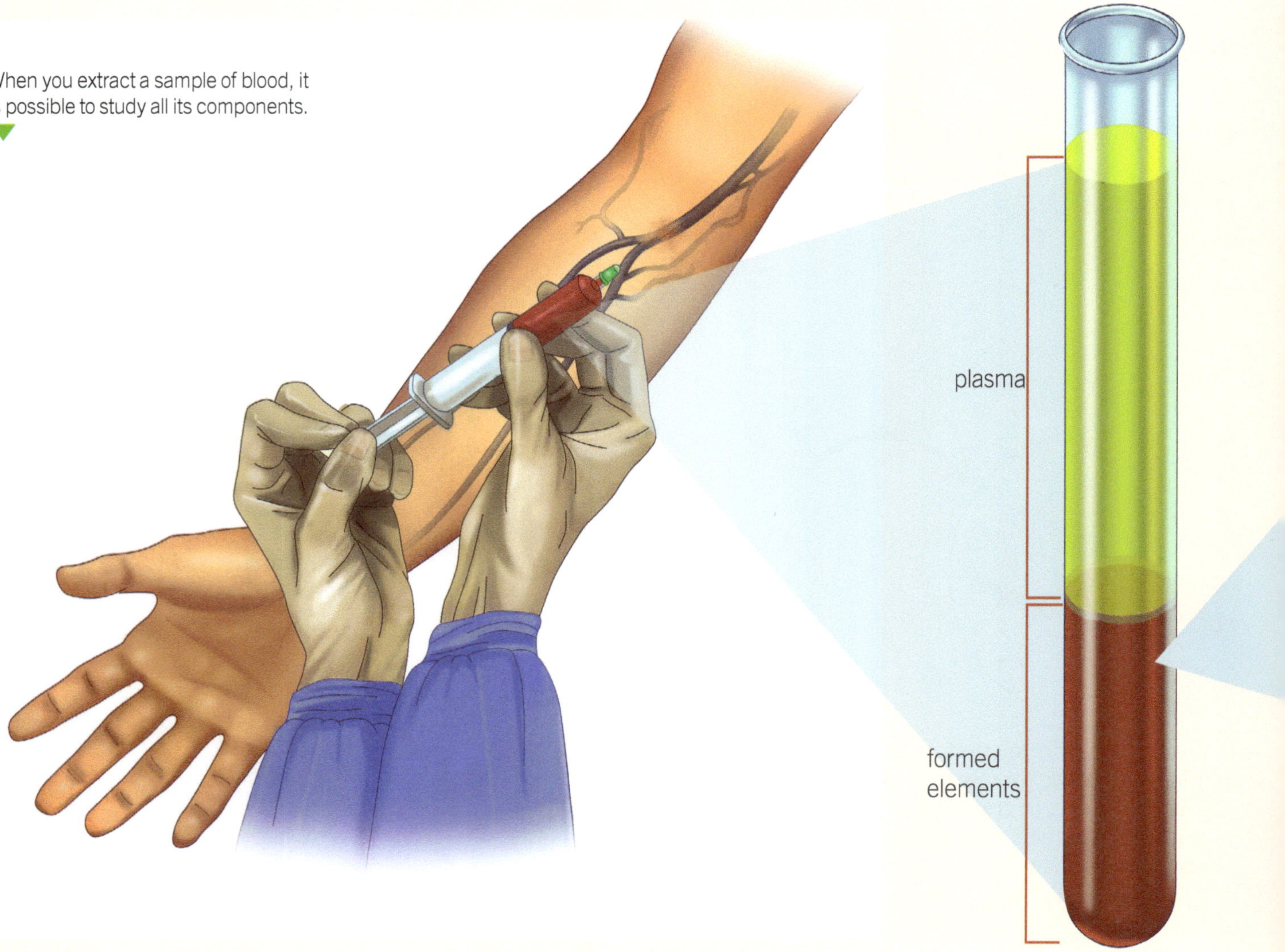

Did You Know...?

Some animals, such as mollusks, have blue blood. Their blood has a substance called hemocyanin, which transports oxygen and turns the blood blue.

Components of Blood

Blood is a tissue that consists of a liquid called **plasma** and a group of cells and cell fragments called **formed elements**. This group consists of **red blood cells**, **white blood cells** and **platelets**.

Did You Know...?

The amount of blood you have in your body changes with age. A baby has about 300 ml, and an adult has about 5,000 ml.

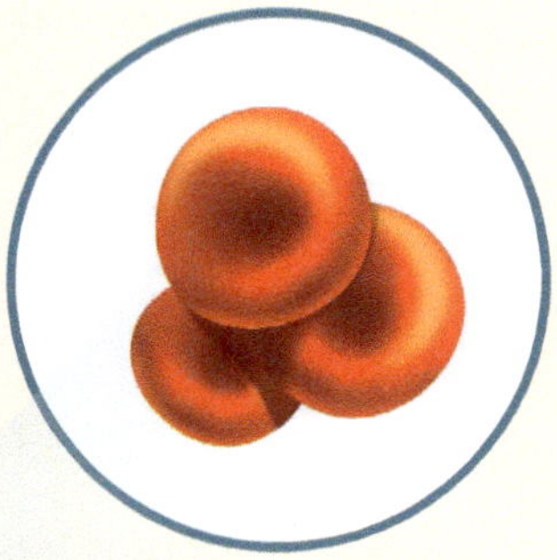

Red blood cells: are the most abundant. They give blood its color and they transport oxygen.

White blood cells: are less abundant than red blood cells. They defend the organism against illnesses.

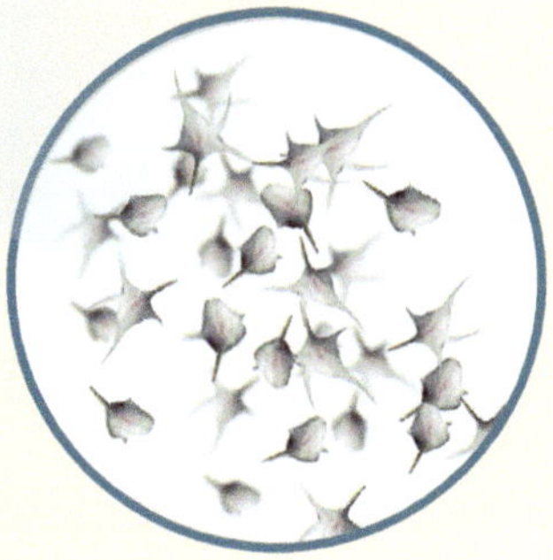

Platelets: are pieces of cells that form a plug, or **clot**. This clot is what stops the bleeding when you cut yourself. This process is called **coagulation**.

Summarizing

The circulatory system has three parts: the heart, blood and blood vessels. One of its functions is to transport nutrients and waste through the body. Blood is a tissue that consists of a liquid called plasma and a group of cells called formed elements. Formed elements are: red blood cells that transport oxygen; white blood cells that protect the organism from illness; and platelets that coagulate to stop bleeding and protect a wound.

Connecting

Blood Vessels

Blood transports substances to all parts of the body. Blood has a defined route through tubes called **blood vessels**.

Blood vessels are tubes that form a **closed circuit** where blood circulates. Have you ever noticed that even small cuts always bleed? That is because we have blood vessels all over our bodies. When we get hurt, sometimes the blood vessels break internally (inside), forming **bruises**, and other times the blood comes out externally (outside). The following image shows the main blood vessels in the body.

Blood vessels are tubes that form a **closed circuit**. This allows the blood to circulate permanently within the body. If the racetrack above represents the blood vessels, what do the cars represent?

Word Focus

Bruises are dark colored spots that form on our skin when the skin is hurt but not broken.

Did You Know...?

If extended in a straight line, the blood vessels of an adult would reach a length of 100,000 kilometers. That is the same as about three trips around the planet.

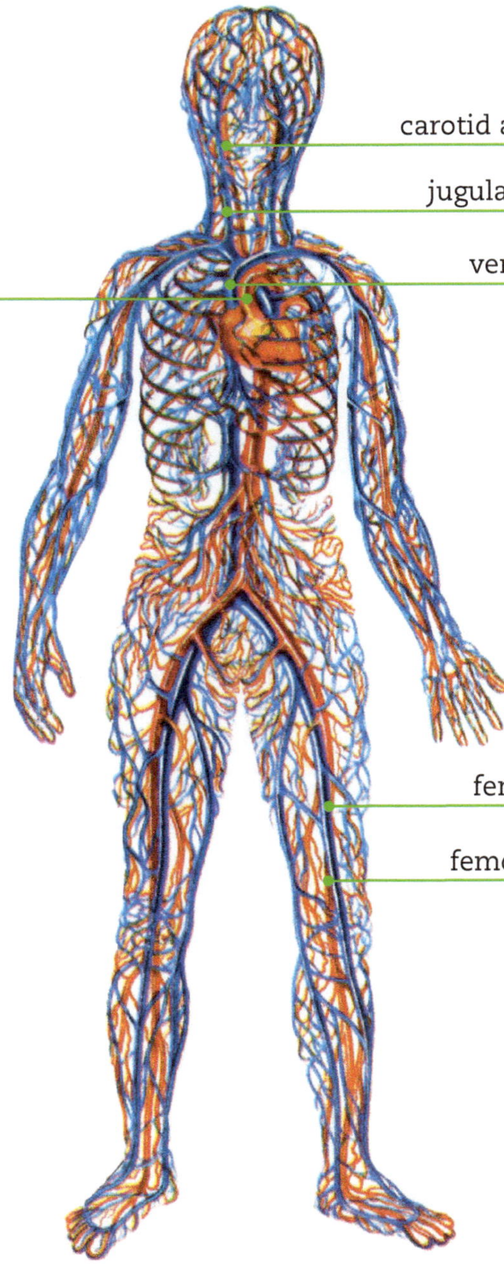

Types of Blood Vessels

The blood vessels in our bodies are classified into three groups: **veins**, **arteries** and **capillaries**.

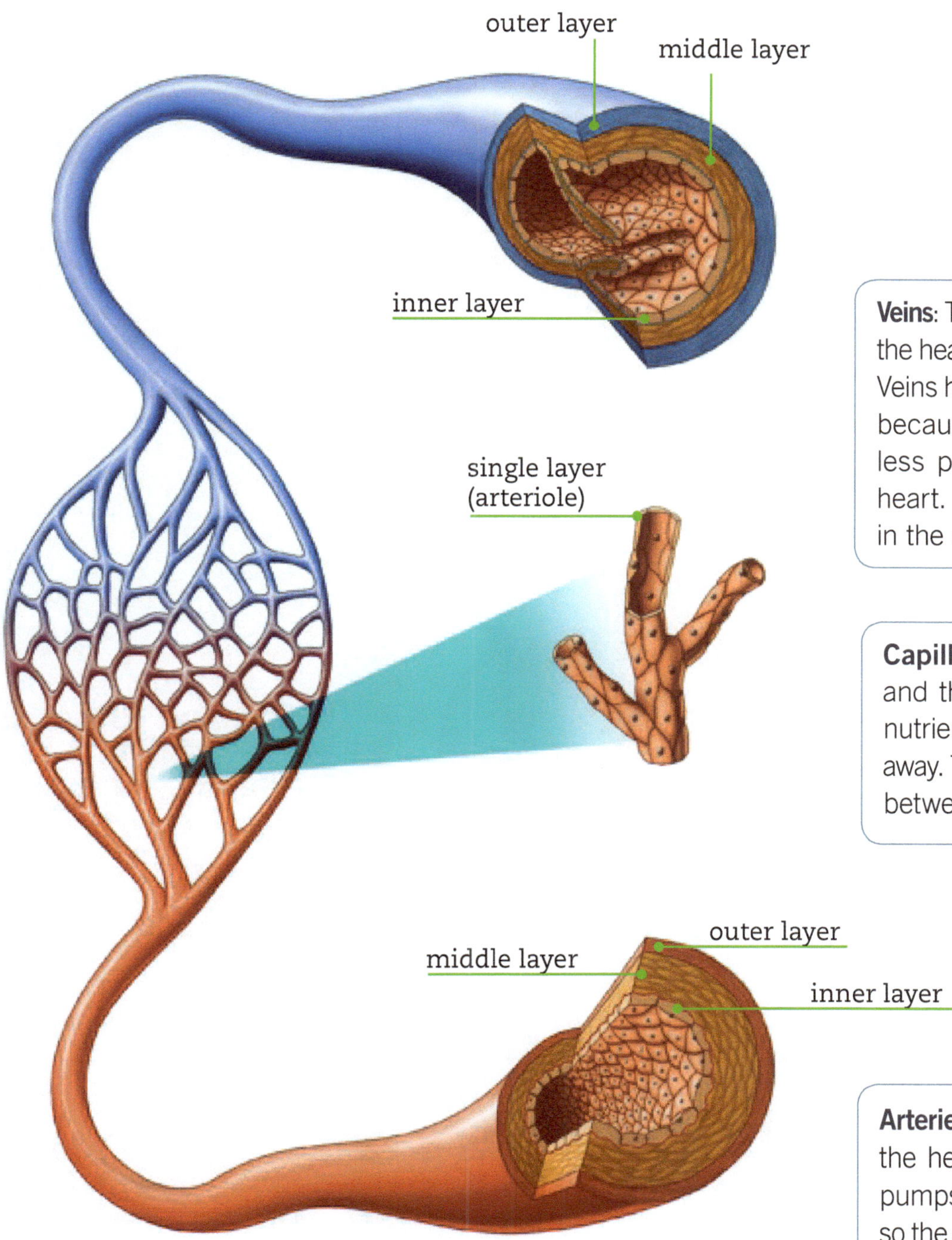

Veins: These move blood from tissues to the heart in the process of circulation. Veins have thinner walls than arteries because the blood circulates with less pressure as it returns to the heart. The veins are shown in blue in the diagram.

Capillaries: These are very small and thin blood vessels. They take nutrients to the cells and take waste away. They are located in organ tissue between the arteries and veins.

Arteries: These move the blood from the heart to the organs. The heart pumps blood with a lot of pressure, so the artery walls are thick, resistant and flexible. They are shown in red in the diagram.

▲ The walls of the veins and arteries have three layers. The walls of the capillaries have only one layer.

The Heart's Function

As you have learned, blood transports nutrients to all the cells in the body, and the blood vessels are tubes in which the blood circulates. But how does the blood move? What pushes it? The answers to these questions are related to one of the most important organs in our body: **the heart**.

The heart is an organ made primarily of muscle tissue. The walls of the heart contract and expand to pump blood through the blood vessels. This movement is called the **heartbeat**. This movement can be felt in some blood vessels as a **pulse**.

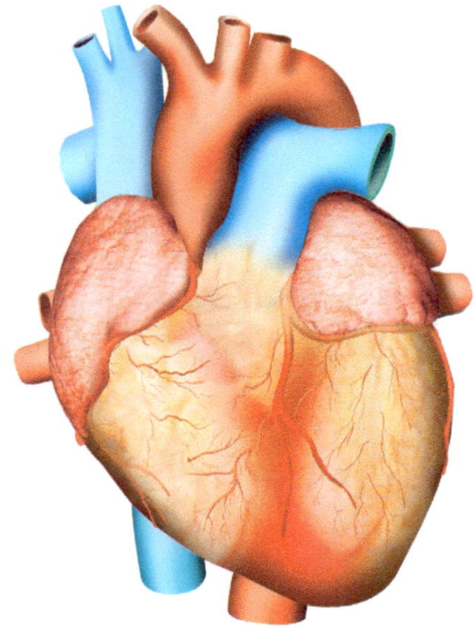

The heart is a muscular organ that causes blood to circulate through blood vessels and the body. Blood continually circulates during the life of an organism.

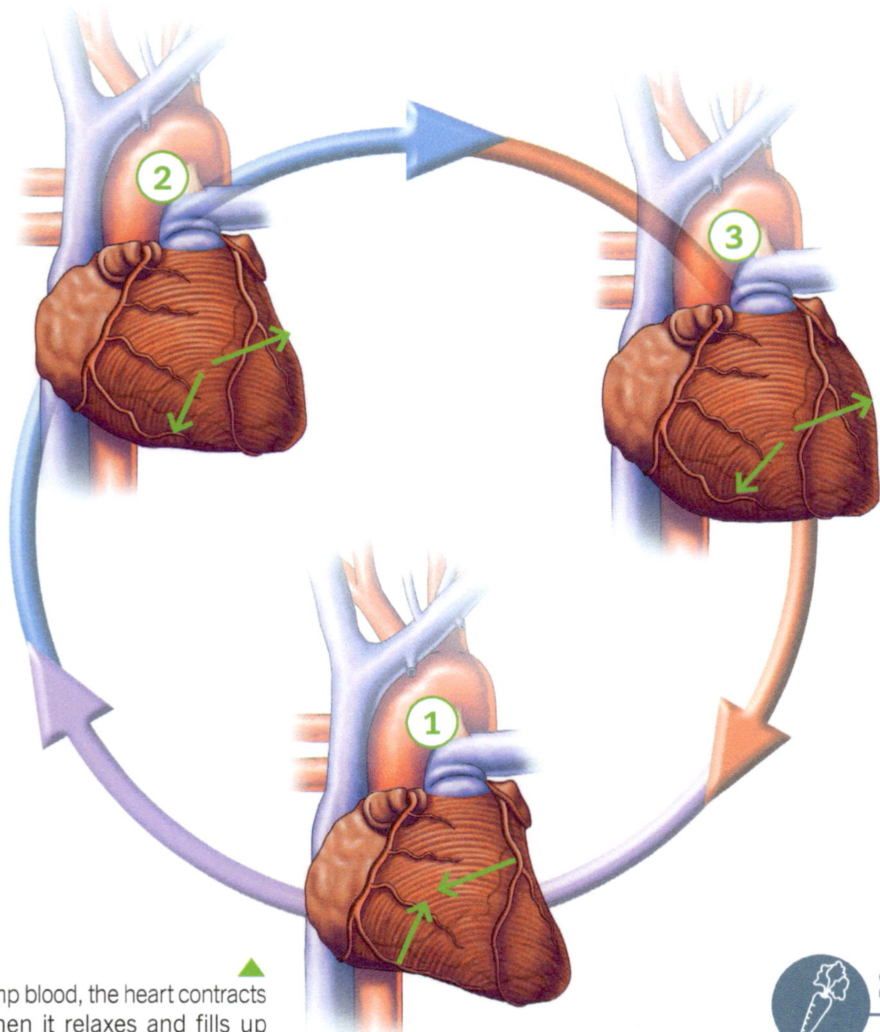

To pump blood, the heart contracts (1). Then it relaxes and fills up with blood (2), which causes it to expand (3). This movement, called the heartbeat, is repeated over and over to move blood through our bodies.

Did You Know...?

The human heart beats about 2,500,000,000 times in a lifetime.

Staying Healthy

Eating low-fat foods and exercising or playing sports helps the heart and keeps it working well.

Practicing

1. Follow the steps below to check your pulse.

- You need a piece of clay and a toothpick.
- Make a small hole in the clay with the toothpick and stick the toothpick in, as shown in image **1**.
- Place your hand on the table and put the toothpick on your wrist, as shown in image **2**, so you can detect movement.

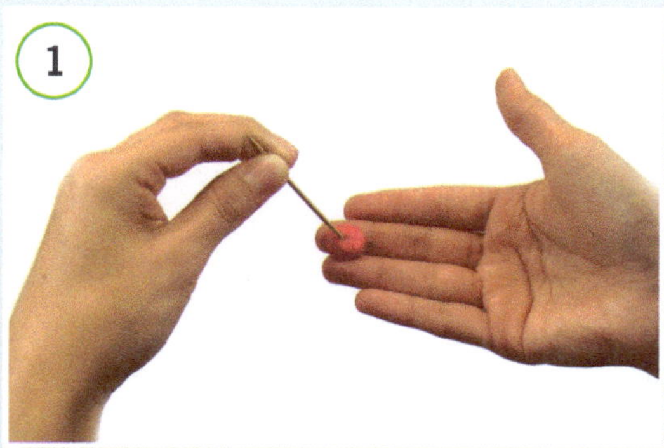

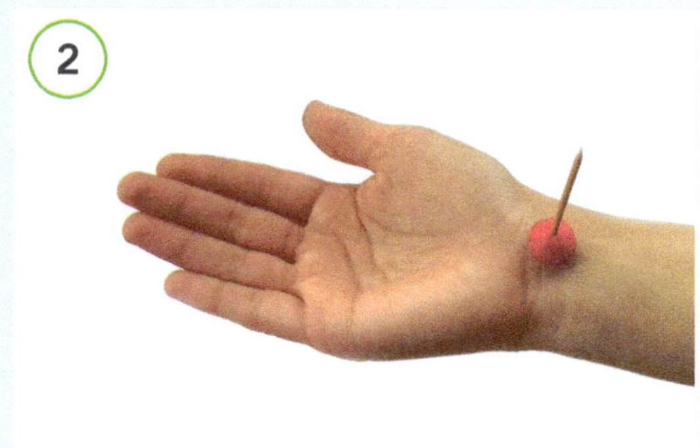

Answer the following questions.

a. What happened to the toothpick? Why? Explain

____

____

b. Why do the results vary when you place the toothpick on different parts of the wrist? Explain

____

c. If your heart beats about eight times in ten seconds, how many times do you think the toothpick will move in the same amount of time? Predict

____

d. What is the connection between the movement of the toothpick, your heartbeat and your pulse? Explain. Infer

____

____

1. Go to **Cutout 4** on **page 169**. Glue each type of blood vessel in the correct box, and then write its name. Identify

Types of Blood Vessels and Their Functions		
	These blood vessels allow substances to move through the blood and toward tissues. Their walls are thin, and they are located between the arteries and the veins.	-------------------
	These blood vessels transport blood from the tissues to the heart. Their walls are thinner than in arteries because the blood flows with less pressure.	-------------------
	These blood vessels transport blood from the heart to the tissues. Their walls are thicker than in veins because the pressure is higher.	-------------------

flows: moves in a steady, smooth way

Summarizing

Blood vessels are tubes that form a closed circuit around the whole body. There are three types of blood vessels: arteries, veins and capillaries. The heart pumps blood through the blood vessels so that it circulates around all parts of the body.

Quiz Yourself

1. Write the words that correspond to the definitions.

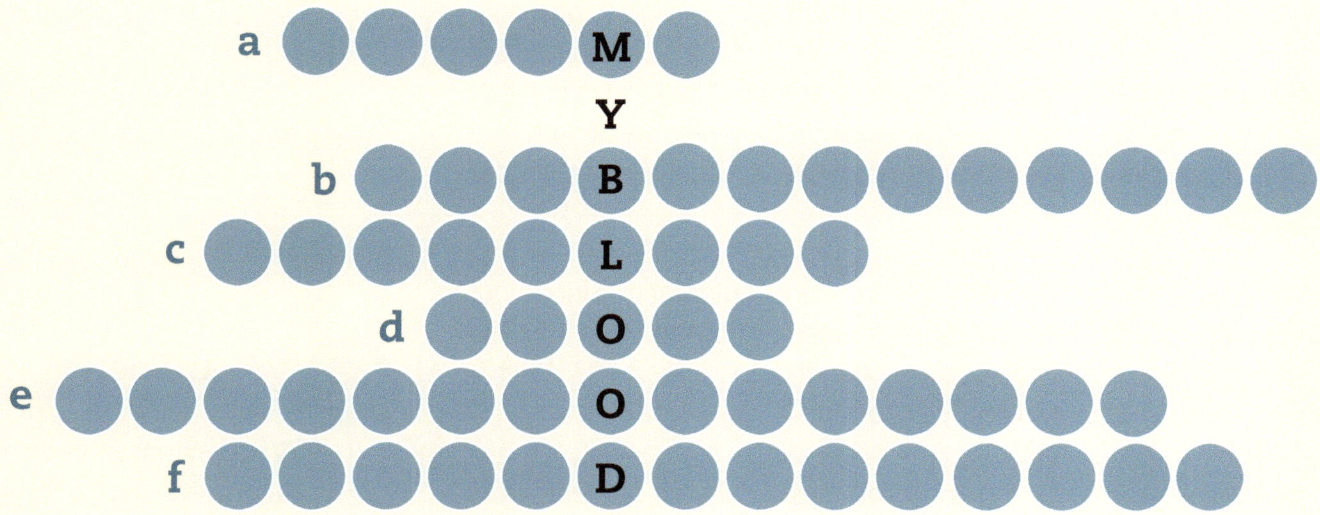

a. The liquid part of blood.
b. Blood cells that transport oxygen.
c. The formed elements that cause coagulation.
d. The plugs that block blood vessels when they break.
e. Cells that defend against illness.
f. The group of cells composed of red blood cells, white blood cells and platelets.

2. Complete the table with the correct definition or concept.

Transports nutrients, oxygen and waste.	
	veins
Transports blood from the heart to the tissues.	
	heart

Section 4 The Respiratory System

Connecting

Respiration

Try holding your breath for a few seconds. It is impossible to hold it for very long. This shows that breathing is an important process for the body. In previous units, you learned that the digestive and circulatory systems are **vital** for human beings since they help us absorb and distribute nutrients. The **respiratory system** is also important for our survival.

maintain

continued existence

The respiratory system is **involuntary** and automatic. Since your birth, you have been breathing all the time without thinking about it. Have you ever asked yourself why breathing is important? What is the purpose of this involuntary action?

Think about your body. You know you need to absorb nutrients from food to survive. It is also necessary to eliminate waste as fecal matter. Similarly, all the cells in your body absorb nutrients and eliminate waste to keep you alive. Through **respiration** our body takes in oxygen from the air. **Oxygen** is transported in the blood to all the cells. In the cells, it is used to generate energy from nutrients. Finally, the cell waste is eliminated as carbon dioxide.

Word Focus

Vital means very important and necessary for survival.

Fun Fact!

Plants and trees take in carbon dioxide and expel oxygen as waste. This is the opposite of humans and animals. Why do you think we need to protect the trees and plants in our environment?

Oxygen and carbon dioxide are very important gases. Oxygen is necessary for survival and is absorbed through the air. Carbon dioxide is waste from the respiratory process and must be eliminated quickly.

Organs of the Respiratory System

The **respiratory system** consists of the **pulmonary airways** and **lungs**.

Pulmonary Airways are respiratory ducts that move air from the outside to the inside of our bodies and vice versa. The airways are the: **nasal passage**, **pharynx**, **larynx**, **trachea**, **bronchus** and **bronchial tubes**.

Lungs are responsible for **gas exchange**. This is the exchange of oxygen and carbon dioxide that occurs within the organism. The lungs are located in the thorax on either side of the heart.

exchange → interchange

either → one or the other

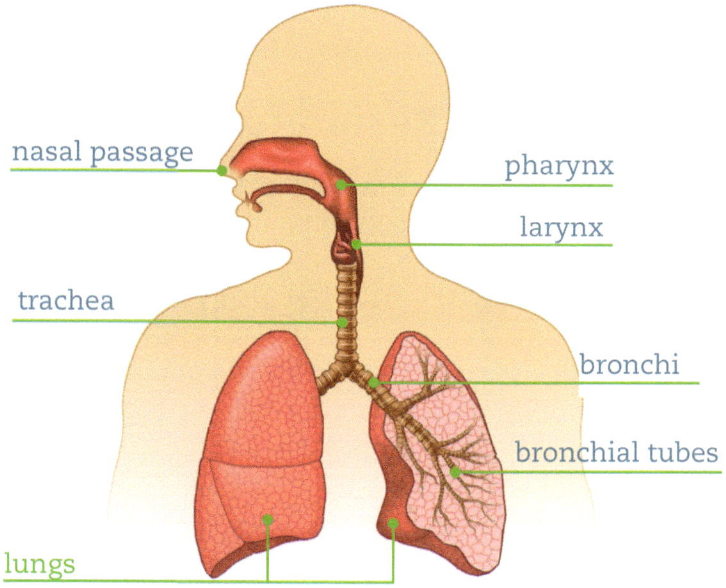

The parts of the respiratory system allow air from the outside world to enter the lungs.

Practicing

1. Color the pulmonary airways **blue** and the lungs **red**. Identify

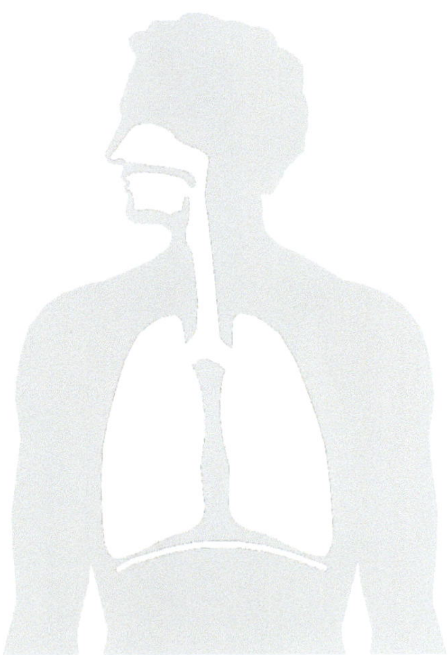

Word Focus

Pulmonary means anything relating to the lungs. Does the word pulmonary look like a word in your first language?

Did You Know...?

Some amphibians, like frogs, use their lungs and their skin for gas exchange, or breathing. Their skin is very thin and has many blood vessels.

Summarizing

Respiration is the process of gas exchange between oxygen and carbon dioxide. The respiratory system consists of the pulmonary airways and the lungs. The lungs are organs located on each side of the thorax and are responsible for gas exchange.

Connecting

The Role of Respiratory System Organs

Imagine you are very small and can float in the air. Let's follow the air you breathe into your body from the exterior to the interior.

The Air's Journey into the Body

1. **Nasal Passage:** The entrance is through the interior of the nose, called the nasal passage. Here air becomes **warm and moist**, and the nasal passage **removes** harmful substances.

2. **Pharynx:** Our journey continues through this muscular tube where the digestive and respiratory systems meet. **Air circulates** from the nasal passage to the larynx.

   journey → expedition

3. **Larynx:** We are now in the home of the **vocal cords**. When air exits, it makes these cords vibrate, which creates sounds. Vocal cords allow us to talk.

   exits → leaves

4. **Trachea:** We continue our journey through this tube. It consists of a series of **cartilage rings** that maintain its shape. As we travel down the trachea, the path divides in two: the bronchi.

5. **Bronchi:** Each bronchus enters a lung and then branches out into many narrower bronchial tubes.

   branches → divides

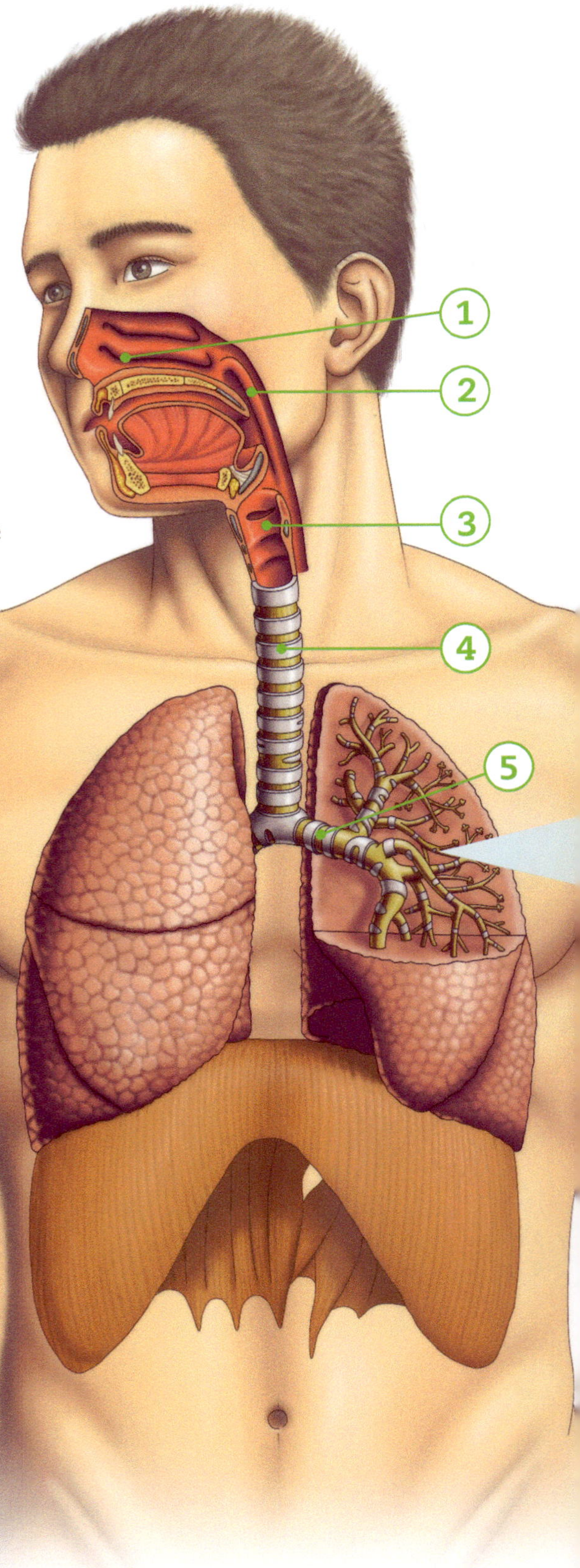

Did You Know...?

The trachea is also called the windpipe.

Fun Fact!

Some animals also have vocal cords, but these are different from human vocal cords. They allow them to make different kinds of sounds. Think of dogs and cats. What sounds do they make? Giraffes do not have vocal cords, so they cannot make sounds.

6 Bronchial Tubes: As we travel through these tubes, they get smaller and narrower. This allows air to reach the whole lung. At the end of the tubes, there are clusters of small sacs.

7 Alveoli: We have reached the end of the respiratory system, the alveoli. These are small clustered sacs, surrounded by capillaries. Oxygen enters the blood to reach all the cells in the body through the alveoli. Carbon dioxide (cell waste) travels through the blood into the alveoli to exit the body. This process is called gas exchange.

close groups

Staying Healthy

Cigarette smoke harms smokers' lungs and the lungs of anyone nearby. Damage includes loss of the elasticity or flexibility in the walls of the alveoli, decreasing the amount of oxygen absorbed by the blood.

Fun Fact!

Did you know that all scientific words come from Latin? We use the Latin singular and plural endings for these words. For example, there can be one bronchus and two bronchi; one alveolus and two alveoli.

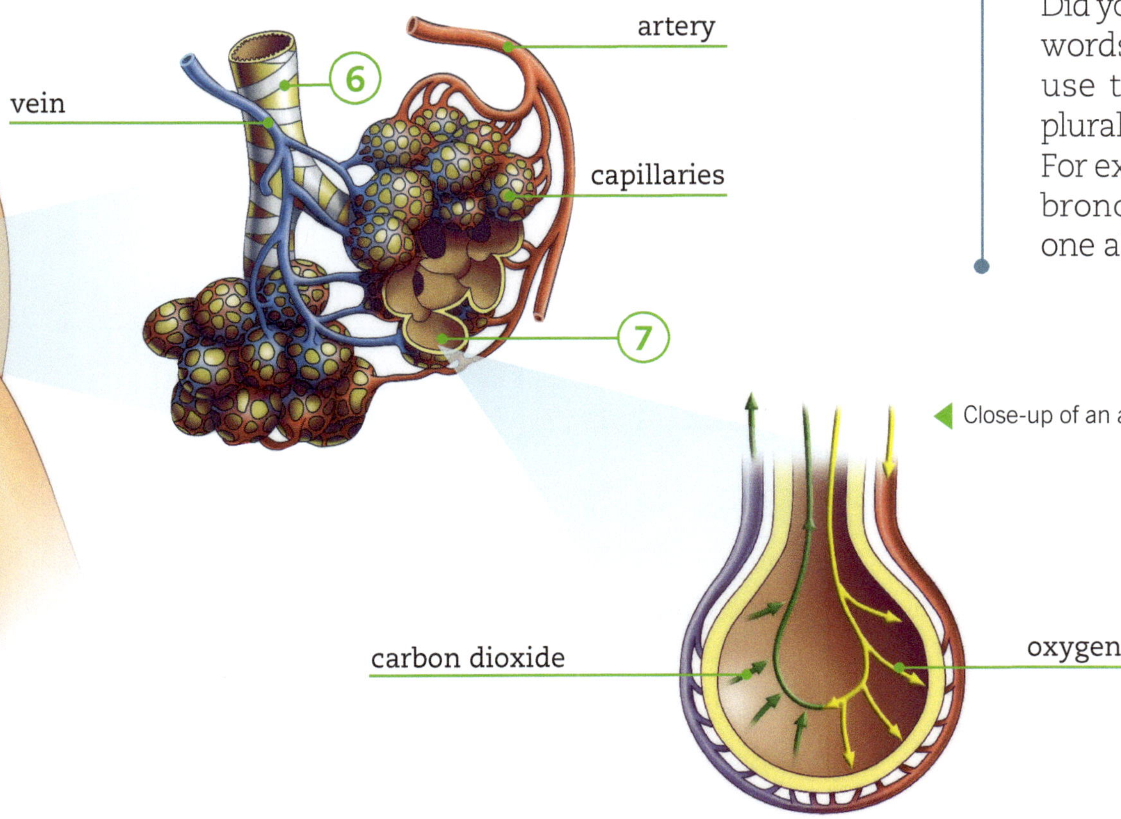

Close-up of an alveolus.

Education through Values

Although some clean vehicles exist, most modes of transportation contaminate the air we breathe. We should try to develop habits that do not contaminate the air. For example, you can ride a bicycle instead of getting a ride in a car. Little things can help make the environment better for everyone!

Exploring

You have now learned about some elements of respiration, such as how air goes from the outside world to the inside of our bodies. Work with your classmates to better understand how air enters and leaves our bodies.

1. Work in groups of four.
2. You will need a pencil, a notebook and a measuring tape.
3. Your classmate stands up and spreads (extends) his or her arms, as shown in the photograph.

Word Focus

Exhale means to breathe out.
Inhale means to breathe in.

4. Your partner **inhales** deeply and holds the air in while you measure around his or her chest, as shown in the photograph.
5. Ask your classmate to **exhale**, and then take another chest measurement.
6. Do the same with the rest of your group and complete the chart.

Name	Measurements of Thorax (cm)		Difference (cm)
	Inhale	Exhale	

7. Get together with your classmates and discuss your results. Answer the following questions.

   a. What happened to the thorax when **inhaling**? Identify

   ____

   b. What happened to the thorax when **exhaling**? Identify

   ____

   c. What is the difference in these movements? Explain. Interpret

   ____

   ____

Understanding Respiration

In the previous activity, we proved that the thorax changes in size when breathing in and out. The thorax is bigger when we inhale and smaller when we exhale. Why? When we inhale, our lungs fill with air. When we exhale, the air leaves our lungs.

Word Focus

Chest is another word for thorax.

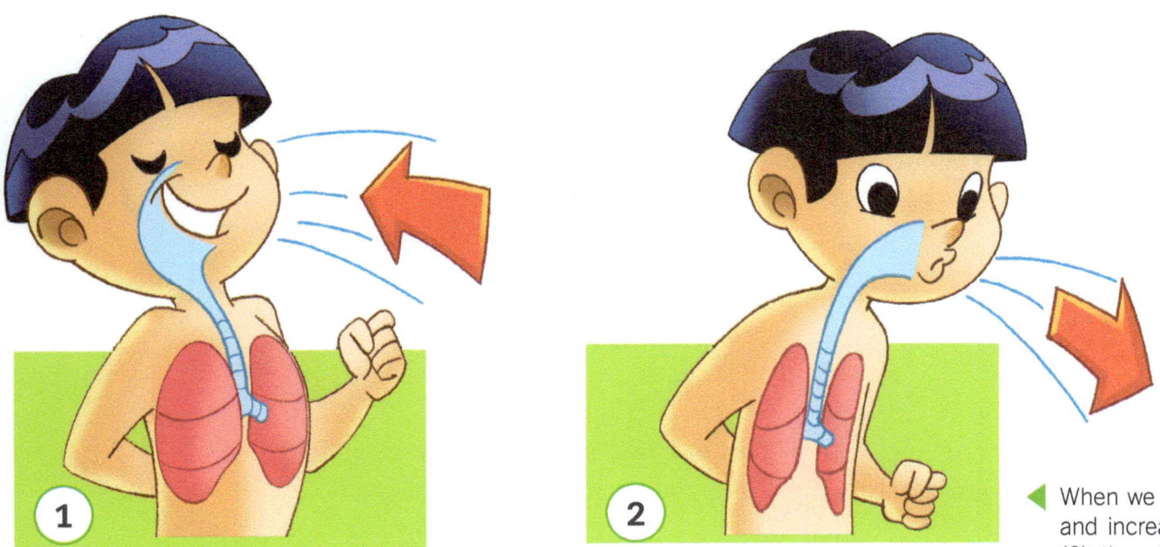

When we inhale (1), our lungs fill with air and increase in volume; when we exhale (2), they decrease in volume.

Practicing

1. Go to **Activity Card 1**. Number the parts of the respiratory system in order from inhaling air through the nasal passage to the alveoli. Identify

2. The chart below shows a child's thorax measurements upon inhalation and exhalation.

	Thorax Measurements (cm)	
Breath 1	63	81
Breath 2	61	83

a. Which numbers represent inhalation? Explain. Infer

____

____

b. Which numbers represent exhalation? Explain. Infer

____

____

c. Why are the changes in the thorax important? Explain. Hypothesize

____

____

Tip

Breathe (v) has the same vowel sound as meat. **Breath** (n) has the same vowel sound as met.

Summarizing

Air enters the body through the pulmonary airways. Then it reaches the lungs, where gas exchange occurs. This exchange consists of oxygen entering the blood and carbon dioxide leaving it.

When we breathe, our thorax changes in size allowing air to enter and exit the lungs.

Quiz Yourself

1. Go to **Cutout 5** on **page 169**. Glue the pictures in the correct boxes and label the parts of the respiratory system. Identify

Tubes that enter the lungs.	Organ where air enters the body.	Sacs where gas exchange occurs.	Large duct that directs air to the bronchial tubes.	Organ that fills with air during inhalation.

2. Look at the following images and write which respiratory movements are shown. Draw an arrow showing in which direction the air is moving. Apply

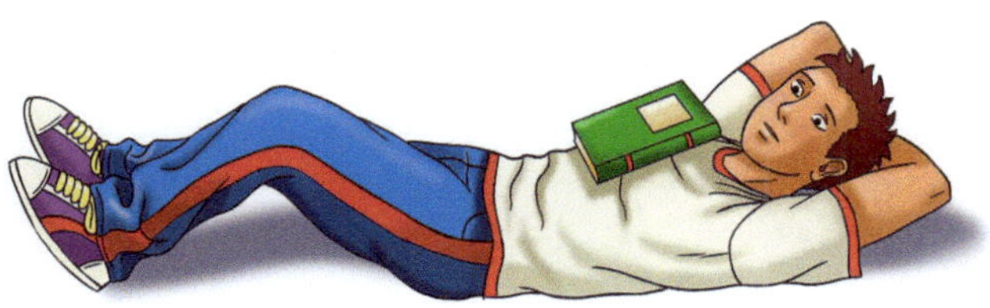

____

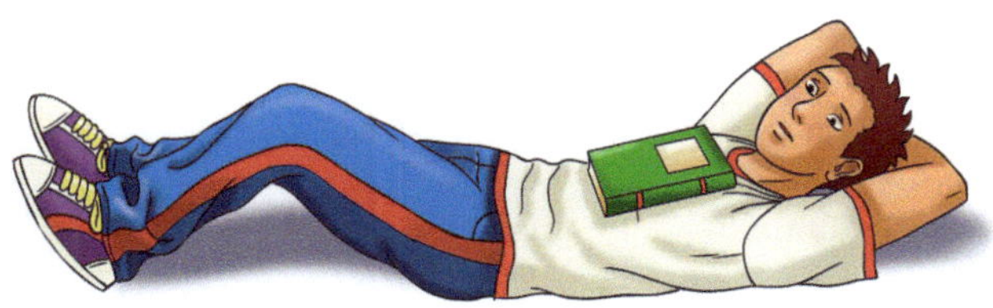

____

3. Explain gas exchange in the alveoli. Reread the **Summarizing** section on **page 50** if you need help. Explain

____

____

____

What Did You Learn?

1. Identify the level of biological organization shown in each image.

points
/ 5

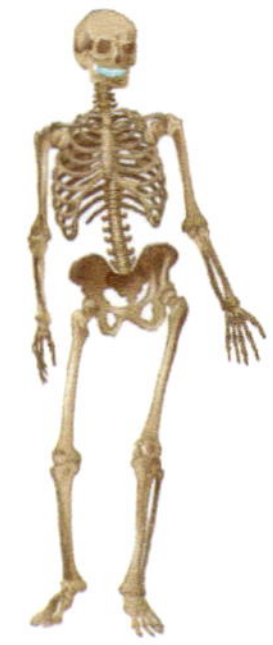

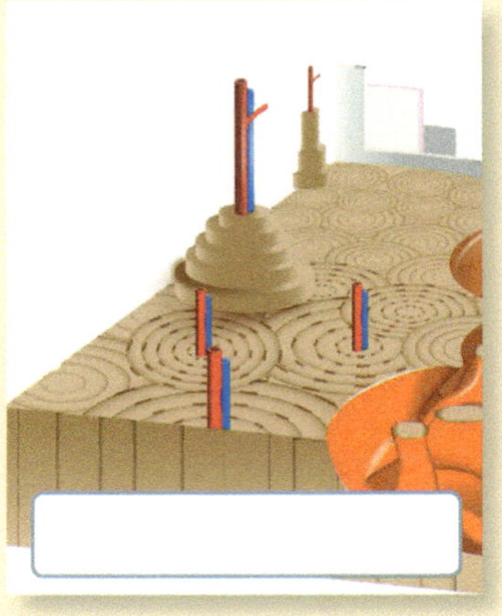

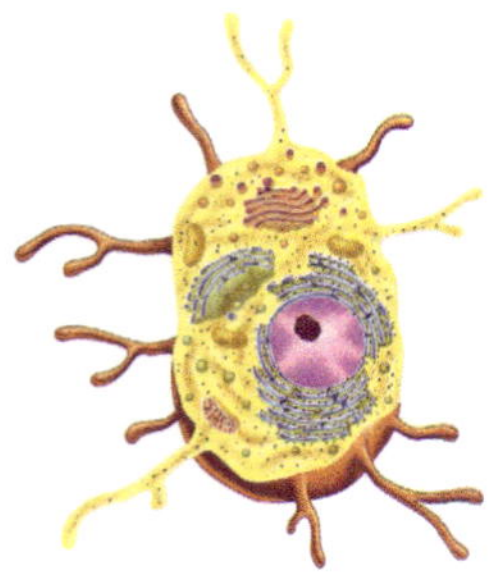

2. Complete the following table.

points
/ 10

Level of Biological Organization	Characteristics of the Level	Examples
Level 1		
Level 2		
Level 3		
Level 4		
Level 5		

3. Match each image with the correct description.

points
/ 4

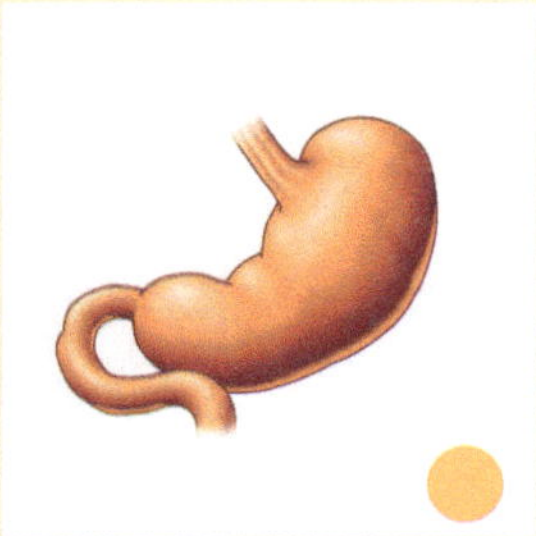
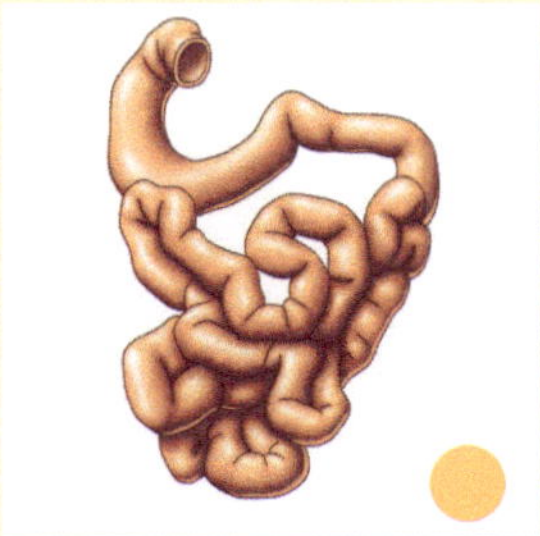
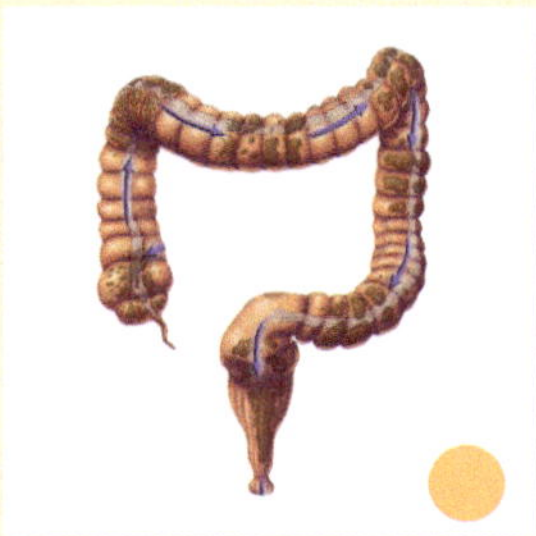
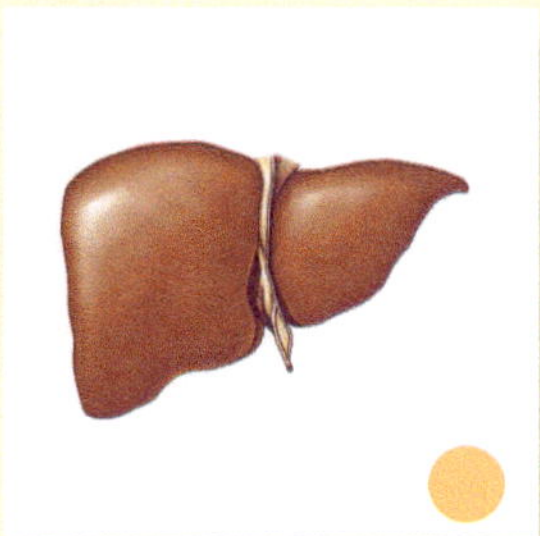

This organ absorbs nutrients.

This organ produces bile to help digestion.

This organ helps eliminate waste.

This organ produces gastric juices to help digestion.

4. Fill in the blanks with the correct words.

points
/ 5

chyme | **pylorus sphincter** | **esophagus** | **mouth** | **egestion**

a. The bolus forms in the ______________________________ before swallowing.

b. The ______________________ is located between the stomach and the small intestine.

c. The bolus passes from the mouth to the stomach through the ______________________.

d. After it passes through the stomach, food is called ______________________.

e. The process of eliminating waste is called ______________________.

5. Complete the table.

points
/ 4

	Veins	Arteries
Are the walls thick or thin?		
Does the blood go to the heart or to the organs?		

6. Complete the diagram.

points
/8

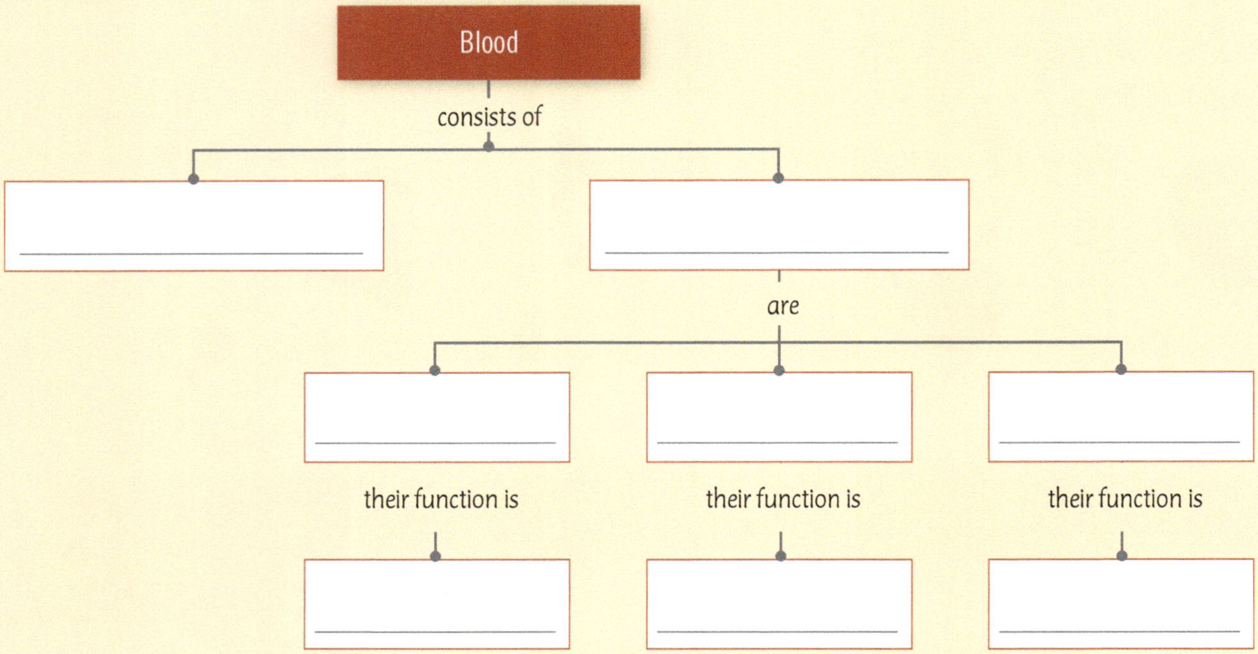

7. Which of the following statements about the human heart is **correct**?

point
/1

A. It expands and contracts to pump blood.
B. It is located under the lungs.
C. It contracts voluntarily.
D. It is a tissue.

8. Complete the following diagram showing the path of air from the nasal passage to the alveoli.

points
/5

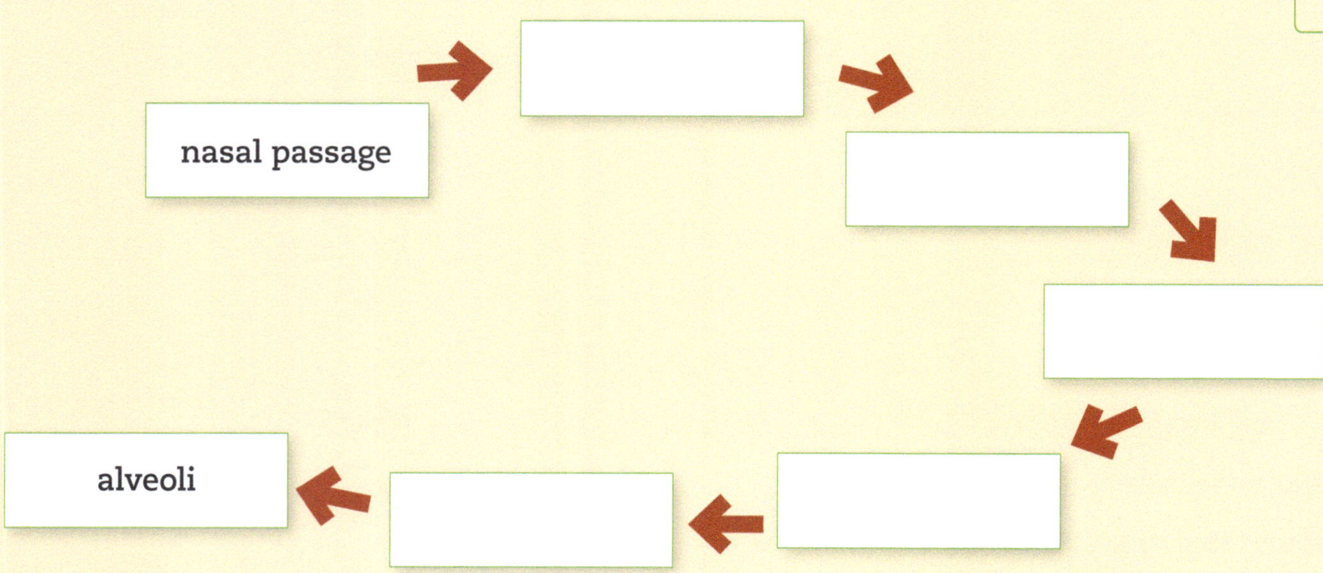

9. Complete.

points
5

a. The movement that forces air out of the lungs is called ______________________.

b. In the alveoli, the absorption of oxygen and elimination of carbon dioxide occurs through

______________________________.

c. The primary organs of the respiratory system are the ______________________________.

d. To allow air to enter the body, we need to ______________________________________.

e. The oxygen we need comes from the ____.

Scientific Skill: Predict

10. The following image shows gastric bypass surgery. This surgery is for people who suffer from severe obesity. Look at the image and answer the question.

points
3

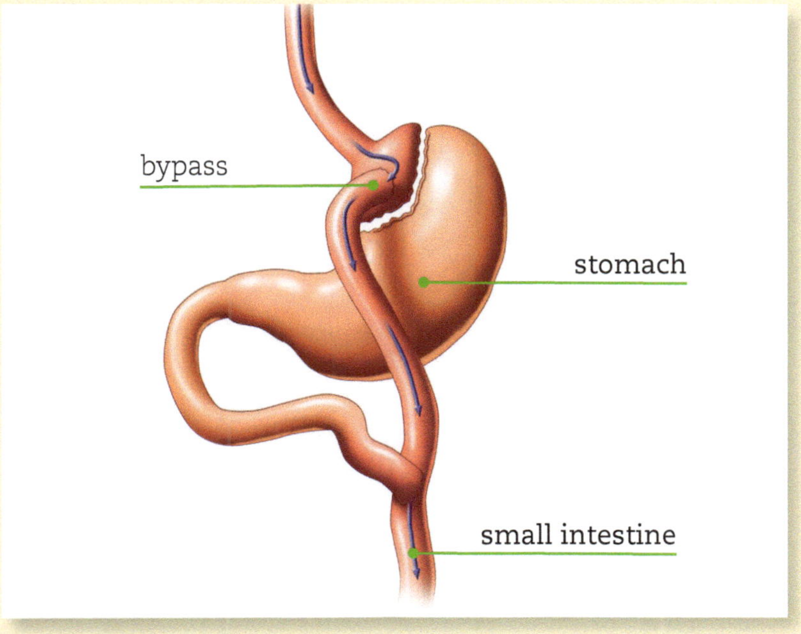

Using what you have learned in this unit, how can people who have this surgery absorb nutrients?

____

____

____

Find Test 1 Study Page

Unit 2

Nutrition and Health

Key Words

- consume
- energy
- diet
- risk
- humid

In this unit you will learn to:

- recognize the importance of nutrients for our bodies.
- identify harmful and beneficial microorganisms.
- plan and study independently.
- develop healthy eating habits.

What Do You Know?

Initial Evaluation

1. Look at the picture. Circle the people that are practicing **healthy habits**.

2. Mark **unhealthy** foods with an ✖ .

3. Mark **healthy** foods with a ✔.

Scientific Skill: Experiment

4. Look and find the children in images (1) and (2). They played in the park yesterday and then had a picnic with their families. This is what happened the next day:

Two classmates decided to find out why only the boy was sick. Each classmate did the following research:

CLASSMATE 1 He interviewed all his classmates and found out who played in the park yesterday.

CLASSMATE 2 She interviewed all her classmates who played in the park yesterday. She found out who washed their hands before eating and who did not.

Using this information, answer:

a. Why do you think the boy is sick? Explain.

____

____

b. Which classmate's method of research into the cause of the illness was better? Explain.

____

____

Nutrition

Connecting

Food Gives Us Energy

Surely you have eaten **food** you do not like, and your parents have said to you "Eat up! It is good for you!" It is normal not to like all foods, but you should always remember the importance of a **healthy diet**.

Have you ever thought about why food is so **important**? Imagine your body is a complex machine that needs fuel, and it needs all its parts to be healthy. Food is fuel for our bodies. It gives us everything we need to stay healthy and keep our bodies moving. That is why eating healthy food in **adequate quantities** is necessary.

fuel: material that produces energy

Remember!

Your diet is everything you usually eat and drink.

Just like a machine, our bodies need fuel to function. Our fuel is food. What happens if you do not have a healthy diet?

Education through Values

There are many organizations that fight world hunger. In many countries, people do not have **enough** food to eat. This makes them more prone to **disease** and **illness**. It is important to be aware of this problem and to support efforts to end it.

prone: susceptible

Food

Food is everything we eat and drink. It supplies the **energy** and **nutrients** necessary to grow and maintain a healthy body. Energy from food makes it possible to talk, write, run, sleep and think. Food also helps heal tissue after an injury and replace tissue as we grow older.

heal → make better

There are many different types of food. They are classified according to their **origin**—for example, if they come from an animal, like meat, or from a plant, like fruit.

▲ The food we eat comes from both animal and plant origins. Which type of food do you eat more of?

Practicing

1. Why is it important for our body to obtain food? Explain

____

____

2. Martin has many foods from different origins in his refrigerator. Help him classify them. Write **A** for foods of **animal origin** and **P** for those of **plant origin**. Identify

☐ eggs ☐ carrots ☐ sausages ☐ tomatoes

☐ lettuce ☐ fish ☐ milk ☐ corn

Summarizing

______________ gives the body the necessary nutrients to function correctly. Food can be classified by its origin as from either ______________ or ______________.

Connecting

Components of Food

What foods do you eat on a daily basis? Things like fruit, milk, bread, meat and cheese all have a **complex mix of nutrients**. Remember that nutrients are substances that give the body energy to live.

Did You Know...?

Nuts are considered an almost perfect food because of the amount and type of the nutrients they contain. They are rich in protein and other substances that contribute to a healthy heart.

Did you know that milk gives you strong bones and helps you grow? It is a well-known fact that milk is full of nutrients.

Nutrients are classified by their function.

Nutrient	Basic Function
Proteins	Help **build body structures**, like muscles, hair and nails.
Carbohydrates	**Give the body immediate energy** for daily activities, like walking or running.
Lipids	Serve as **energy reserves** when there are no immediate sources of energy.
Vitamins and Minerals	Help **regulate body functions**, like blood coagulation. Minerals are also part of some structures, like bones.

Water is also considered a nutrient—it does not give the body energy, but it is vital all the same. Next, we will learn about each of these nutrients.

Proteins

Every time you eat meat or drink milk, you **consume** a large amount of **protein**. Proteins have many functions, but primarily they **build and repair body structures**. All parts of the body, especially muscles, partly consist of proteins.

→ basically

Foods that have a large amount of protein usually come from animals, like meat, milk and eggs. Some foods from plant origin are also rich in protein—for example, legumes, like beans and lentils.

▲ Proteins help build and maintain body structures throughout your body, from the cells to the tissues and organs like your skin or your stomach.

Practicing

1. Write the name of the nutrient that matches each description. Infer

Description	Nutrient
Bears **lose weight** when they hibernate because they use the stored energy from these nutrients.	
We need these nutrients to maintain all the structures in our bodies, such as our muscles.	
We need the energy from these nutrients to walk, run and study.	
If we do not have these nutrients, our bones become **weak**.	

Summarizing

______________ consists of a complex mix of nutrients. They are classified into four groups: proteins, carbohydrates, lipids, and vitamins and minerals. ______________ help build and maintain body structures, like muscles.

Connecting

Carbohydrates

Look at the image.

having a large amount

What do these foods have in **common**? They may look different, but they have an important similarity: they are both rich in **carbohydrates**.

Carbohydrates are essential nutrients in any **diet**. They supply the body with **immediate energy** that is used during daily activities.

Carbohydrates are found in many types of food and have different characteristics. There are sweet carbohydrates, like honey, sugar and fruit. Others, like bread, pasta and potatoes, are not sweet.

These nutrients are a source of energy that is used **immediately**—for example, before competing in a marathon, athletes eat foods rich in carbohydrates. Running a marathon uses a lot of energy, so it is important that the body is prepared.

Word Focus

The word **diet** can refer to a change in eating habits by limiting certain foods. It can also refer to the things you eat daily. Healthy dietary habits give you more energy and can help you live longer!

These foods are rich in carbohydrates.

Explore and discuss.

One of the most important carbohydrates is **starch**. You can use **Lugol's iodine** to see if a food has starch. When mixed with starch, it turns dark blue.

Do this activity to test different foods for starch.

1. Collect the following supplies:
   - a paint tray
   - grated apple
   - flour
   - milk
   - cooking oil
   - Lugol's iodine
   - a dropper
2. Which foods do you think contain starch?
3. Put a different food in each space of the paint tray. Then add five drops of Lugol's iodine to each. Observe the color changes and answer: which foods have starch? Explain.

Practicing

1. Alex is going to play in a championship basketball game for his school team. His coach told him he needs a lot of energy. What type of food should he eat to prepare for the game? Explain your answer. Apply

____

____

Tip

Go to page 29 in Unit 1 to review the uses of Lugol's iodine.

Summarizing

______________________ are a source of immediate energy. One of the most important dietary carbohydrates is ______________.

Exploring

Lipids

Have you ever heard that certain foods clog (block) your arteries? These foods have many **lipids** or a **high fat content**.

Do this activity to test different foods for lipids.

1. Collect the following supplies:
   - peanuts
   - nuts
   - noodles
   - a spoon
   - craft paper
2. Draw four circles on the paper and label each with a different food.
3. Put the foods in the circles. Then use the spoon to crush (break up) them.
4. Remove the foods, and observe the paper against light.
5. Lipids can be identified because they leave stains (marks).
6. Use your observations to answer: Which foods have lipids? Is it healthy to eat a lot of these foods?

The principal function of lipids is to supply the body with energy. However, unlike (different from) carbohydrates, lipids give the body **energy to store**. This energy is stored in the **adipose tissue** as body fat. It is used when there are no sources of immediate energy—in other words, carbohydrates.

Word Focus

Obesity is the excessive or abnormal accumulation of body fat. It is harmful to a person's body and general health.

Lipids are found in many foods, like red meat, oil, margarine, mayonnaise and avocados. It is fine to eat lipids in **moderation**, but eating them in **excess** can cause health problems, like **obesity**. To avoid negative consequences, limit the amount of foods you eat that are high in lipids.

Foods high in lipids should be eaten in moderation. Which of these foods do you eat on a regular basis?

Vitamins and Minerals

Vitamins and minerals are substances that help **regulate body functions**. Minerals are also part of some **structures**, like bones and teeth.

The body requires lower quantities of vitamins and minerals than of the other nutrients, but they are still very important. They can be found in many foods but are principally in fruits and vegetables. In the following chart, you will learn about a few **essential vitamins and minerals**, their functions and their sources. After you finish reading the chart, complete the blanks with the names of the foods.

Vitamins and Minerals		
Name	**Function**	**Food Sources**
Vitamin B	Contributes to the functions of the nervous, digestive and muscular systems—for example, it maintains the structure of nervous system cells.	 ________ ________
Vitamin D	Helps the body absorb calcium, which strengthens bones and teeth.	 ________ ________
Iron	Forms part of the red blood cells and has an important role in oxygen transportation.	 ________ ________ ________
Calcium	Helps bones and teeth grow and helps blood clot.	

Vitamins

Minerals

Connecting

Nutritional Composition of Foods

The **nutritional composition** of a food is the **amount and variety of nutrients** it contains—for example, meat has a lot of protein, while bread has a lot of carbohydrates and little protein. This information helps us decide what foods we need to eat.

A Balanced Diet

benefit

Do a piece of candy and a piece of fruit have the same **nutritional value**? Definitely not! Every food has a different nutritional composition. That is why you need to have a **balanced diet** in order to be healthy.

A balanced diet means getting an adequate amount of nutrients by eating the right foods. If you meet the nutritional needs of your body, you will stay healthy. Everybody's needs are different and depend on things like age, body mass (weight), height and physical activity.

It is very important that you pay attention to what you eat and exercise regularly. If your body has more energy than you need, you gain weight. This can be harmful to your health.

A balanced diet includes a variety of foods that contain all the nutrients a person needs. Is your diet balanced?

Staying Healthy

Playing sports and exercising regularly help maintain healthy bones and muscles and a healthy heart. Activities like these also **burn** energy and prevent weight gain.

Challenge

Calculate your Body Mass Index score with this formula:
weight (kg) / (height x height (m)) = BMI

The Food Pyramid

The food pyramid is a **guide** to help us choose the quantity and types of foods to eat. The pyramid shows the different food groups and recommends **daily portions**. The bottom of the pyramid shows foods that should be eaten the **most**. The top shows foods that should be eaten the **least**.

every day

infrequently

5th Level: foods that should rarely be eaten, like sugar, honey, cakes and candy.

4th Level: foods that should be eaten in **small amounts**, like oils, butter and nuts. These foods contain a lot of lipids, especially those of animal origin.

3rd Level: foods that should be eaten **2–3 times a day**. This level is divided into two groups: dairy products (milk and cheese) and other proteins (red meat, fish, eggs and legumes, such as beans and lentils).

2nd Level: foods that should be eaten **3–5 times a day**. This level is divided into two groups: fruits and vegetables. These foods are rich in vitamins and minerals.

1st Level: foods that should be eaten **3–8 times a day**, like potatoes, pasta, rice, bread and corn. These foods are rich in carbohydrates.

The base of the pyramid shows two necessary components for a healthy life: water and physical activity. People your age should drink **4–6 glasses of water and exercise for at least half an hour daily.**

Word Focus

A **serving** or **portion** is the amount of food that should be eaten by a person at a meal and has the nutrients necessary for a healthy diet according to the food pyramid. The size of a portion can also depend on the type of food and the age and physical activity of the person.

The food pyramid gives **suggestions** about how to maintain a balanced and healthy diet. Think about your daily diet. Do you follow the recommended portions of the food pyramid? If you do not, you should start. You will be healthier!

Let's Check!

1. Go to **Cutout 6** on **page 171**. Match and glue the foods in the boxes according to the nutrients they contain. Then describe the function of each nutrient.

points
/ 8

carbohydrates	proteins	lipids	vitamins and minerals
Function:	Function:	Function:	Function:

2. Match each food with the correct level of the food pyramid.

points
/ 5

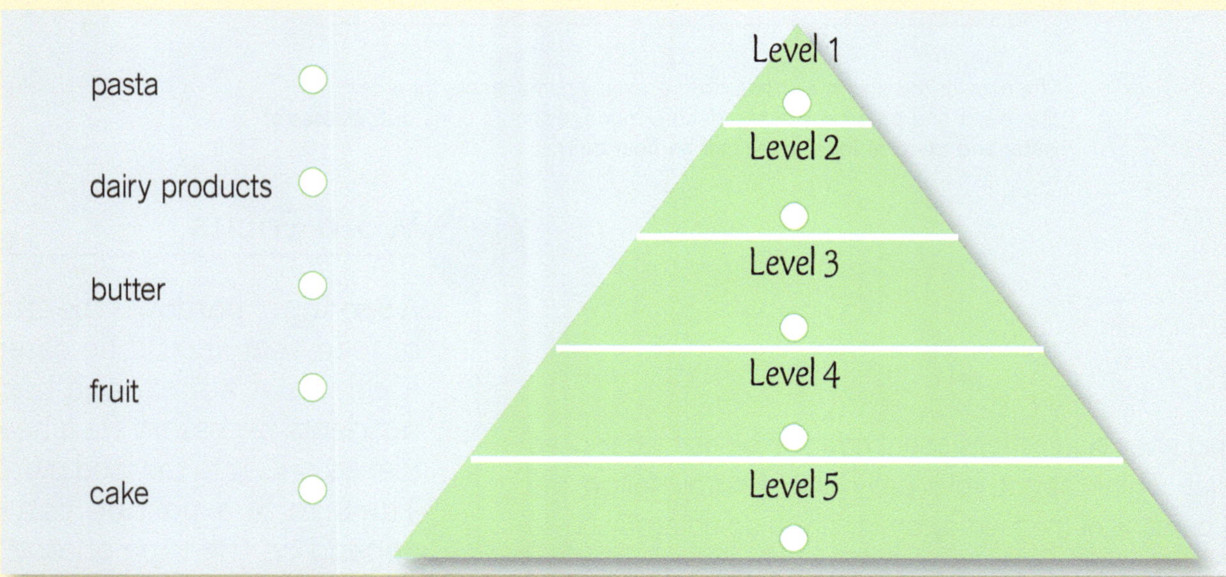

3. Use **Cutout 7** on **page 171** to complete the food pyramid on **Activity Card 2**. Decide which nutrient is most common in each level. Identify

points
/ 8

____

____

a. Give an example of a balanced diet. Explain

____

____

____

4. Go to **Cutout 8** on **page 173**. Use the foods to put together examples of a **healthy** and an **unhealthy meal**. Each lunch box should have the same amount of food. Explain your choices on the lines below.

points
/ 8

____

____

____

____

____

____

Microorganisms

Connecting

Health and Illnesses

Do you think you are healthy? This question might make you think about your diet and exercise routines or simply whether or not you have any health problems. These ideas are not wrong, but they are incomplete because they only take into account **physical** health. However, health also includes **mental** or **psychological** health—for example, when you are unmotivated, you have less interest in doing daily activities like studying or playing with friends, and this can affect your health.

incorrect

Word Focus

Physical: of the body or tangible and concrete.
Mental: of the mind.
Social: of the people, places and things around you.

Your social surroundings also affect your health. A good quality of life, shelter, water and waste disposal are all necessary in order to be healthy. Being **healthy** includes your **physical**, **mental** and **social well-being**. In other words, what is needed is a **balance of the body**, **mind** and **surroundings**. What happens if something changes this balance?

protection from the weather

To be healthy means to have a balance between your body and your surroundings. When this balance is changed, you can become sick.

When we have the flu, we feel down. Sometimes we have a fever or a cold that affects our health. This means we feel sick or ill. **Illnesses** are defined as **changes that affect our organism's balance in a negative way**.

Illnesses or diseases can be transmitted in many ways: through a wound, contaminated water or food, the air or an animal or insect bite.

Staying Healthy

There are certain illnesses that we can avoid through vaccines, good hygiene, healthy eating and routine medical checkups.

inspections

Types of Illnesses

How many times have you been sick in your life? It is hard to count how many times you were sick or remember why because it is normal to get sick once in a while.

difficult

Illnesses can be classified in different ways, one being their origin or source:

growing old

Degenerative diseases are caused by the **deterioration** or aging of an organ. Alzheimer's disease is degenerative. It affects the brain by causing progressive memory loss.

Infectious diseases are caused by microorganisms. They act fast and are very **contagious**. The common flu is an example of an infectious disease.

Deficiency diseases are caused by the lack, or **deficiency**, of necessary nutrients. One example is anemia, which is caused by a lack of iron and vitamin D.

Parasitic diseases are caused by **parasites** that live inside or outside our bodies and have negative effects. For example, taeniasis is caused by a type of tapeworm that stays in the small intestine and affects the absorption of nutrients.

Word Focus

Microorganisms are the smallest living beings on earth. They are not visible to the **naked eye** but can be seen with a microscope.

Practicing

1. Classify each illness according to its origin. Identify

	Type of Disease
Rickets is characterized by soft bones because of a lack of vitamin D.	
A group of students has lice. These insects feed on blood, causing irritation and wounds on the scalp.	
Damien has a cold. He feels weak and sneezes often. His sister, who was taking care of him, woke up with similar symptoms.	
Tom's grandfather has Parkinson's disease. This disease causes degeneration of parts of the brain.	

skin of the head

Summarizing

Being ____________________ means having a balance between the body, the mind and surroundings.

______________________________ change the balance in your body and negatively affect it.

Connecting

Microorganisms: Bacteria, Fungi and Viruses

What is the smallest thing you can see? It could be the tip of your pencil or a grain of salt. However, there are some things we cannot see with the naked eye, such as microorganisms. These are very small and are only visible through a microscope.

extremity

Bacteria and **fungi** are the most studied microorganisms. Despite the fact that **viruses** are not considered to be alive, they are still considered microorganisms because of their small size. All three cause illnesses and diseases.

However, bacteria and fungi also benefit our body. For example, the **human microbiome** defends our body from harmful bacteria.

Bacteria

Bacteria are the smallest and the most abundant living organisms on the planet. Bacteria can be found everywhere: the air, the water, the ground, our bodies, close to volcanoes and even in places as cold as Antarctica. Bacteria are all unicellular, but there are many different types.

Type of Bacteria	Shape
Coccus 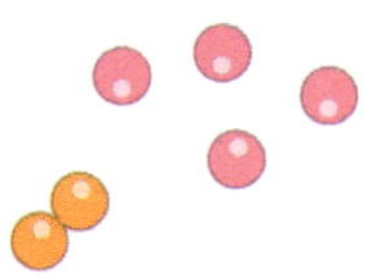	spherical
Bacillus 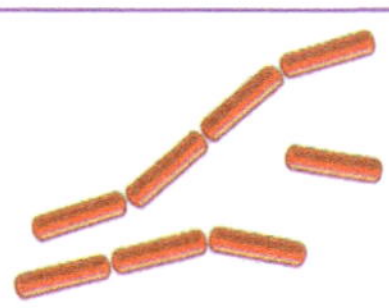	rod shaped (cylinder)
Spirochetes 	coiled (spiral shaped)
Vibrio 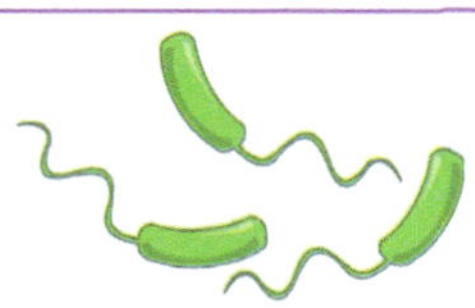	comma shaped

Word Focus

The **human microbiome** refers to the microorganisms that live on our skin and in our bodies. They protect us from **foreign** microorganisms.

The **microscope** is an optical science instrument that magnifies small objects using lenses.

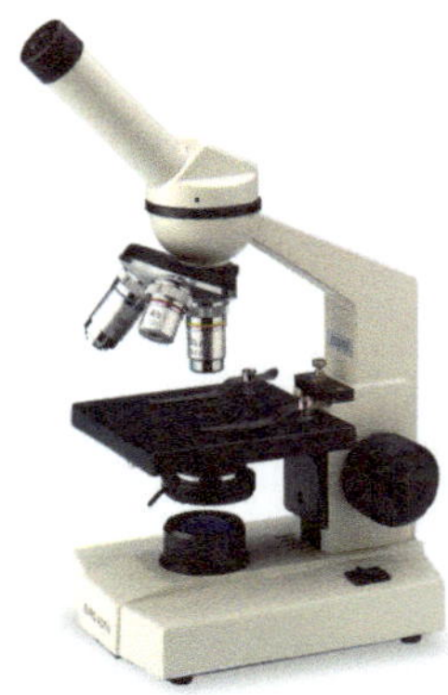

Fun Fact!

Today, scientists disagree on whether or not a virus is alive. Until they can agree, viruses are not considered living things.

Fungi

humid

Fungi are organisms that grow in damp areas. They can be **unicellular** or **multicellular**. Yeast is an example of a unicellular fungus, and mushrooms are multicellular.

a fungus used to make bread

Fungi are similar to plants because they grow from soil and do not move. However, they do not make their own food. Fungi absorb nutrients from **decomposing** plants and animals.

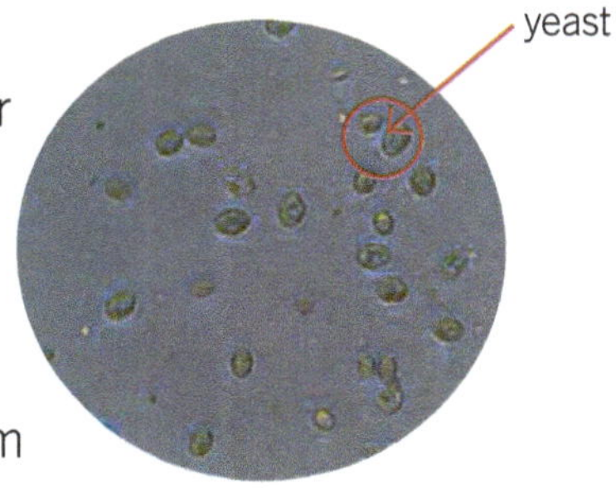

Yeast is a microscopic, unicellular fungus that is used, amongst other things, to make bread.

Viruses

Viruses have such unique characteristics that it is still debated whether they are alive or not. One characteristic is that they depend on another organism to survive. Viruses **infect** cells and multiply, producing more viruses that infect other cells.

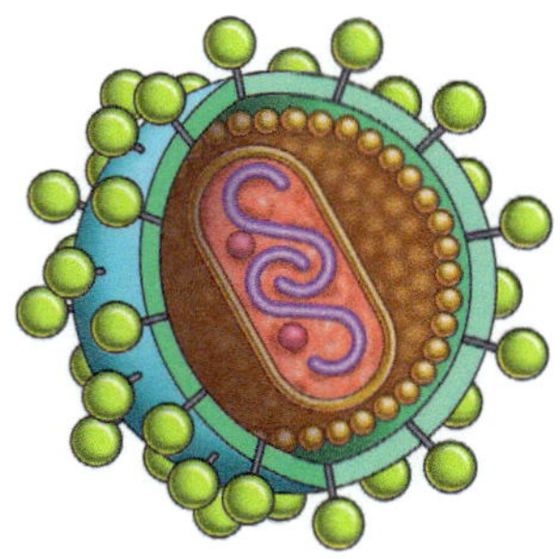

Representation of the AIDS virus.

Practicing

1. Identify which microorganism matches each description. Recognize

"I do not know if I am a living organism because I need another organism to live."	
"I am unicellular and come in different shapes. I am sometimes with others like me. You can also find me in many places, including in many living beings."	
"I am usually confused with a plant, but I absorb my nutrients from other organisms. I grow in damp environments and am unicellular or multicellular."	

Summarizing

The most studied microorganisms are ______________ and ____________. ______________ are unicellular and can be grouped according to their shape. Fungi are ______________ or ______________ organisms that absorb nutrients. It is uncertain whether ______________ are microorganisms because it is still debated whether or not they are alive.

Connecting

Harmful Microorganisms

Infectious diseases are responsible for more than **thirteen million deaths** a year. What do you think is the cause of these deaths? Microorganisms are the cause. Despite their size, microorganisms are capable of harming organisms and are sometimes fatal.

Fun Fact!

The writer Edgar Allen Poe often wrote about tuberculosis in his stories. His most famous story about this illness is "The Masque of the Red Death."

Harmful Bacteria

Some illnesses caused by bacteria are:

Cholera is caused by consuming food contaminated with Vibrio cholerae bacteria. The bacteria stays in the large intestine and causes diarrhea and nausea that lead to dehydration. If it is not treated, it can be fatal.

Typhoid Fever is primarily caused by consuming food—like eggs, cheese or vegetables—that are contaminated with Salmonella typhi bacteria. It produces abdominal pain, fever and diarrhea.

Tuberculosis is caused by Mycobacterium tuberculosis bacteria. It is an airborne disease affecting the lungs. It can cause a cough, fever, shivering and weight loss.

uncontrollable trembling

Cholera is a highly contagious illness caused by ingesting food or water contaminated by bacteria.

Harmful Fungi

These organisms cause mycosis or fungal infections characterized by irritation, redness and itchiness of the skin. An example is:

need to scratch

Ringworm is a fungus that affects the skin. Ringworm is caused by prolonged humidity of the skin, a wound or lack of hygiene. The most common ringworm is athlete's foot. It causes a burning sensation and a bad smell on the bottom of the foot and in the space between toes.

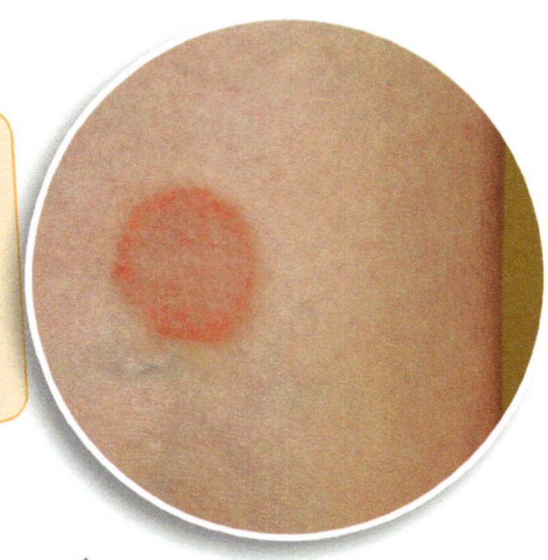

Ringworm can affect different parts of the skin, such as the arms.

Harmful Effects of Viruses

Some examples of illnesses caused by viruses are:

Chicken pox is very common in young children. It is characterized by red, itchy bumps all over the body. Although it is not a very dangerous illness in children, it is very contagious, and it can be passed to another person two days before the symptoms appear.

AIDS is one of the most serious diseases and is responsible for the deaths of more than three million people a year. AIDS is caused by HIV (Human Immunodeficiency Virus), which attacks the cells that protect the body. This weakens the person's immunity to other diseases. Treatment exists but only to prolong life because a cure for AIDS has not yet been found.

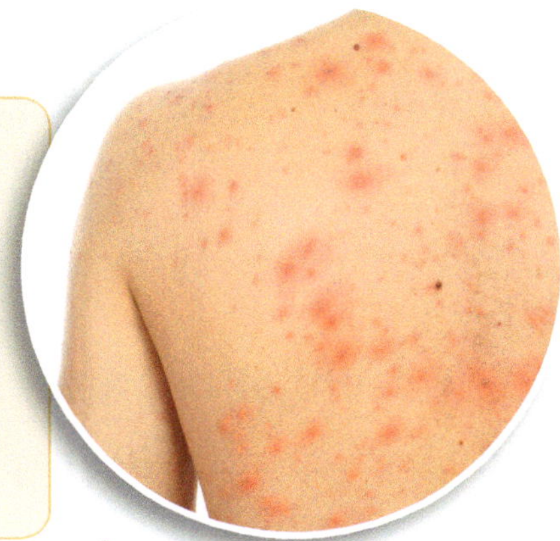

Chicken pox is characterized by the appearance of red bumps all over the body.

bumps → protuberances

Practicing

1. Complete the table with the missing information. Identify

Type of Microorganism	Illness / Disease	Effects
	typhoid fever	
fungus		Burning feeling on feet and bad odor.
	cholera	
	AIDS	
		Red spots on the skin.

odor → smell

2. Ian has chicken pox. His doctor recommended he stay home and prohibited his classmates from visiting him. Why did the doctor make these recommendations? Explain. Apply

____

____

Word Focus

Affect means to influence something. **Effect** is the result or outcome of a situation.

Summarizing

Microorganisms responsible for illnesses are:

______________ and ______________. Although it is debated whether or not they are alive, ______________ produce illnesses and therefore are included in this group, too.

Connecting

Beneficial Effects of Microorganisms

Microorganisms have many negative effects on our health, but they can also be beneficial. Our bodies are home to many beneficial bacteria. Throughout history, humans have learned to use these microorganisms in food, to improve health and in other areas.

Did You Know...?

Yogurt has probiotic bacteria that help and protect your own intestinal flora.

Beneficial Effects of Bacteria

As mentioned, **beneficial bacteria** live on our skin and inside our bodies.

An example is the **human microbiome**, which is found on the skin in the nose, stomach and intestines. It stops harmful microorganisms from invading the body and causing illnesses.

Some **bacteria** that reside in our large intestine help with the production of **vitamin K**. Vitamin K is crucial for our body since it allows blood to coagulate.

Bacteria are also used by human beings to create medicine, like insulin. **Insulin** is naturally made by the pancreas and works to regulate sugar absorption. There are some people, like diabetics, who have problems producing insulin. Some diabetics have to inject insulin because their bodies do not produce enough.

Bacteria also help with the **production** of foods like cheese and yogurt. The production of yogurt involves at least two types of bacteria. They change the composition of milk and give yogurt its consistency and flavor.

Lactobacillus bacteria present in yogurt.

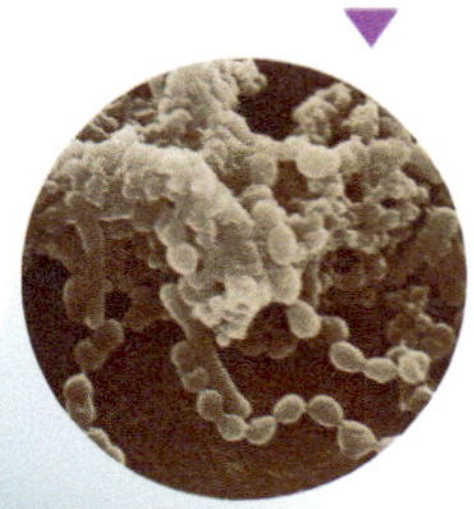

Yogurt is made with beneficial bacteria.

Beneficial Effects of Fungi

Fungi, unicellular fungi in particular, are also used to **help people and improve health.**

perceived

About a century ago, Alexander Fleming, an important Scottish scientist, studied bacteria. His samples became contaminated by **fungi**. He observed the bacteria and realized that although they had died, the fungi remained alive. From this accidental experiment, he deduced that fungi are able to kill bacteria, and he discovered **penicillin**, the first **antibiotic**. An **antibiotic** is a substance that can kill bacteria, and it is created by a microorganism. Antibiotics are very efficient in treating bacterial illnesses.

Fungi are also used in some foods. A common example is the yeast used to make bread rise. The microorganisms use the sugar in the bread and produce carbon dioxide. The carbon dioxide then makes the bread rise.

go up

Tip

One fungus, two fungi
One bacterium, two bacteria
One virus, two viruses

Practicing

1. Mark the images that show the **positive effects** of microorganisms in humans. Identify

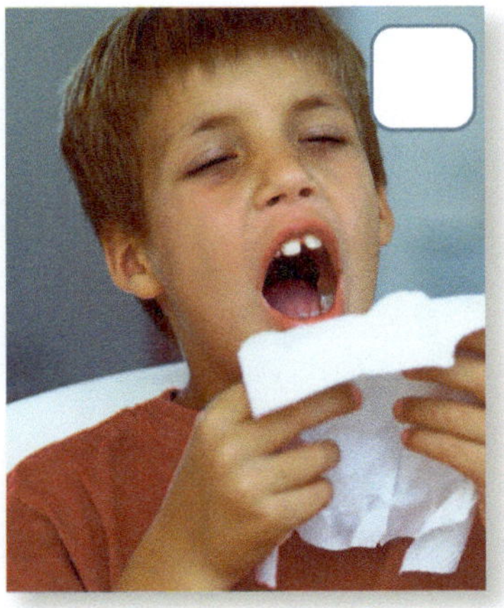

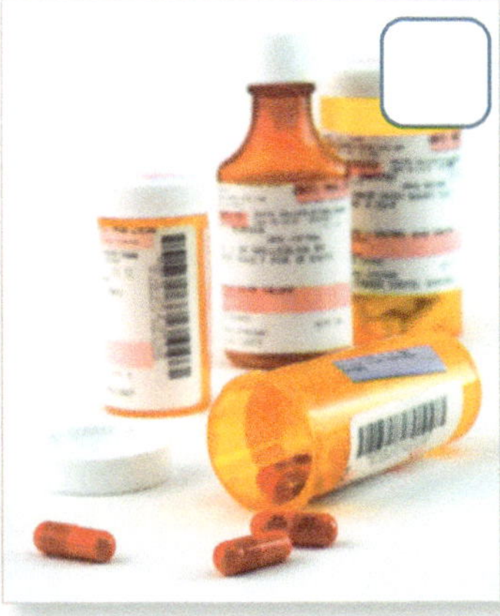

Summarizing

Some microorganisms, like ____________________ and ____________________, have positive effects on the human body.

Connecting

Taking Care of Your Body

To stay healthy and avoid getting sick, it is necessary to have good **hygiene**.

Healthy daily habits include rest, exercise, sleep and eating well. If we want to stay healthy and avoid infectious diseases, good hygiene should also be a daily habit. Having good hygiene means you clean and take care of your body. Some habits you should have are:

rest → repose

Did You Know...?

When you shower, the number of bacteria on your body decreases from approximately 15,000 to 6,000.

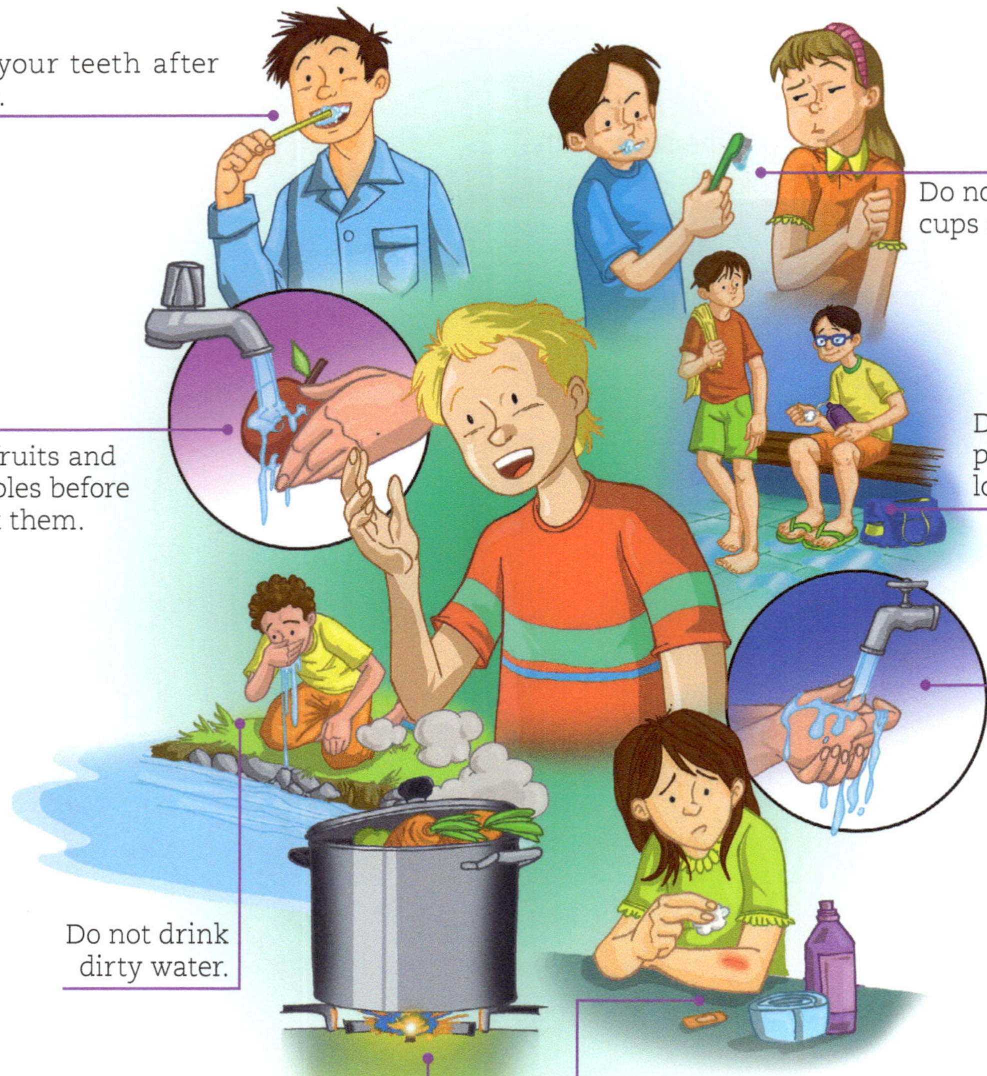

By following these rules, you can avoid infectious diseases. What else can you do to avoid getting sick?

Quiz Yourself

1. Read the sentences. Mark the microorganism that matches each description.

Bacteria	Fungi	Viruses	
☐	☐	☐	They exist in different shapes: spherical, rod shaped and coiled.
☐	☐	☐	They absorb other organisms for nutrients.
☐	☐	☐	They need another organism to live.
☐	☐	☐	They are all unicellular and can be classified by their form.
☐	☐	☐	They can be unicellular, like yeast, or multicellular, like fungus.
☐	☐	☐	It is still unclear whether or not they are alive.

2. Form groups of three people. Find **Activity Card 3** and go to **Cutout 9** on **page 175**. Test your knowledge of harmful and beneficial microorganisms.

3. Chris and his brother Nicholas are playing in their yard. When they decide to eat, Nicholas takes an apple out of the fruit basket and eats it. Chris washes his hands and the apple before eating it.

a. Which brother has a greater chance of getting sick? Explain your answer.

____

____

4. What habits can prevent you from getting sick?

____

____

____

Scientific Skill: Experiment

Where Fungi Grow

Basic Framework

Fungi grow in **humid** places—for example, in the shade of trees in parks and gardens. These are places where sunlight cannot reach. They prefer warm, wet places that provide the necessary nutrients, and even grow in decomposing food.

Observation

Marcus looked at the oranges on the ground in his backyard. After it rained, fungi started to grow on their peel. The oranges his mom picked before it rained did not have any fungi.

Why did the oranges left outside grow fungi?

____

____

Before the rain.

After the rain.

Research Question

How does humidity affect the growth of fungi?

Hypothesis

Mark the hypothesis you think is correct.

☐ Humidity **helps** fungi grow.

☐ Humidity **does not** help fungi grow.

Word Focus

Humidity is the amount of moisture in the air.

Predictions

How will humidity affect the growth of fungi on food?

____

____

____

A science experiment is a scientific method used to verify a hypothesis. To conduct a successful experiment, it is important to think about the **variables**, **the supplies** and the **process**. Now we will do a science experiment to answer this question: does humidity help fungi grow on food?

Experimental Procedure

Which Variables Can You Control?

In an experiment, you need to determine what **factors** or **variables** might affect the results. In this case, there are two variables: humidity is the **independent variable**, and growth of fungi is the **dependent variable**. Which of the variables do you think affects the experiment?

☐ humidity ☐ fungi growth

In an experiment, one variable can be manipulated to observe its effects. This is called the independent variable. The dependent variable changes as a result of the manipulation of the independent variable. The **control** variables are not manipulated or changed in anyway.

What Supplies Do You Need?

For any experiment, you need supplies to create the correct **conditions** to observe an event. In this experiment, you want to see if fungi will grow on food. Here is a list of possible supplies.

Mark the supplies you think are **necessary**:

☐ measuring tape ☐ piece of wood ☐ water ☐ lightbulb ☐ bread

☐ bleach ☐ storage bag ☐ jar ☐ tongs

One or Two Storage Bags?

You need two storage bags to do this experiment. In the first bag, you will **manipulate** the independent variable (the humidity). In the second, the independent variable will not change. The second bag is called the **control group**. A control group is necessary to see if the manipulation of the independent variable really is what caused the results, and not some indeterminate factor.

Science Lab

What Process Do You Follow?

Once you have your supplies, you need to determine the **experimental procedure** you will use in your experiment. The procedure is a **step**-by-step description of how to conduct the experiment with the supplies. Complete the procedure:

Having a procedure is fundamental to a successful experiment. Remember to follow each step and instruction carefully.

1. Use a __marker__ to label the __storage bags__ 1 and 2.
2. Take a piece of ________ and use the __tongs__ to dip it in the __________ in the __measuring cup__. Then put the __________ in __storage bag 1__ and close it immediately.
3. Next, use dry __tongs__ to put another piece of ________ directly into __storage bag 2__, and close it immediately.
4. Put both __storage bags__ in a dark place at room temperature for six days.
5. Write down your observations in **Results.**

Results

Mark your answers on the table and describe your observations.

Day	Storage Bag 1		Storage Bag 2		Observations
	Are there any changes to the bread?		Are there any changes to the bread?		
1	yes	no	yes	no	
2	yes	no	yes	no	
3	yes	no	yes	no	
4	yes	no	yes	no	
5	yes	no	yes	no	
6	yes	no	yes	no	

Interpreting and Analyzing the Results

1. What happened to the bread in **storage bag 1** over six days?

___

2. What happened to the bread in **storage bag 2** over six days?

___

3. Did **storage bag 2** work as the control group for the experiment? Explain.

___

___

Conclusions

1. Was your hypothesis **verified**? Explain.

___

___

2. What factor made the fungi grow on the bread? Explain.

___

___

3. What other factor could have affected the growth of fungi?

___

4. In the experiment, if the bread were replaced with a rock, would the **same results** occur? Explain.

___

___

5. How can you **relate** this experiment to fungi that form on the body? Explain.

___

___

What Did You Learn?

1. Write the name and principal nutrient of each food on the plate.

points
/ 5

a. What nutrients are not present in high quantities on the plate?

____

b. Why do you think these nutrients were not present on the plate?

____

2. Make sentences by matching each food with its function.

points
/ 4

A	B
Pasta	builds different structures in the body.
Meat	gives immediate energy.
Lettuce	becomes fat to be used as energy later.
Oil	regulates different functions within the body.

3. A scientist observed some samples with his microscope. Then he wrote his observations in the following table.

points ___ / 9

a. Go to **Cutout 10** on **page 177**. Glue the microorganisms in the correct boxes.

b. Write the positive and negative effects each microorganism has on the human body.

Sample	1	2	3
Where is it from?	Near a volcano.	From a domestic animal.	Under a tree.
Observation	A long cell that looks like a pole.	Cannot survive without the animal.	Absorbs food to grow.
Image			
Positive Effects			
Negative Effects			

Unit 3

Electricity

Key Words

transform

efficient

predict

device

safety

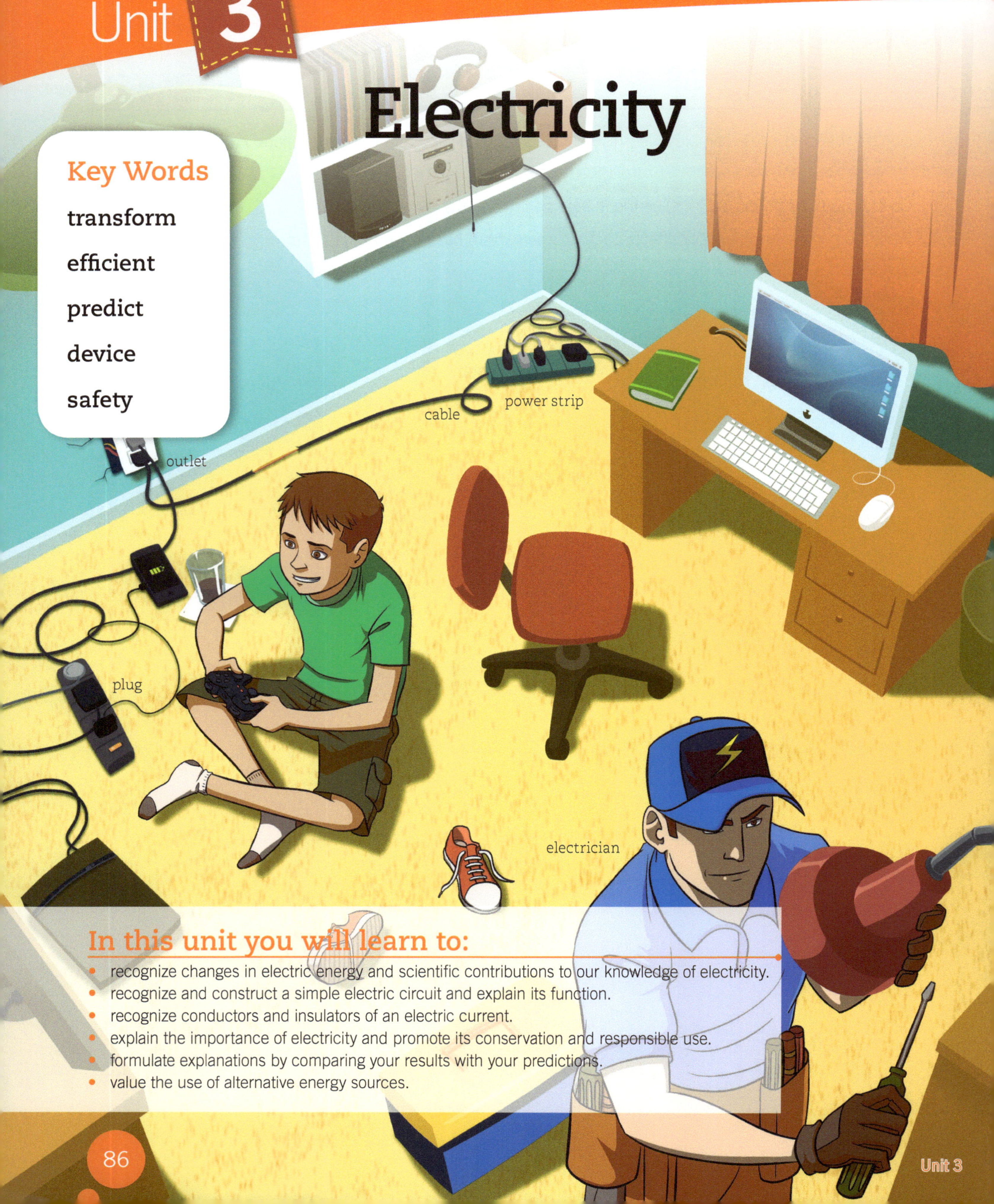

In this unit you will learn to:

- recognize changes in electric energy and scientific contributions to our knowledge of electricity.
- recognize and construct a simple electric circuit and explain its function.
- recognize conductors and insulators of an electric current.
- explain the importance of electricity and promote its conservation and responsible use.
- formulate explanations by comparing your results with your predictions.
- value the use of alternative energy sources.

What Do You Know?

Initial Evaluation

1. Mark all the objects that need electricity with a ✔.

2. Mark dangerous situations with an ✖.

Scientific Skill: Compare predictions with results

3. Look at the photograph and answer the questions.

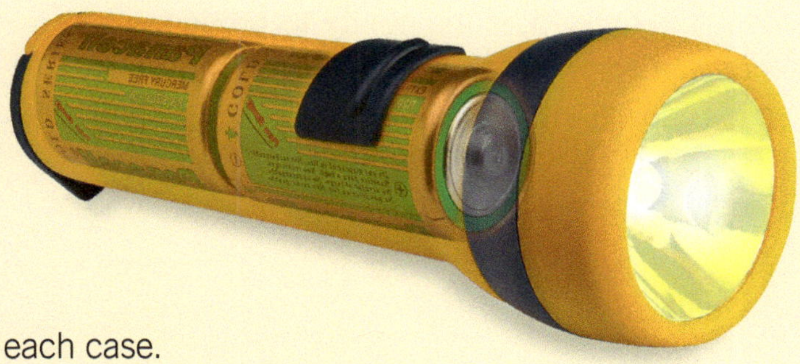

a. Make a prediction for each case.

Case 1: Would the flashlight turn on if it had only one battery?

____

Case 2: Would the flashlight turn on if one of the batteries were placed backward? → in the wrong direction

____

Case 3: Would the flashlight turn on if there were a piece of copper between the batteries? → a red-brown metal

____

b. Collect a flashlight, two batteries and a piece of copper. Test each of the cases above. Record your results in the table.

	Case 1	Case 2	Case 3
Does the flashlight turn on?			

c. Compare your results with your predictions. Are they the same? Explain why or why not.

____

____

____

Section 1

Electric Energy

Connecting

Energy in Our Surroundings

Do you need energy to open and close your eyes? Yes, you do! You even need energy to sleep. All living things need energy to complete their vital functions. This energy comes from nutrients in food. Energy is also needed for a TV to turn on or a car to start.

Energy can be found in many places. It is defined as the **ability to produce changes in the properties or movements of a body or an object**—for example, it is used when you go from walking to running or turn on a fan.

fan → ventilator

hiker → walker

Read about the different forms of energy in the chart below.

Form of Energy		Example
Gravitational potential	Found in objects or people when they are at a certain height.	A hiker on a mountain or a glass on a table.
Chemical	Contained in chemical substances.	Food, coal, wood or batteries.
Kinetic	Found in bodies or objects in motion.	A car driving on the road.
Wind	Generated by the wind.	A flag moving in the wind.
Electric	Produces the movement of electric charge through a conductor.	A television, computer or microwave.
Thermal	Produced by heat.	A stove, a heater or hot water.
Hydraulic	Generated by the movement of water.	Dams and reservoirs.
Light	Emitted by objects in the form of light.	A lightbulb or the sun.
Sound	Transports sound.	A guitar.

Renewable Energy Sources

Where does the electricity come from to turn on the TV? Electricity powers all the electric devices in our homes, like our televisions, stereos and video game consoles. A lot of electricity comes from nonrenewable sources, such as petroleum, coal and natural gas. However, it is now possible to generate electricity from various renewable sources, like the wind, ocean or sun. Electric energy is produced by electricity generators. The principal generators of renewable energy are:

Fun Fact!

China is home to the largest wind farms in the world.

Principal Renewable Energy Generators

Hydroelectric dams use **gravitational potential** energy. Water is contained in a large **reservoir** at high altitude. When it falls, it turns giant wheels that generate electric energy.

reservoir: man-made lake that stores water

Wind farms use the **kinetic** energy of the wind to move the blades of wind turbines and generate electric energy.

Geothermal energy plants use the heat from the earth's core to generate electric energy.

core: center

Solar energy plants use the **radiant** energy of the sun. Chemical reactions in solar panels turn this natural energy into electric energy.

radiant: relating to rays or waves

Education through Values

Our population has grown and technology has advanced in recent years, increasing the need for electricity. It is now necessary to find alternative energy sources that do not harm the environment, like solar and wind power.

Changes in Electric Energy

What happens when we use electric energy? Once the energy reaches our houses, it is used to power electric devices. These devices **change** the electric energy into a different form of energy. Read the examples below:

When electric energy makes a lamp work, it turns on a lightbulb, which emits energy in the form of light and heat. This means electric energy is transformed into light and thermal energy.	electric energy →  → light and thermal energy
A stereo uses electric energy to play music. It transforms electric energy into sound energy.	electric energy →  → sound energy
An electric fan uses energy to turn its blades and make wind. This process transforms electric energy into kinetic and wind energy.	electric energy →  → kinetic and wind energy

Practicing

1. Complete the sentences with the words. Identify

light and thermal energy | wind energy | hydroelectric dams | the sun

a. ______________________ produce energy from falling water.

b. ______________________ is an alternative energy source.

c. Solar power plants use the energy of ______________________.

d. The electric energy that turns on a lamp transforms into ______________________.

2. Write the change in energy related to each device. Recognize

Original Energy Source	Device	Energy Change
electric energy	electric motor	
	electric stove	
	computer screen	
	toaster	

Summarizing

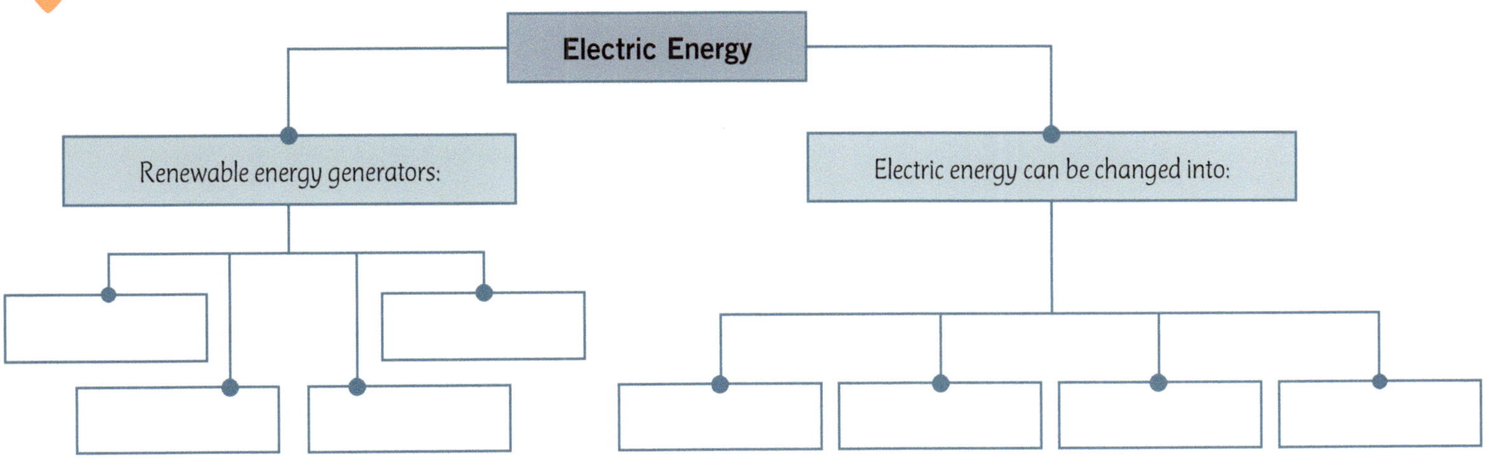

Connecting

Electricity: The Important Scientists

Our current knowledge of the properties of electric energy is due to the contributions of many scientists who investigated electricity over the centuries. Read about their contributions below:

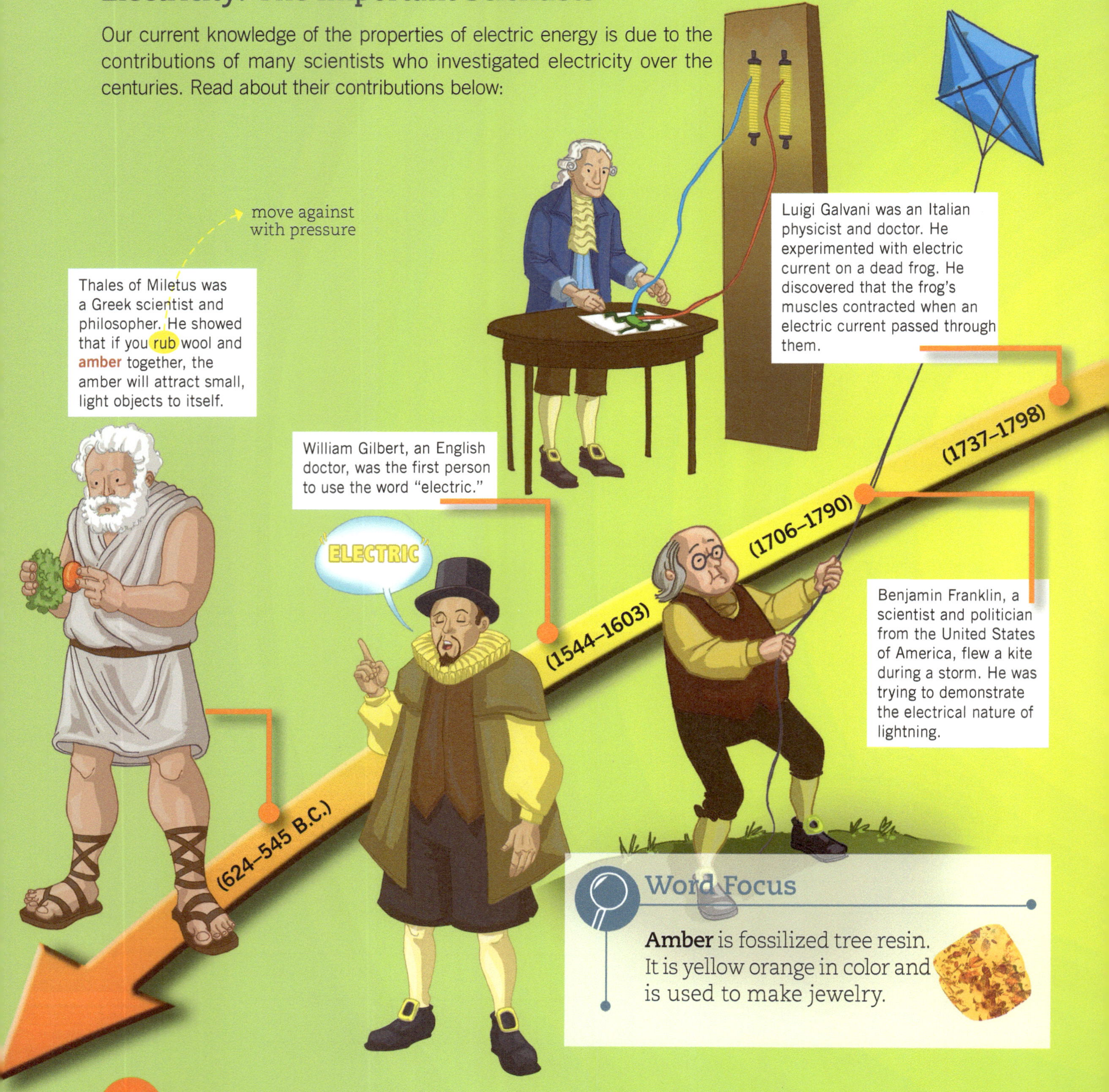

rub: move against with pressure

Thales of Miletus was a Greek scientist and philosopher. He showed that if you rub wool and **amber** together, the amber will attract small, light objects to itself.

William Gilbert, an English doctor, was the first person to use the word "electric."

Luigi Galvani was an Italian physicist and doctor. He experimented with electric current on a dead frog. He discovered that the frog's muscles contracted when an electric current passed through them.

Benjamin Franklin, a scientist and politician from the United States of America, flew a kite during a storm. He was trying to demonstrate the electrical nature of lightning.

Word Focus

Amber is fossilized tree resin. It is yellow orange in color and is used to make jewelry.

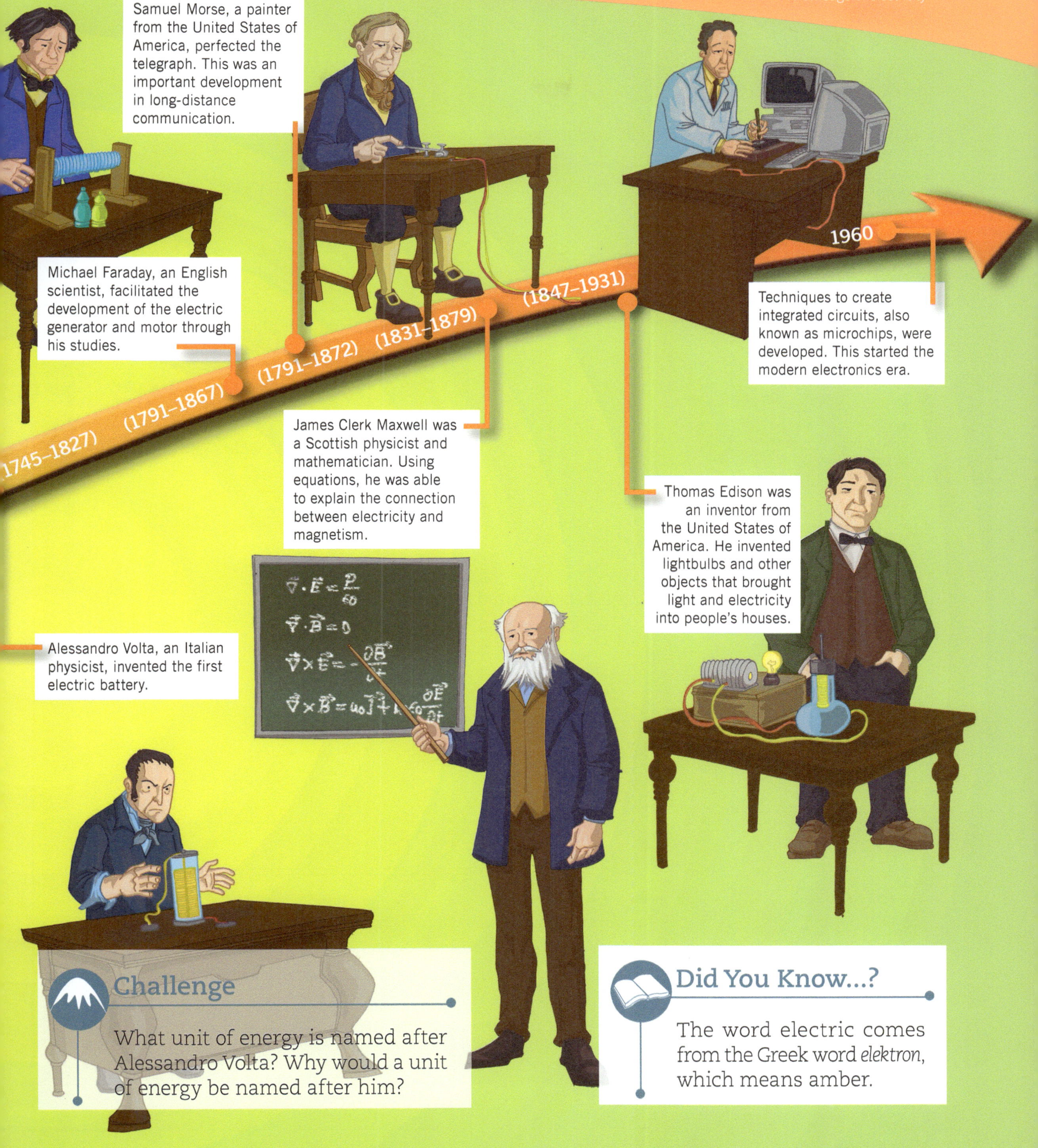

Alessandro Volta, an Italian physicist, invented the first electric battery.

Michael Faraday, an English scientist, facilitated the development of the electric generator and motor through his studies.

Samuel Morse, a painter from the United States of America, perfected the telegraph. This was an important development in long-distance communication.

James Clerk Maxwell was a Scottish physicist and mathematician. Using equations, he was able to explain the connection between electricity and magnetism.

Thomas Edison was an inventor from the United States of America. He invented lightbulbs and other objects that brought light and electricity into people's houses.

Techniques to create integrated circuits, also known as microchips, were developed. This started the modern electronics era.

Challenge

What unit of energy is named after Alessandro Volta? Why would a unit of energy be named after him?

Did You Know...?

The word electric comes from the Greek word *elektron*, which means amber.

Practicing

1. Match each scientist with his scientific contribution. Associate

James Clerk Maxwell ◯	◯ Described the connection between electricity and magnetism.
Michael Faraday ◯	◯ Demonstrated lightning is a form of electricity.
Thales of Miletus ◯	◯ Observed that amber attracts objects when rubbed.
Alessandro Volta ◯	◯ Created the first electric battery.
Benjamin Franklin ◯	◯ Developed the first electric generator and motor.
Thomas Edison ◯	◯ Invented lightbulbs.

2. How do the discoveries of these scientists help modern-day scientists study electricity? Explain. Apply

____

____

Summarizing

Scientific Contributions	

Quiz Yourself

1. Name the different types of energy studied in Section 1.

- ______________ • ______________ • ______________
- ______________ • ______________ • ______________
- ______________ • ______________ • ______________

2. Match each energy generator **A** with its description **B**.

Column A	Column B
wind farm	Uses the heat that is generated and stored in the earth.
geothermal power plant	Uses the gravitational potential energy of water in a reservoir.
hydroelectric dam	Uses heat and light energy from the sun.
solar energy plant	Uses kinetic energy from the wind.

3. Look at the following images of electric devices. Remember that they all transform electric energy into a different type of energy. Write the form of energy that they produce below each image.

iron

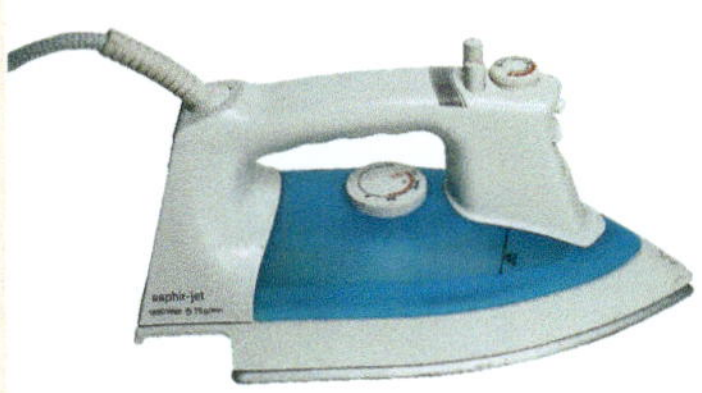

TV

hair dryer

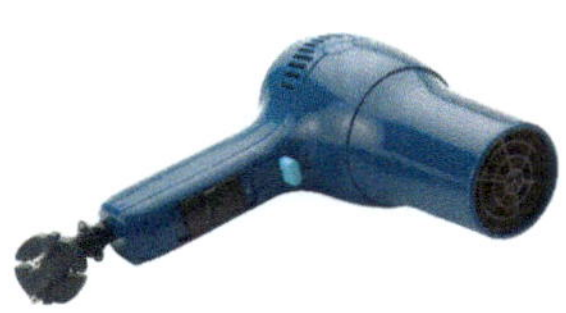

blender

4. Give three examples of scientific contributions to the study of electricity.

- ______________________________
- ______________________________
- ______________________________

Section

2 Electric Circuits

Connecting

Electric Current

Look at the following images.

computer

refrigerator

toaster

microwave

Did You Know...?

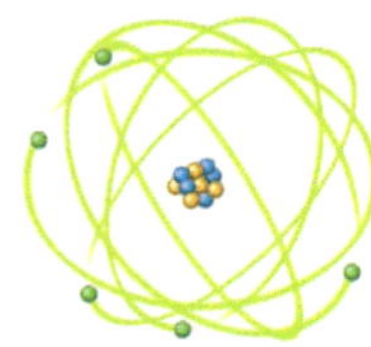

All physical things consist of small particles called atoms. Atoms consist of smaller units called protons, electrons and neutrons. Protons have a positive charge, electrons have a negative charge, and neutrons have no charge. **Nuclear** energy comes from splitting the nucleus, or center, of an atom.

breaking into parts

What do these devices have in common? They all need an electric current to work, but what is an electric current? **An electric current is the movement of electric charges inside a material**. The electric charges that move through devices are negative charges. The charges transport energy, which is transformed by each device into another type of energy.

Word Focus

Electric charge is an electrical property of particles. The charge can be positive or negative. Positive and negative usually mean good and bad, but in the study of electricity, they are simply opposites.

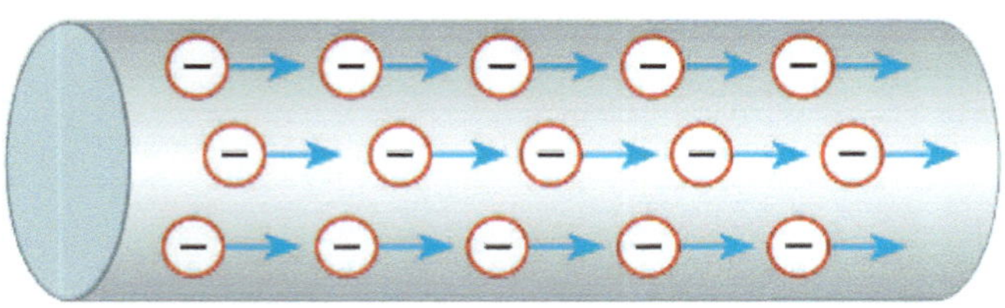

The negative electric charges move in the same direction in an orderly manner.

Different Types of Electric Currents

Electric currents can be classified into two groups:

Direct current: In this type of current, the electric charges travel in the same direction, and the current always maintains its **polarity**. Batteries generate a direct current.

Alternating current: This type of current continually changes direction. The electric charges do not always circle in the same direction, so the current's polarity varies. The electricity in our homes is alternating current.

Word Focus

Polarity is a characteristic that differentiates the two sides of a direct current battery. Each side is called a pole, which can be positive or negative.

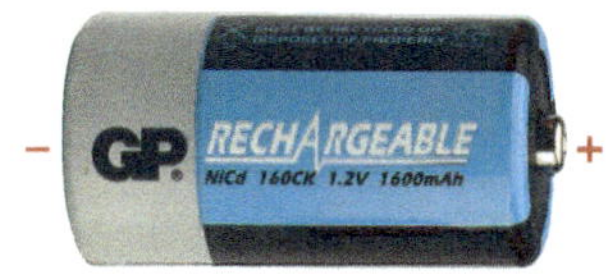

Practicing

1. What is an electric current? Explain

____

____

Did You Know...?

In most countries, the alternating current changes its polarity 50 times per second.

2. Complete the table. Describe

	Direct Current	Alternating Current
Description		
Example		

Summarizing

Electric Current

- direct current
  - example: ____________
- ____________
  - example: The current that we use in our houses.

Connecting

Electric Circuits

How can a television remain **off** even when it is plugged in? That is the function of the **electric circuits** inside the TV. An electric circuit is a **system in which an electric current circulates**. This circuit **transforms electric energy into a different form of energy**. A simple electric circuit has these basic elements:

connected by a plug

Word Focus

A conductor is any material that allows electric charges to move freely within it.

1. **Electric cables** are cords with small wires inside them. The wires are **conductors**. The electric current circulates within these wires.
2. A **generator** is an energy source that produces an electric current. Each side of the generator is called a pole, and one pole is negative and the other positive. A battery is a type of generator.
3. **Receptors** change the electric energy into another type of energy. Lightbulbs are receptors because they change the electric energy to light and thermal energy. Another example is the electric motor, which changes electric energy into kinetic energy.
4. A **switch** is used to open and close the circuit.

The elements of a circuit can be combined in different ways. However, they should be **closed** so that the current can circulate.

Circuit Symbology

Electric circuits can be represented by symbols. The most commonly used are:

Part	Electric cable or wire	Generator	Switch	Receptor
Symbol				

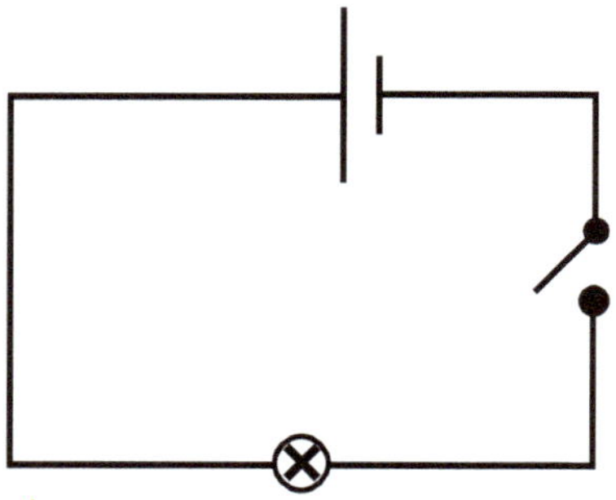

This is a symbolic representation of the circuit above.

Series Circuit

In a series circuit, the current **passes through each part of the circuit in the same direction**. The circuit has receptors connected by the same electric cable, so the same current passes through each of the receptors.

This type of circuit is not used very often because it can have problems. For example, if one receptor is damaged, the current cannot pass to the next receptor, and the circuit stops working. A flashlight is an example of a series circuit.

Did You Know...?

Christmas light cables used to be series circuits, so if one light burned out, they all turned off. Nowadays, Christmas lights use a parallel circuit, so when one burns out, the others stay on.

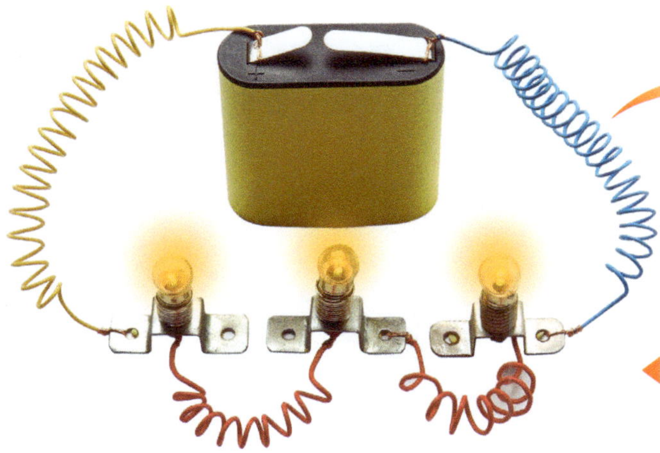

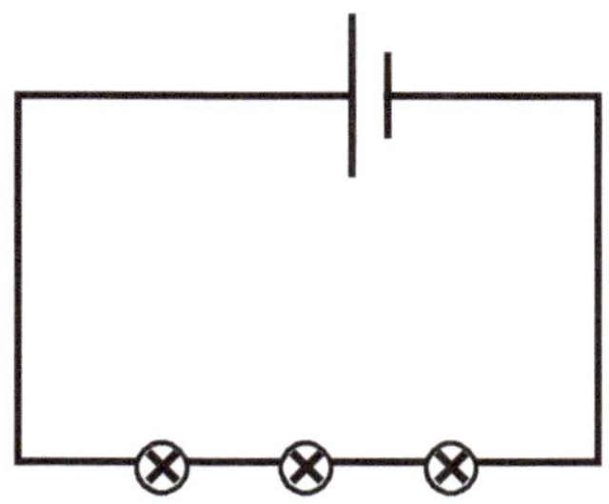

series circuit

Parallel Circuit

In a parallel circuit, **the current passes through electric cables that split and go in different directions**. The current that passes through each receptor is different.

This type of circuit is used often. It is useful because if one of the parts has a problem, the electric current still reaches the other parts and the circuit still functions. The electric **outlets** in our houses are parallel circuits.

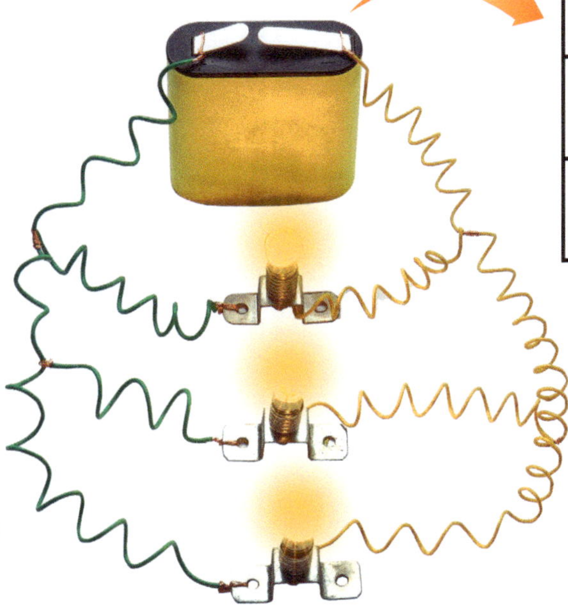

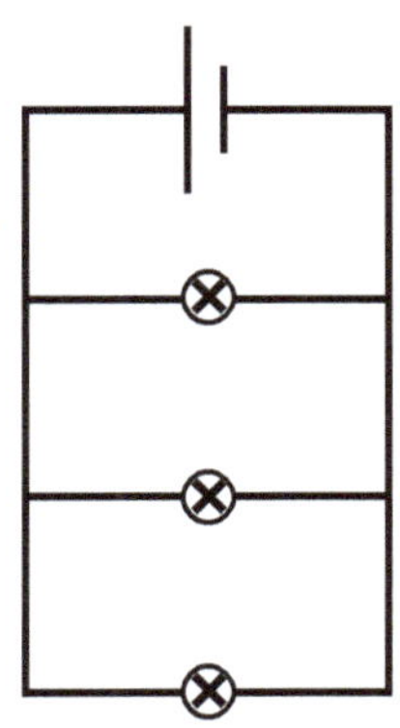

parallel circuit

Connecting

Electric Circuits in Our Homes

If one lightbulb in your house burns out, do all the others turn off, too? The answer is no because the network of circuits in your house is **parallel**. If one receptor stops working, the others continue to work. In every house, the electricity network consists of several electric circuits.

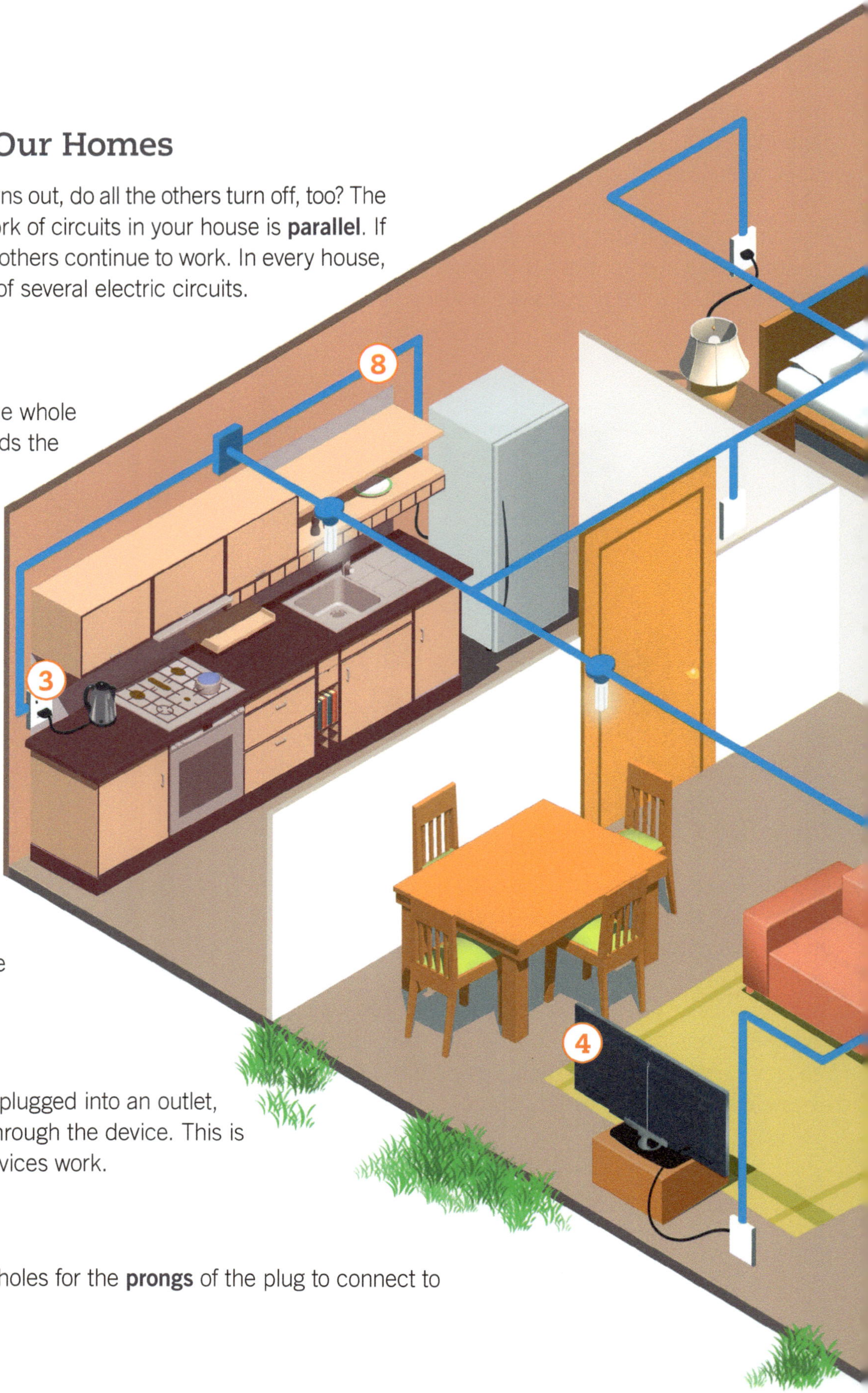

1. The **outlet box** connects the whole electricity network and sends the electric current to all the different circuits.

2. The **electricity meter** is located outside the house, or in large buildings there is usually a meter room. The meter measures how much energy is used in each home.

3. Many electric devices connect to the electricity network through **outlets**. An outlet connects a device to a circuit.

4. When an electric device is plugged into an outlet, current starts to circulate through the device. This is what makes our electric devices work.

5. Modern outlets have three holes for the **prongs** of the plug to connect to the current.

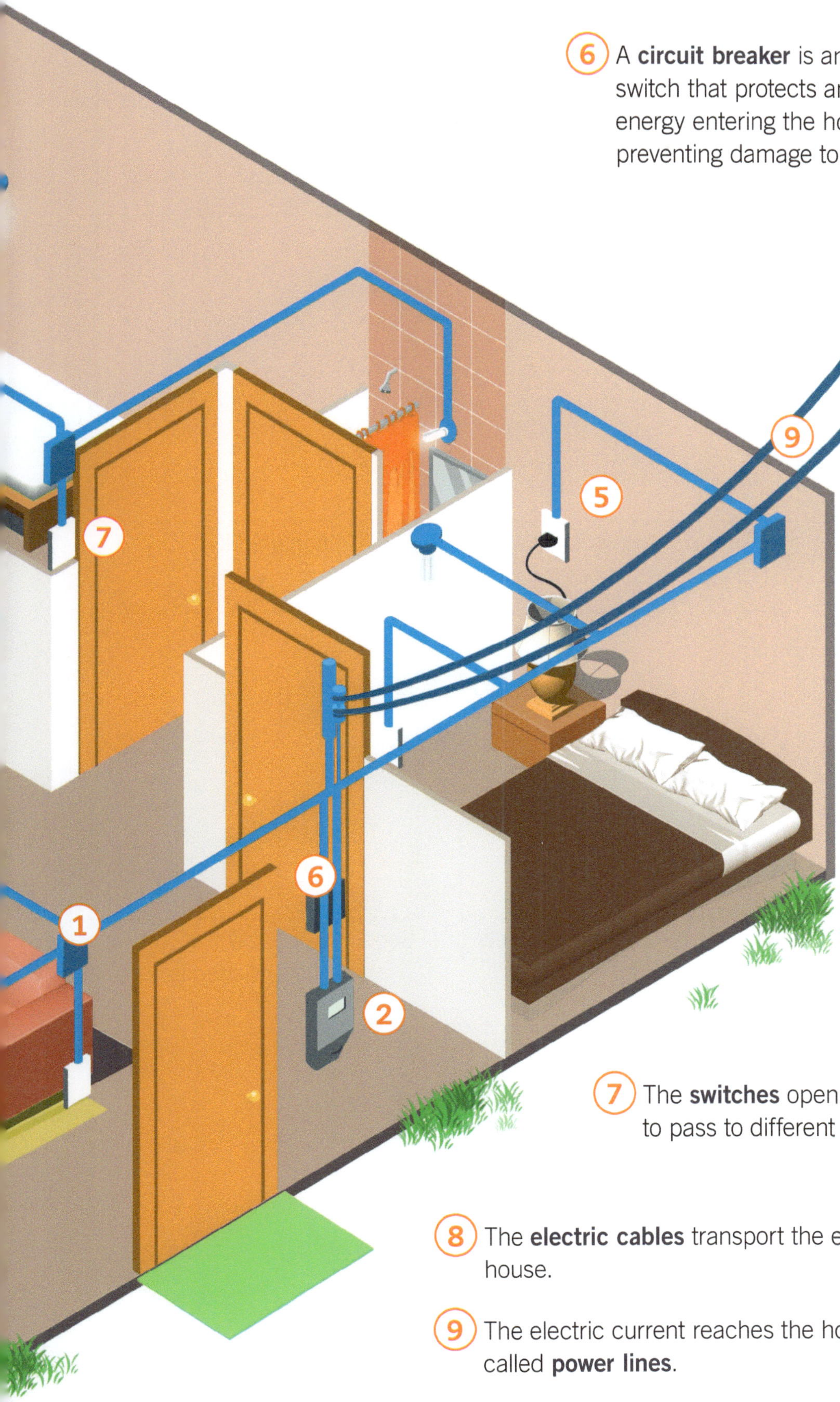

6 A **circuit breaker** is an automatically operated electrical switch that protects an electric circuit. It disconnects the energy entering the house when there is a short circuit, preventing damage to the whole electricity network.

malfunction or error

Did You Know...?

Electricity can be measured in **volts**, and each country uses a different voltage in their homes. Common voltages include 120 (Canada, USA), 127 (Mexico), 220 (much of Asia, South America and Africa) and 230 (much of Europe). Make sure to take an **adaptor** when you travel!

7 The **switches** open or close to allow current to pass to different parts of the house.

8 The **electric cables** transport the energy throughout the house.

9 The electric current reaches the house through cables called **power lines**.

Practicing

1. Go to **Cutout 11** on **page 179**. Glue each component of the home electricity network in the correct box. Identify

Measures the use of electricity.	Opens or closes to allow current to pass.	Transports electricity.
Where you plug in an electric device.	Electrical switch that protects against short circuits.	Sends electric current to all the different circuits.

Summarizing

Home Electricity Network

components:

outlets				

Quiz Yourself

1. Look at the circuit and answer the questions:

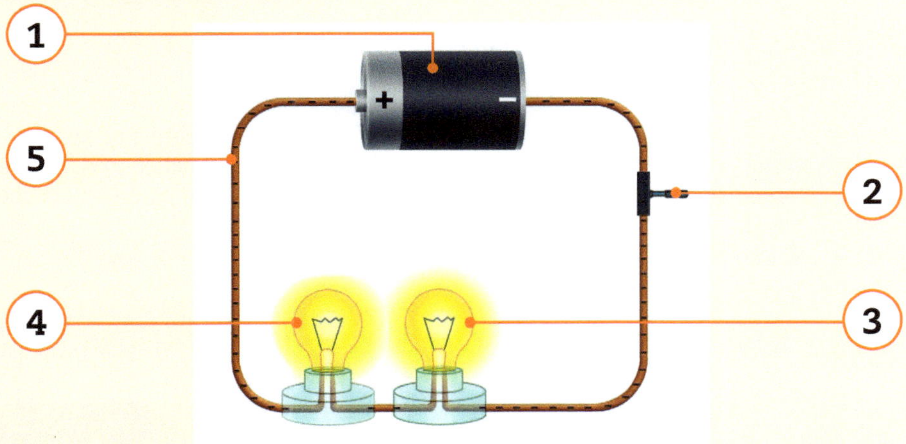

a. Write the name of each component.

1: ______________________________

2: ______________________________

3: ______________________________

4: ______________________________

5: ______________________________

b. Explain how this type of circuit functions.

____

____

c. What would happen if one of the lightbulbs burned out? Explain.

____

____

2. What are the similarities and differences between a simple electric circuit and a home electricity network?

____

____

____

Scientific Skill: Compare predictions with results

Series and Parallel Circuits

Basic Framework

In groups of three, write the **basic framework** for this activity.

The **basic framework** is the theory of an experiment. It should contain the scientific concepts necessary to develop the experiment. To create a basic framework, find information in reliable sources, like your textbook or other science books and journals. In this experiment, the important concepts are series and parallel circuits.

dependable

Observation

Look at the following situation:

When a lightbulb burns out in your house, do the others keep working? Why or why not?

____

____

Research Question

What happens when a series circuit receptor is damaged? What if the same happens to a parallel circuit receptor?

Hypothesis

Mark the hypothesis you think is correct.

☐ In a series circuit, if one of the receptors is damaged, the others **stop** working. In a parallel circuit, if one of the receptors is damaged, the others **continue** working.

☐ In a series circuit, if one of the receptors is damaged, the others **continue** working. In a parallel circuit, if one of the receptors is damaged, the others **stop** working.

Predictions

1. Look at the diagrams of the following circuits.

circuit 1	circuit 2
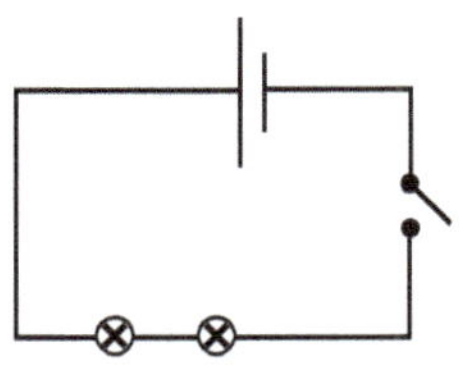	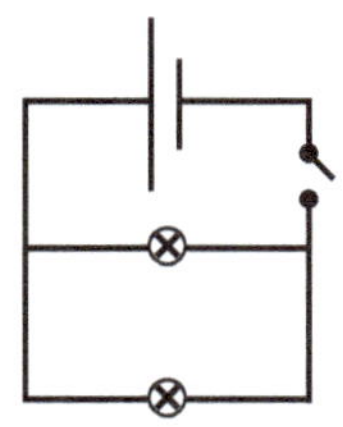

a. What would happen if one of the lightbulbs in **circuit 1** were disconnected? Would the other stay on?

___

b. What would happen if one of the lightbulbs in **circuit 2** were disconnected? Would the other stay on?

___

Experimental Procedure

1. In groups of three, collect the following materials:

- 1 nine volt battery with connector
- 1 meter of electric cable
- 2 portable light sockets
- 2 six volt lightbulbs
- 1 switch
- 1 set of pliers

2. Put together **circuit 1**. Press the switch and observe what happens.
3. Turn off the lights and take out one of the lightbulbs. Press the switch again and observe what happens.
4. Then put together **circuit 2**. Press the switch and observe what happens.
5. Turn off the lights, and take out one of the lightbulbs. Press the switch again and observe what happens.
6. Record your observations in the **Results** section.

circuit 1
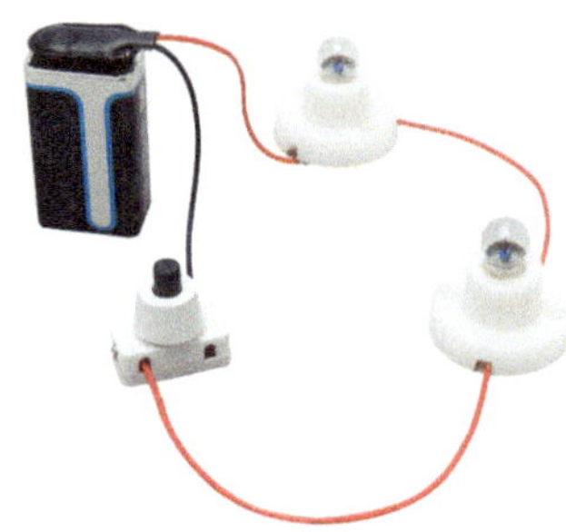
circuit 2
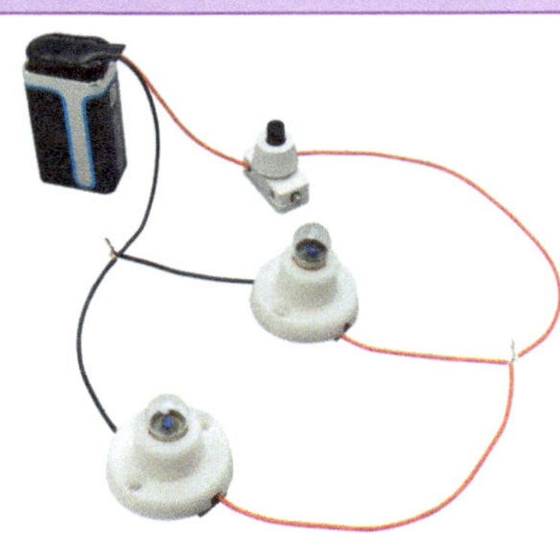

Results

The **results** are what you observed during the experiment. Recording and reviewing results allows you to prove or reject your hypothesis. You should also record the relationship you discovered between the variables. In this case, you should record the type of circuit and what happened when you disconnected one of the receptors. The results should be organized using charts, tables or diagrams.

1. Draw a symbolic representation for each of the circuits you made.

circuit 1	circuit 2

2. Record your observations for each circuit before and after disconnecting the lightbulbs.

Before Disconnecting the Lightbulb	
circuit 1	circuit 2

After Disconnecting the Lightbulb	
circuit 1	circuit 2

Interpreting and Analyzing the Results

1. What happened when one of the lightbulbs was disconnected in **circuit 1**?

___

2. What happened when one of the lightbulbs was disconnected in **circuit 2**?

___

3. What type of circuits are they?

circuit 1: ___ **circuit 2:** ___

4. Compare your results with your predictions. Are they the same? If your results are different from your predictions, why do you think that is?

___

___

Comparing predictions with results proves, through experimentation, whether your hypothesis was correct or not.

Conclusions

1. What happens to a series circuit when one of the receptors stops working?

___

___

2. What happens to a parallel circuit when one of the receptors stops working?

___

___

3. Did you prove your hypothesis? Explain.

___

___

4. Use the results of your experiment to explain why home electricity networks use parallel circuits.

___

___

Let's Check!

1. Mark the devices that transform electric energy. Write the new form of energy below each device.

points ___ / 8

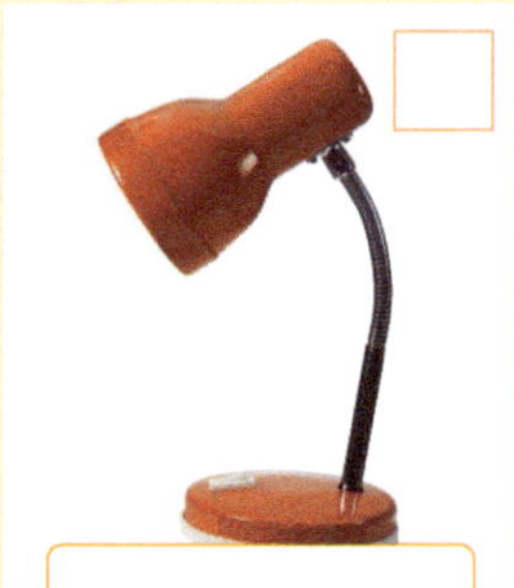

2. Use the time line to record some principal contributions of scientists to the study of electricity.

points ___ / 6

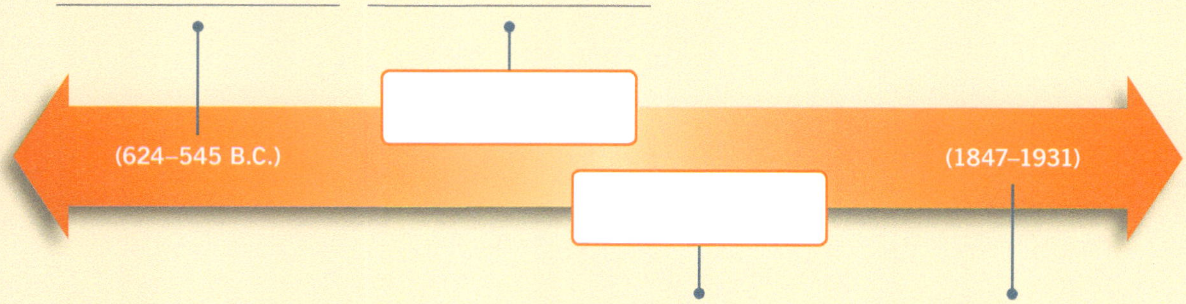

3. Match each image with its description.

points
/4

Receives and transforms electric energy into another type of energy.

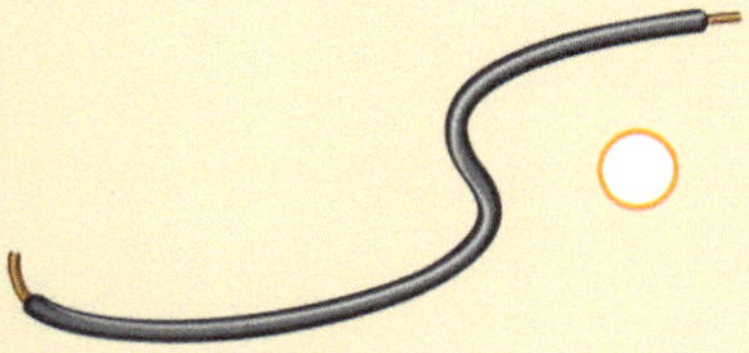

Used to open and close a circuit.

Transports the electric current and is a conductor.

A source of electric energy. It has one positive and one negative pole.

4. Look at the images. For each one, write whether the remaining lightbulbs will still work if one is removed. Explain why or why not in each case.

points
/2

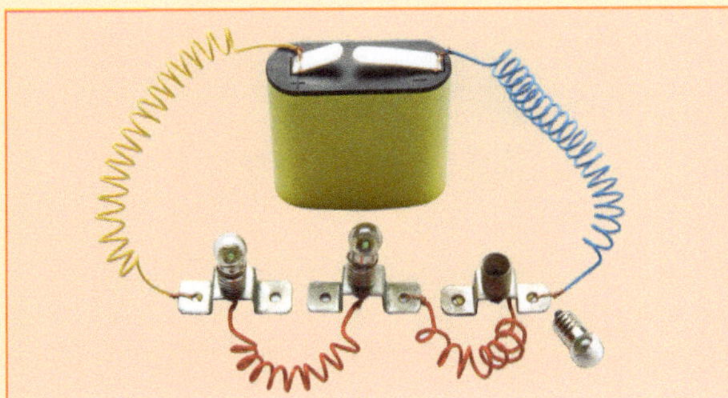

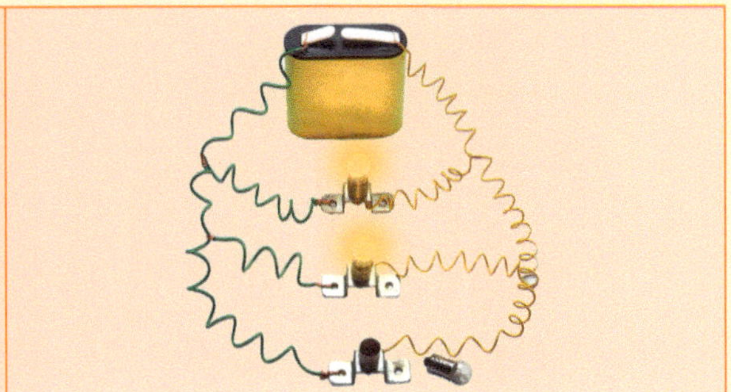

Conductors and Insulators

Exploring

Conductors and Insulators of Electricity

As we learned in the last unit, an electric current transports energy from one place to another. However, some materials conduct the current better than others. What are some of these materials?

To answer this question, form groups and do the experiment.

1. Collect the following supplies:
   - 1 nine volt battery with connector
   - 5 twenty centimeter electric cables
   - 1 portable light socket
   - 1 six volt lightbulb
   - 1 switch
   - 2 sets of electrical pliers
   - 10 different materials (a metal pen, an eraser, a rubber band, a piece of paper, a paper clip, a piece of cloth, a pencil, a strip of copper and an ice cream stick)

2. Put together the following circuit:

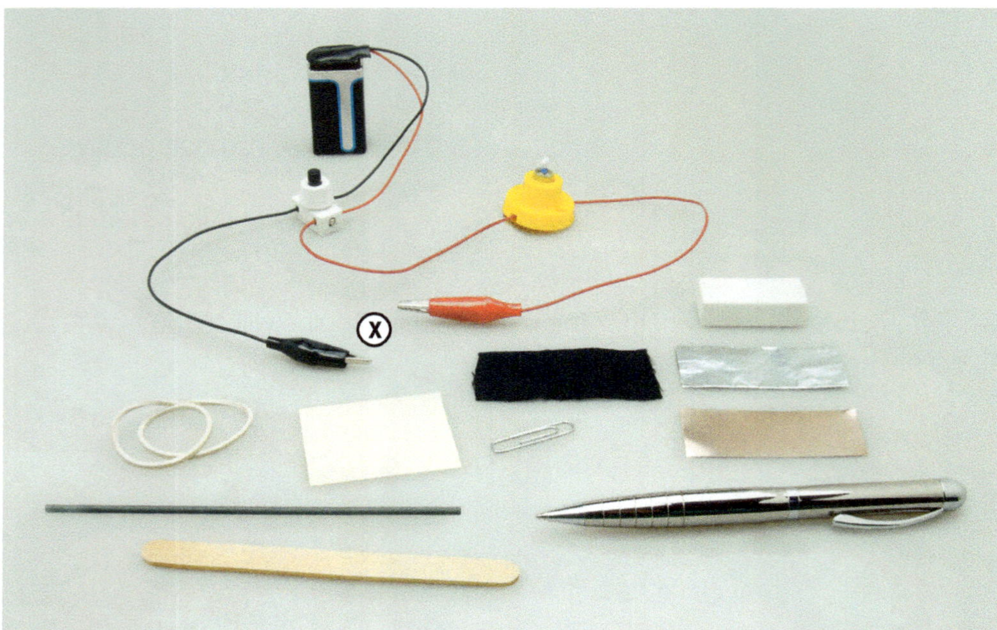

3. If you were to place each material in the place marked ⓧ, with which materials do you think the lightbulb would turn on? Write your predictions below.

____

____

____

____

4. Place each of the materials in the spot marked ⓧ.

5. What happened to the lightbulb with each material? Did it turn on or stay off? Complete the table with your results. Mark the correct answer with a ✔.

Material	The lightbulb turned on	The lightbulb stayed off

6. What are the characteristics of the materials with which the lightbulb turned on?

____

____

7. What are the characteristics of the materials with which the lightbulb did not turn on?

____

____

Fun Fact!

The first lightbulb was invented in 1879 by Thomas Alva Edison.

The lightbulb turned on every time the circuit was completed with a material that conducted the electric current. These materials are called **electrical conductors**. The lightbulb did not turn on when the circuit was completed with materials that did not conduct the electric current. These materials are called **electrical insulators**.

Connecting

Objects can be classified as **conductors** or **insulators** according to their capacity to conduct an electric current.

Conductors

Conductors are materials that allow **electric charges to move freely within them**. Examples are copper, aluminum, iron, silver, gold and other metals.

Insulators

Insulators are bad conductors and **resist the electric charges that move through them**. They do not allow charges to move freely. These materials are used to avoid electricity-related accidents. Examples are wool, wood, rubber, plastic, glass and cotton.

Fun Fact!

In between conductors and insulators, there are **semiconductors**. These are materials that are not good conductors but do not resist electricity, either.

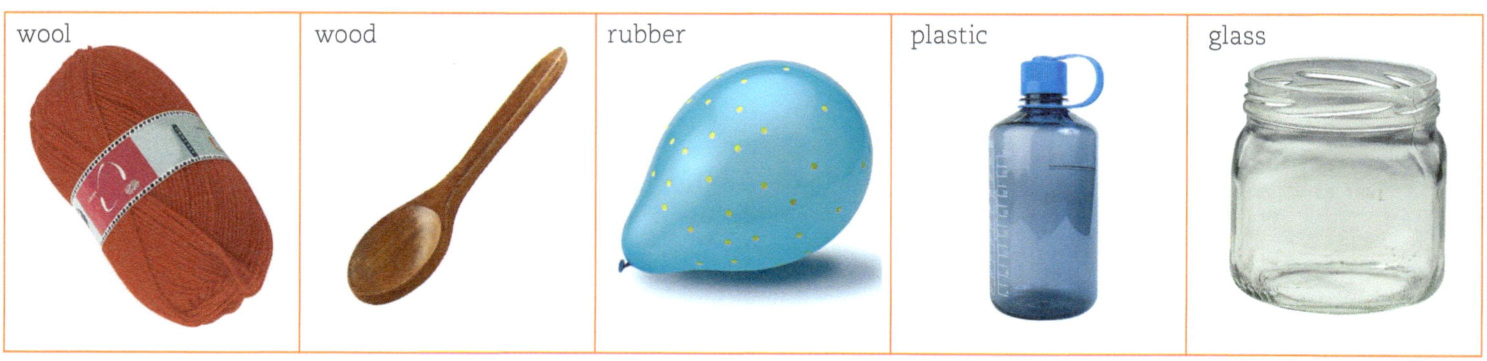

Components of a Circuit: Conductors and Insulators

Electric circuits are made using both conductors and insulators.

The poles of a battery are conductors. They allow electric charges to circulate.

The inside of a light socket is metal, which makes it a conductor. The electric current can easily circulate from the socket to the lightbulb.

The lightbulb also has a metal part at the bottom that serves as a conductor.

The switches contain conductors that permit current to pass when the switches are closed.

The switches are covered in plastic (an insulator) to keep the current inside.

security, protection

Electric cables always have conductive materials inside.

The cables are covered by an insulator, usually plastic, for safety.

Daily Uses of Conductors and Insulators

Conductors and insulators are useful when building and designing many of the things we use every day.

Pliers

Pliers are tools used to cut wires. Their handles are covered in rubber, an insulator. This allows them to be used with a lower risk of **electrocution**.

handles: the parts that you hold

Word Focus

Electrocution is when someone is hurt by an electric shock. Be careful when you use electric devices.

See **page 116** for important safety tips to remember when dealing with electricity.

Voltage Tester

This tool is a screwdriver that is completely insulated except for the tip. It is used to find electric currents. Inside, it has a small electric circuit with a lightbulb. When it makes contact with an electric current, the lightbulb turns on.

These testers have a switch and only work when turned on.

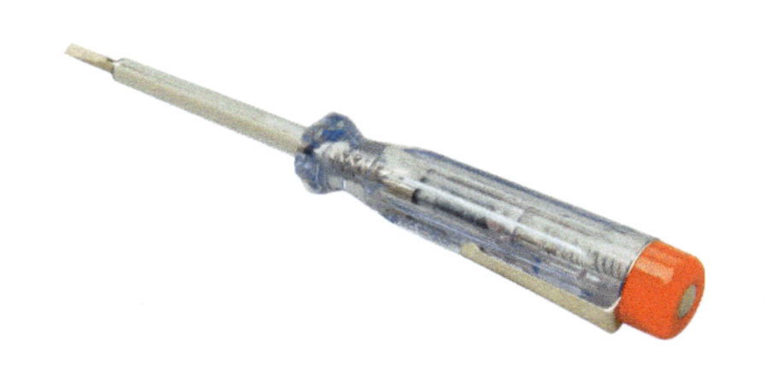

Plug

The prongs of a plug are conductors, but the part of the plug that you hold is insulated.

Practicing

1. With which materials, when placed in spot A, would the light turn on? Mark yes or no. Apply

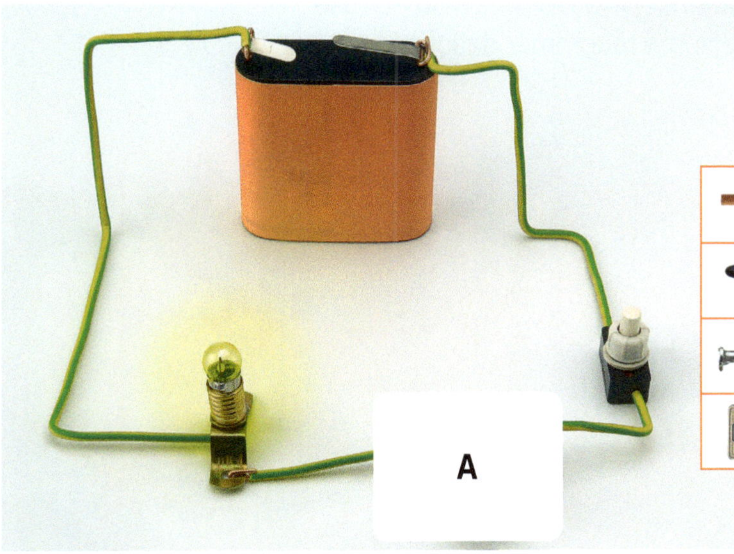

	Yes	No

a. Why does the lightbulb turn on with these materials? Explain

____

____

b. Which components of the circuit are conductors and which are insulators? Explain. Explain

____

____

Summarizing

Materials can be

- conductors
  - examples:
    - ____________
    - copper
- ____________
  - examples:
    - plastic
    - ____________

Connecting

Safe Ways to use Electric Devices

Electricity is very important and useful for humans. However, if we do not use it carefully, it can be very dangerous. Here are some recommendations to help avoid accidents when using electricity.

When connecting or disconnecting a plug to an outlet, always touch the covered part and never the metal prongs. When disconnecting, pull the plug and never the cable.

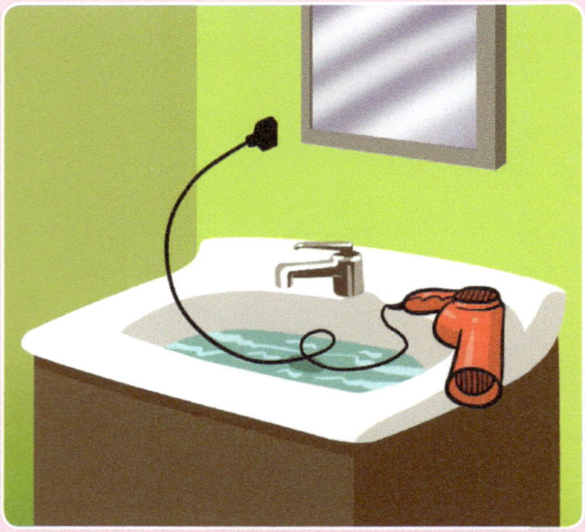

Never use electric devices in water or when your hands are wet. Water is a conductor of electric current.

Do not put electric cables below rugs or in places where people can trip over them.

floor coverings

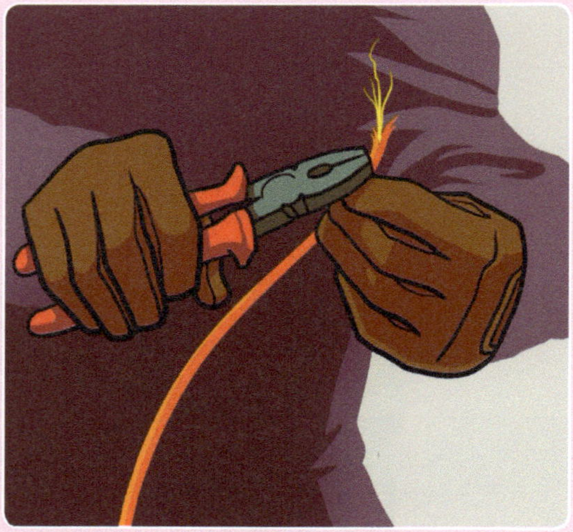

Let a professional handle electric repairs. Do not try to fix broken cables or wires yourself.

manage, control

Unplug a lamp before changing the lightbulb. → remove from an outlet

Take precautions so that children do not stick objects or their fingers into outlets. → insert

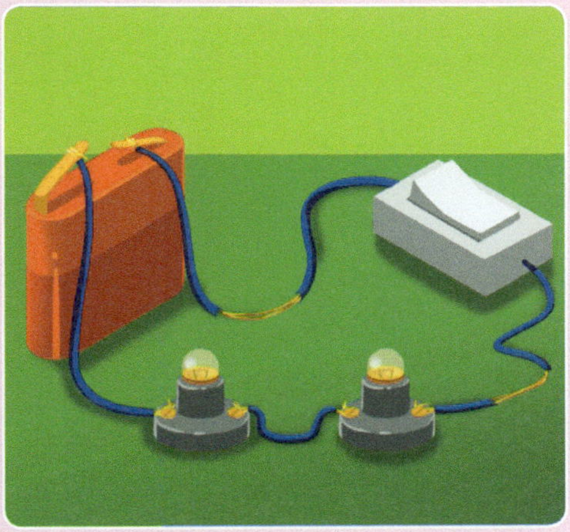

When you put together a circuit, follow all the teacher's instructions. Remember:

- do not leave wires uncovered.
- do not touch the circuit with wet hands.

Do not connect too many plugs to one outlet. The outlet could get hot and start a fire.

Did You Know...?

To prevent accidents in companies or public places, this sign is used as a warning:

Staying Healthy

Respecting safety recommendations helps prevent accidents such as electrocution.

Practicing

1. Go to **Cutout 12** on **page 181**. Glue the situations in the correct boxes. Classify

Safe Electricity Use		

Dangerous Electricity Use		

Summarizing

Safety recommendations when using electric devices:

-
-
-
-
-

Quiz Yourself

1. Identify the conductors with a **C** and the insulators with an **I**.

2. People who repair electric connections in light or phone cables need to wear special clothing and take safety precautions. One precaution is wearing rubber gloves and shoes with rubber soles. Use this information to answer the following questions.

soles: the bottom part of a shoe

a. Think about what you've learned about the conduction of electric current. What kind of material is rubber?

____

____

b. Why do they take these safety precautions?

____

____

____

What Did You Learn?

1. Identify the form(s) of energy in each of the images.

points
/4

2. Mark the devices that need electric energy to function. Then write which type of energy the electric energy is transformed into.

points
/6

☐ 	☐ 	☐ 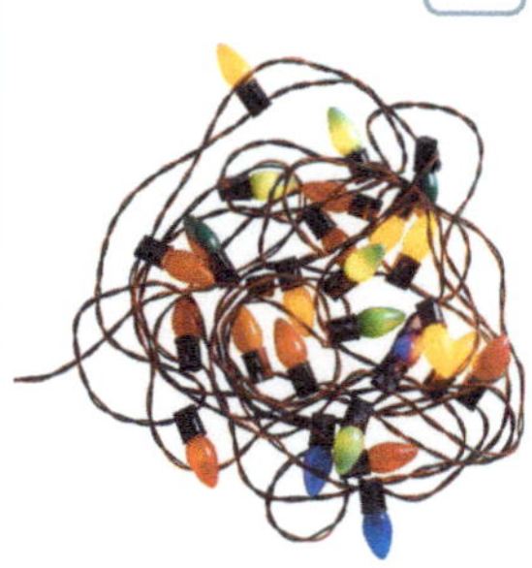	☐ 

3. Name three important contributions to the study of electric energy.

points ___ / 3

- ____________________.
- ____________________.
- ____________________.

4. Write the name and function of each part of the circuit.

points ___ / 8

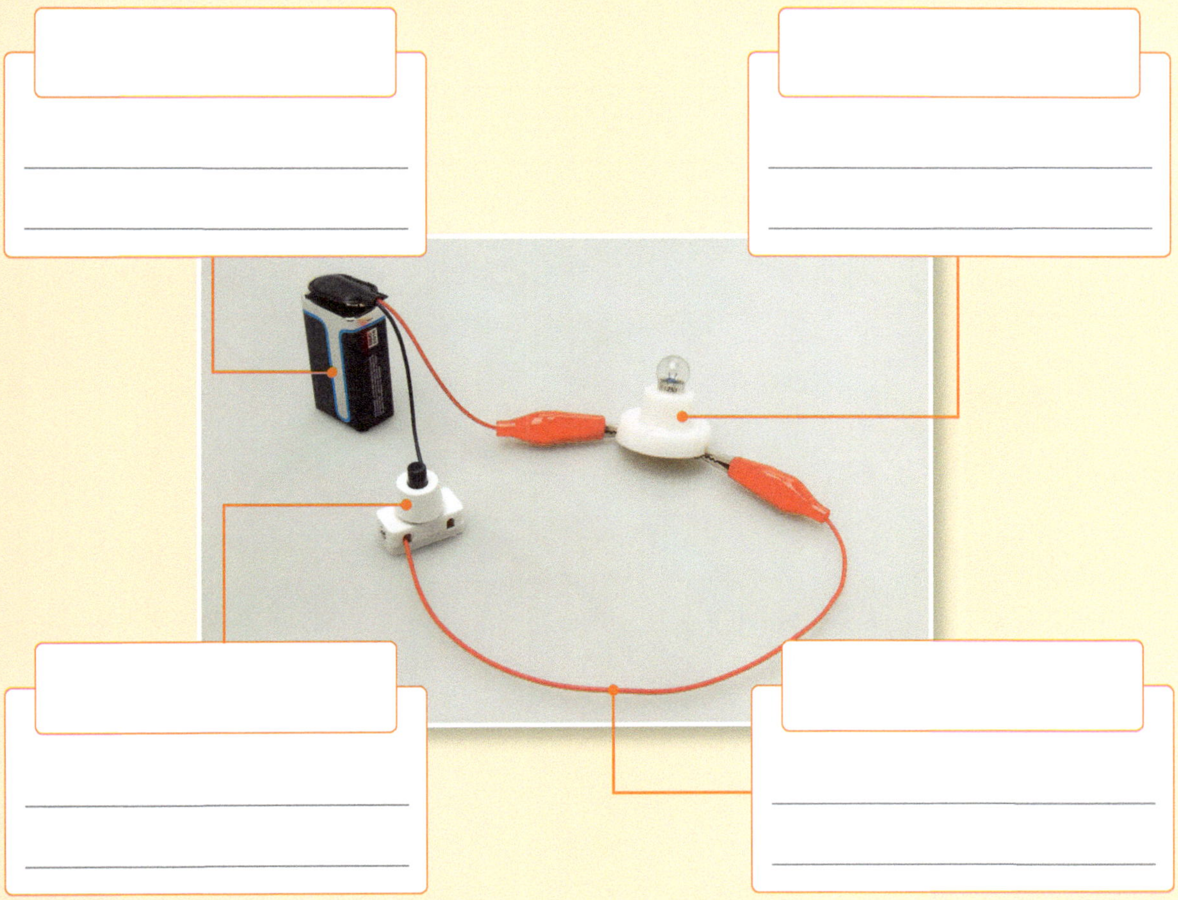

5. In a home electricity network, this device stops the electric current when there is an error:

point ___ / 1

A. A high-tension tower.
B. An electricity meter.
C. A circuit breaker.
D. A switch.

6. Classify the objects as insulators or conductors.

points
/ 8

Examples	
Conductors	Insulators

  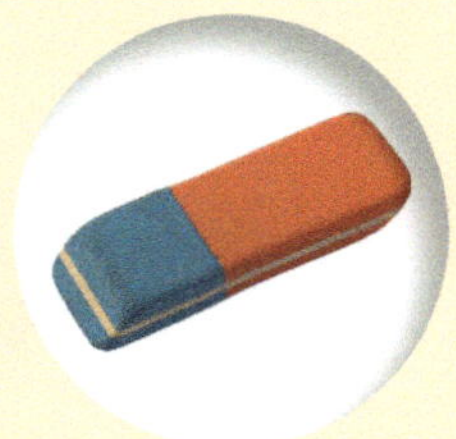 

7. Match each phrase in column **A** with a phrase in column **B**.

points
/ 5

A	B
Ryan is watching television. ◯	◯ She should not touch electric devices.
Sonia's hands are wet. ◯	◯ He should turn off the lights.
Kevin left his room. ◯	◯ She should close the door.
Julie is playing with a metal clip close to an outlet. ◯	◯ He should turn it off when he is done watching.
Tara took an apple out of the refrigerator. ◯	◯ She should stop because she could electrocute herself.

8. Look at the image and answer the questions:

points
/ 6

a. What would happen if you replaced the battery in a circuit with a lemon? Would the lightbulb turn on? Make a prediction.

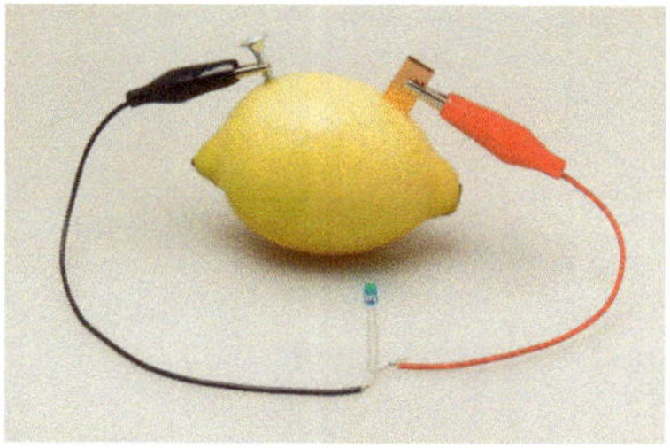

b. Collect the following supplies:

- 3 lemons
- 3 metal screws
- 3 pieces of copper
- 1 LED
- 50 centimeters of electric cable

c. Build this circuit.

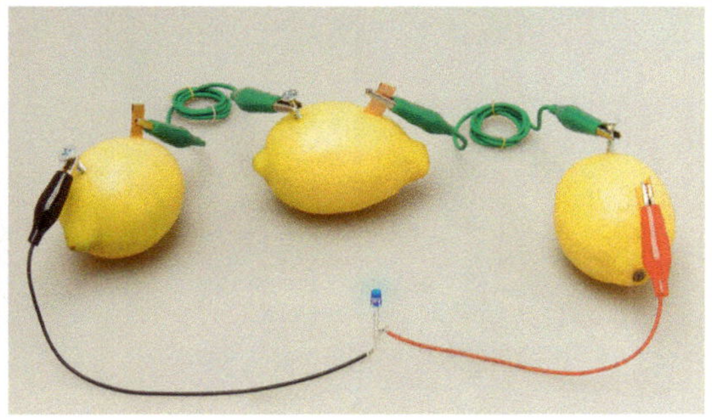

When you place a screw and a piece of copper inside a lemon, a chemical reaction is produced, electrons move, and electricity is generated.

d. Record your results.

e. Compare your predictions with your results. Are they the same? Explain.

Find Test 3 Study Page

Unit 4

Hydrosphere

Key Words

- salt water
- fresh water
- shallow
- deep
- reserve

In this unit you will learn to:

- describe the distribution of water on earth.
- analyze and describe characteristics of oceans, seas and lakes.
- communicate evidence and conclusions of an experiment.
- value water as a fundamental part of life.

What Do You Know?

Initial Evaluation

1. Look at the image. Write the letter that corresponds to each stage of the water cycle in the circles.
   - **A.** Water from the ocean evaporates slowly because of the sun's rays.
   - **B.** Water vapor forms clouds that move with the help of wind.
   - **C.** Water falls to the ground in the form of rain, snow or hail.
   - **D.** Water falls to the ground and becomes part of rivers or lakes, stays frozen or soaks into the earth.
   - **E.** Water returns to the oceans through rivers, both above and below the ground.

2. In what state is the water (solid, liquid or gas) at each stage of the cycle? Write the stages in the boxes.

3. Mark the activities that contaminate water with an ✖ and the activities that protect water with a ✔.

Scientific Skill: Communicate and represent evidence

4. A group of researchers conducted a study to analyze the amount of wildlife present in two zones of a river. The first zone corresponded to the flow of water through a nature reserve, and the second zone corresponded to the flow of water through the surrounding areas.

   a. Mark the data from the study that should be communicated by the researchers.

   - ☐ Basic Framework
   - ☐ Research Question
   - ☐ Inferences
   - ☐ Predictions
   - ☐ Interpreting and Analyzing Results
   - ☐ Conclusions

   b. What other research steps do you think should be recorded? Explain.

   ____

   ____

   ____

   ____

Water on Earth

Connecting

Land and Water

What does the earth look like from space? Imagine boarding a spaceship and traveling far from earth. On your trip, you could observe the planet from a great distance as you've never seen it before. This picture shows how earth looks from space.

When you see earth from space, you will notice that it is almost completely blue. What covers almost the entire planet? You know the answer: water. From space, earth seems to be covered only in water.

Our planet, also called the "blue planet," is **mostly covered in water**, which is a **fundamental** resource for living things. Why do you think scientists have tried to research whether there is water on other planets? The answer is simple: they are looking for other places in the universe that can support life, and water is essential for life. Think, for example, of an animal that cannot find any water for many days. What will happen? The animal will probably have serious health problems as water is vital for all living things on earth.

High-resolution image of earth. Taken from the satellite *Suomi* on January 4, 2012.

Did You Know...?

All the water on our planet has not always been there. Scientists think that when earth was still forming millions of years ago, a large amount of water vapor condensed to form **torrential** rainfall on earth.

Challenge

Make a physical representation of the earth using a ball, cotton balls for clouds and any other materials you choose. Mark important geographic locations on your earth. Hang it up in your classroom.

The Hydrosphere

Water is everywhere, and sometimes we do not even notice. It forms an important part of our bodies and the bodies of animals and plants, and it is in our food and the air we breathe. However, we usually recognize it coming out of the tap or in oceans, lakes and rivers.

How much water is there on earth? Three-fourths of earth's surface is covered in water.

Water on our planet is distributed in clouds, seas, oceans, streams, lakes, rivers, underground rivers, polar caps and glaciers. These bodies of water make up the **hydrosphere**. In the hydrosphere, water can exist in a solid state, like **icebergs** or glaciers; a liquid state, like the ocean; or as a gas, like water vapor in the air we breathe.

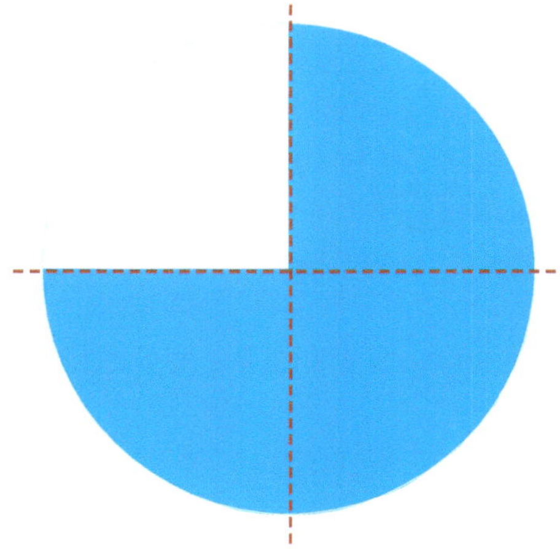

If we represent earth's surface as a circle divided into four equal parts, the three shaded parts symbolize the part of earth that is covered in water.

Word Focus

An **iceberg** is a very large piece of ice floating in water, generally the ocean.

Water is present in its three states in nature.

Education through Values

Although there is plenty of water on earth, human beings can only use a limited amount of it. This is why we should respect the environment and keep our water clean.

Different Types of Water on Our Planet

You have probably accidentally tasted seawater. What did it taste like? The taste of seawater is very different from river water or the tap water in your house. This implies that water on earth is not always the same and that many different types of water exist.

indicates

Water on our planet is classified into two large groups: salt water and fresh water.

Salt water is much more abundant than fresh water. It is estimated that about 97 percent of water on earth is salt water, while only 3 percent is fresh water. Salt water is found in oceans, and fresh water is found on land in rivers, lakes, **lagoons**, **polar ice caps**, glaciers and groundwater. Only some of these sources can be used by humans. Other sources of fresh water, such as the ice on top of tall mountains (glaciers), are not available for use. The following charts show the distribution of salt water and fresh water on earth.

Did You Know...?

Fresh water is the opposite of salt water. It has much less salt and needs to be cleaned before it is safe to drink.

Distribution of Water on Land

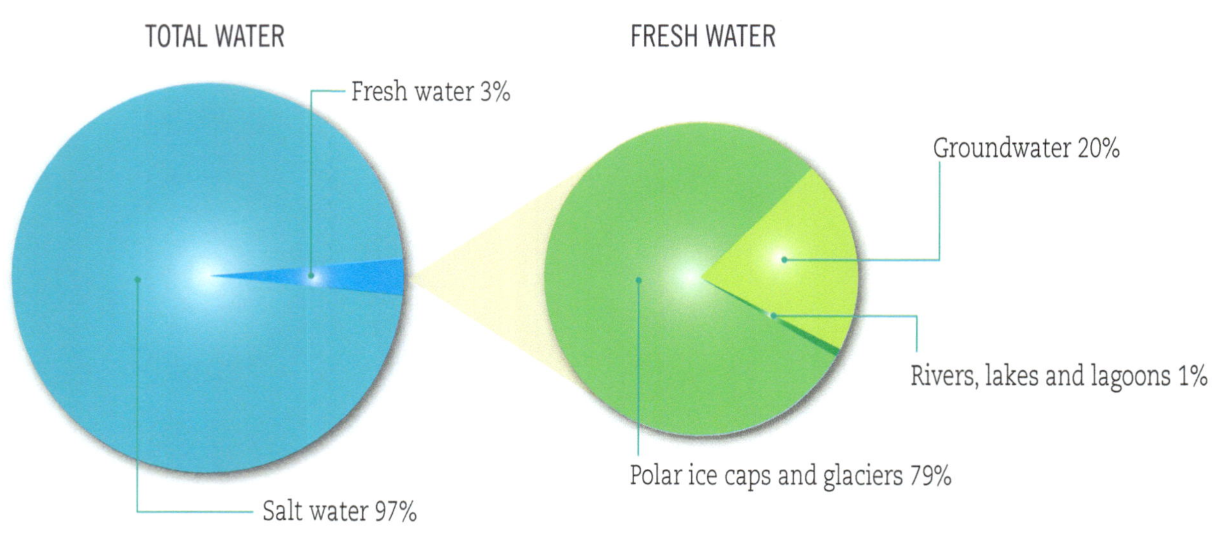

The amount of fresh water on our planet is small. It is found mostly in a solid state.

As you can see, there is much less fresh water than salt water. Also, the fresh water available to human beings is even less because we cannot use the water in polar ice caps or glaciers. This is why it is so important not to waste or pollute our freshwater supply.

Practicing

1. The following box represents earth's surface. Color the part that is covered in water. Identify

2. Write **F** in the box if the image shows fresh water and **S** if it shows salt water. Identify

3. Create a chart to show the distribution of fresh water and salt water on earth. Describe

Summarizing

Three-fourths of our planet is covered in ________________________.

Water is fundamental for all ______________________________.

Water is classified as ____________________ or ____________________. Salt water is much more abundant than fresh water.

Connecting

The Distribution of Water on Land

Imagine your class uses a special vehicle to travel from the top of a mountain to the ocean shore. Then you dive into the depths of the earth before flying high into the atmosphere. On this trip, you can discover how water is distributed on our planet.

shore → coast

Word Focus

Infiltrate is to slowly soak into the crust of the earth.

1 You begin the journey in the solid reserves of fresh water in the form of ice. These reserves are very important and are primarily found in polar areas, but they also exist at the top of high mountains. These mountains store a great natural reserve of fresh water.

2 You continue the journey over the large amounts of fresh water flowing on the surface of the earth in the form of **rivers**. Rivers usually begin as a trickle of water in hills or mountains and travel until they reach the ocean. Sometimes, water accumulates in certain areas of the surface without going to the ocean. These accumulations form **lakes** and **lagoons**.

trickle → small flow

3 As we go to the depths of our planet, we find **groundwater**. This water is absorbed from the surface of the land through rivers, lakes or when it rains. This process is called **infiltration**. This water is fresh and generally clean, which makes it important for human use and also represents a natural reserve for the future.

4

In the atmosphere, we find water either as vapor or in tiny drops that form clouds. This is an important natural reserve that humans use when it falls in the form of precipitation.

Did You Know...?

The Pacific Ocean is the largest and deepest ocean in the world. At one point it is 11,000 meters deep!

Challenge

One of the most important sources of fresh water is found in large deposits of groundwater called **aquifers**. Research the importance of aquifers to people. Think of a creative way to present what you learn to your class.

5

After traveling through all the places where water exists, you will reach the most abundant reserve of all: the oceans. These are large bodies of water that cover earth and represent the largest reserve of water. These huge masses of salt water separate the continents from one another. Shallower bodies of water close to the coast are called seas. not as deep

Connecting

The Water Cycle

Think of raindrops falling on a rainy day. They come from the atmosphere, but how do they get so high in the sky? Why do they fall when they do? When the rain stops, what happens to the water that accumulates on the ground? Where does it go? The answers to these questions are related to the **hydrologic** or **water cycle**.

The water cycle is a set of processes and transformations that allow water to move through different parts of the hydrosphere. In this cycle, water that falls from the sky as precipitation reaches the ground and forms rivers. It then **infiltrates** the land to form part of the groundwater. Other precipitation falls directly into the ocean. From these places, water evaporates into the atmosphere before falling again as rain, hail or snow. The water cycle is as follows:

1 **Evaporation** ▸ Because of the heat of the sun's rays, water in oceans, rivers and lakes evaporates and changes its state from liquid to gas. Then water rises into the atmosphere in the form of vapor.

2 **Condensation** ▸ Water vapor goes high up into the atmosphere and cools when it meets areas of low temperature. This causes it to form tiny water drops that make up clouds.

3 **Precipitation** ▸ When clouds accumulate a large amount of water, it falls to the ground as rain. If this happens in cold areas, it falls as snow or hail.

4 **Surface Runoff** ▸ This is the movement of water across land as rivers. This water comes from melting ice on mountains or from rain and continues to the ocean.

5 **Infiltration** ▸ Part of the water that falls on land is absorbed into the lower layers of the ground, forming underground rivers and traveling to the ocean or replenishing groundwater reserves.

filling again

6 **Transpiration** ▸ Water that evaporates from plants in the form of vapor.

The Importance of Water for Living Things

Have you ever heard that you should drink around six glasses of water a day to stay healthy? Do you follow this advice? Maybe you have never measured the amount of water you drink daily, but it is important that you begin to think about it because water is vital for human beings.

Why is water so important? Why should we drink it? The answers to these questions are related to the characteristics of water that make it a necessary substance for life.

Staying Healthy

Remember to drink six to eight glasses of water daily.

not be affected by

Water is a substance that can withstand a lot of heat and cold without changing temperature. This property means human beings can live in different climates without harm because our bodies are almost 60 percent water.

Water acts as a lubricant that allows different body parts to move. For example, bone joints are surrounded by a liquid that consists mostly of water. It protects them from rubbing against each other when they move.

occur

The primary chemical reactions that permit the existence of life take place in the water in our cells. It is thought that life on earth evolved in water millions of years ago.

becomes lined

In human beings, water helps maintain soft, healthy skin. As it ages, the body naturally loses water, and the skin wrinkles. Water inside plants maintains the shape and structure of the leaves and stems.

In living things, water acts as a mode of transportation for different substances. For example, in animals, blood consists mostly of water and transports many different elements to all parts of the organism.

Did You Know...?

As we age, the amount of water in our body decreases. A baby's body is 70 percent water, an adult's body is 60 percent water, and an elderly person's body is only 55 percent water.

Education through Values

Water is a very important and scarce resource, so we should ensure that it is used properly. For example, a person can use more than 100 liters of water during a normal shower. That's a lot!

rare, difficult to find

How can you use less water to help care for the environment?

Practicing

1. Look at the image and complete.

a. Write the stages of the water cycle in the boxes. Identify

b. Using the picture, describe how fresh water and salt water are distributed on earth. Describe

____

____

c. Why is water important to human beings? Give three examples to explain. Explain

____

____

____

Summarizing

Water from the hydrosphere is distributed in different ways in different places: glaciers, ____________, rivers, lakes, lagoons, ____________ and the water in the atmosphere.

The water cycle, or hydrologic cycle, allows water to circulate in nature. The processes are: ____________, condensation, ____________, runoff, infiltration and ____________.

Water is a fundamental substance for all ____________. For example, it maintains body structures, lubricates moving body parts and keeps our ____________ soft and healthy.

Quiz Yourself

1. Draw a diagram to represent the distribution of water on earth.

2. Complete the table with the required information about the hydrosphere.

Water on Our Planet	
What are the different types of freshwater reserves?	
Where can salt water be found?	
Why is water so important for human beings?	

3. With a partner, go to **Activity Cards 4** and **5**. Play the water cycle game.

Section 2

Characteristics of Oceans, Seas and Lakes

Connecting

Differences between Fresh Water and Salt Water

1. With four classmates, find the following materials: 1 transparent plastic cup, 1 raw egg, 1 spoon, 3 tablespoons of salt and some water.
2. Fill the cup with water and place the egg inside. What happens?
3. Take the egg out of the water, and add the salt. Stir the water until the salt dissolves completely.
4. Place the egg in the cup again. What happens?
5. Discuss the results with your group.

raw → uncooked

Stir → mix a liquid

Did You Know...?

Seawater can be changed into fresh water through a process called **desalination**, in which salt is taken out of the water.

As you saw in the activity, it is easier for an object to float in water with salt than in water without salt. Now imagine that you are given two cups of water. One cup contains seawater, and the other cup contains water from a lake. How could you distinguish each type of water? As you are probably thinking, seawater tastes very different from lake water. However, what is the scientific difference between salt water and fresh water?

Characteristics	Salt Water	Fresh Water
Where can we find it?		
Salinity	Has a greater amount of dissolved salt.	Has a smaller amount of dissolved salt.
Physical State	Is found mostly in a liquid state.	Is found as a liquid, solid or gas.
Abundance	Forms the majority the water that exists on the planet (97 percent).	Forms a small part of the water that exists on the planet (3 percent).

As you can see, salt water and fresh water are different in many ways. The primary difference is in the quantity of dissolved salt or minerals they contain.

Types of Water in Oceans, Seas and Lakes

We have discussed seas and oceans, but what is the difference between the two? Oceans are huge, deep masses of salt water that separate the continents. Seas are shallower areas of water close to the coast that are sometimes partially enclosed by land. Water in seas and oceans, unlike fresh water, has a large quantity of dissolved minerals. The most prominent mineral is **sodium chloride**, commonly known as salt.

surrounded

In contrast, lakes are bodies of fresh water that are completely surrounded by land. They are much smaller and shallower than oceans and are generally connected to rivers that provide them with water. Although the majority of lakes have fresh water, there are some exceptions, such as Qinghai Lake in China, the Dead Sea in the Middle East and the Caspian Sea in Asia.

Did You Know...?

Lake Budi in Chile is the only saltwater lake in South America.

Practicing

1. Describe the characteristics of the water in each picture. Describe

____

____

____

____

____

____

Summarizing

Water from lakes is fresh and has a ____________________ quantity of dissolved minerals. Water from oceans and seas has a ____________________ quantity of dissolved minerals and is salty.

Connecting

Characteristics of Oceans and Seas

Have you ever imagined what the bottom of the ocean is like? Oceans occupy large areas and can be very deep in some parts. The deepest areas are called deep-sea trenches, which range in **depth** from 7,000 to over 11,000 meters. The deepest known trench is the Mariana Trench in the Pacific Ocean, which has a depth of 11,033 meters.

trench → channel

It is not easy to live in the deepest parts of the ocean, where the water temperature can reach below 0 °C. These are very cold, dark places because sunlight cannot reach them. At 1,000 meters under the surface of the ocean, there is absolute darkness, so many animals that live below this depth do not have eyes.

If we could observe the bottom of the ocean without water, we would not see a flat plain. Instead, we would see something similar to earth's surface, with mountains, volcanoes and plains. In the image, you can see the bottom of an ocean that separates two continents.

Challenge

The marine life in the Mariana Trench is very different from the life in the rest of the ocean. Research and then draw a picture of your favorite marine animal from this trench. Why do you like it?

Word Focus

Seismic activity is the movement of earth's plates. This movement causes earthquakes and volcanic eruptions.

Islands in the middle of the ocean are underwater landmasses that emerge from the bottom of the ocean. Islands near the coast are parts of the continent separated by submerged land.

Continental shelves are extensions of continents that have been covered by water. These areas are commonly referred to as **seas**, for their proximity to a continent and shallowness.

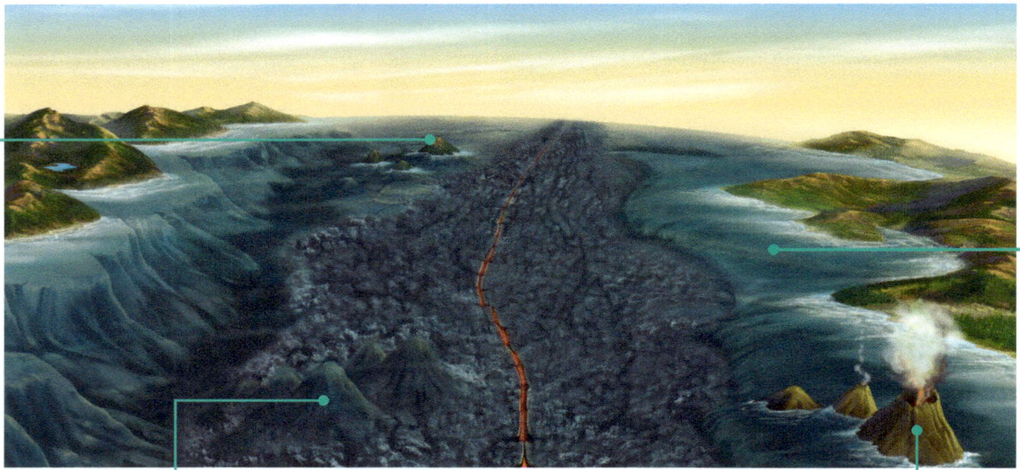

On the bottom of the ocean, **oceanic ridges** can be found. These are underwater mountains, and they often experience high levels of volcanic and seismic activity.

ridges → long, narrow mountaintops

Some underwater volcanoes emerge from the ocean floor and form sets of islands, or archipelagos, like the Hawaiian Islands.

Effects of Water Conditions on Living Things

Have you heard of sea monsters? There are many stories about them based on ancient beliefs. Although there is some truth to the stories—as there are indeed some giant animals in the ocean—none of them are monsters as people used to believe.

certainly

Diverse forms of life are distributed throughout the ocean, no matter how deep or cold it is. Three key factors affect the types of life forms that develop in different parts of the ocean: **light**, **temperature** and **pressure**. Pressure is related to depth and indicates the force that water exerts on the organisms that live in it.

in every part of

These three factors determine which living things can survive in each area of the ocean. We can generally say that as the water becomes deeper, light and temperature decrease while pressure increases.

Did You Know...?

Ancient maps show our past belief in sea monsters. Sea monsters were included on the maps so that travelers could take precautions when traveling through the areas.

conviction that something is true

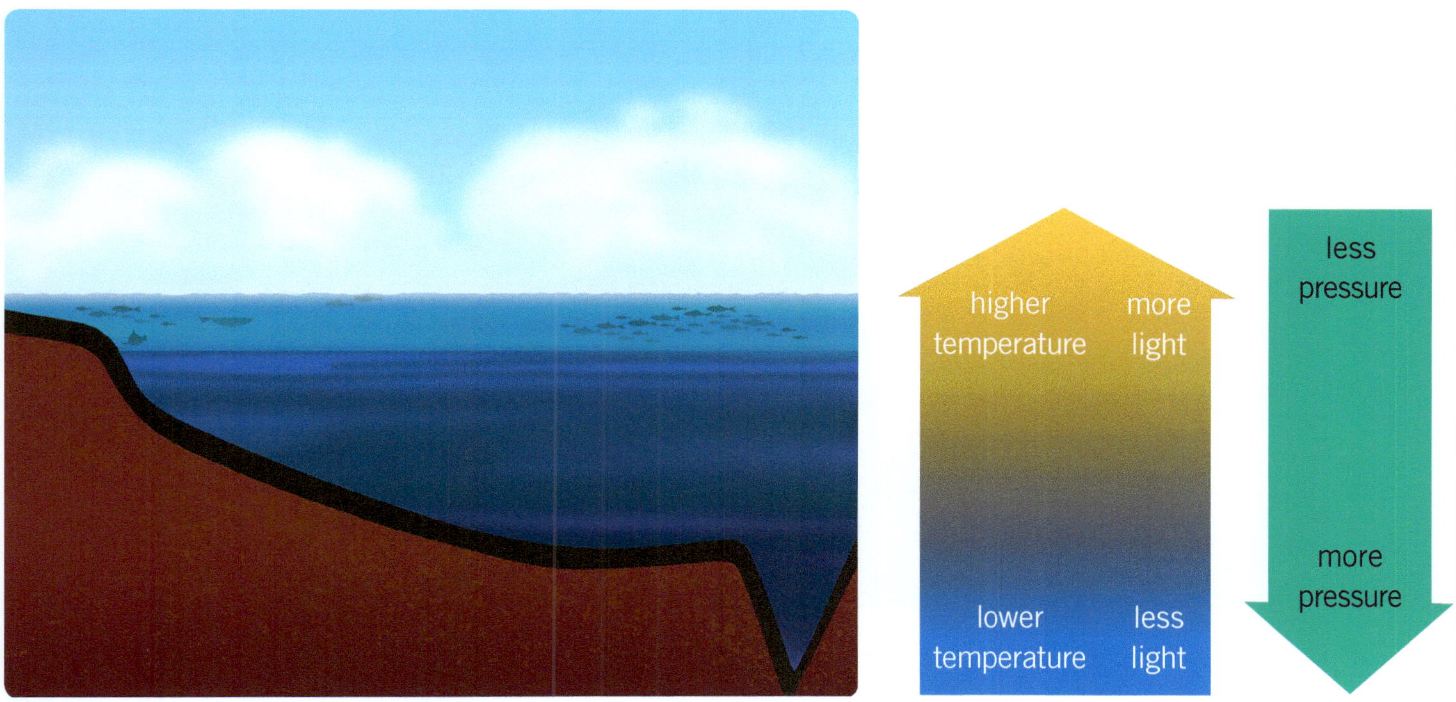

The **diversity** of living things varies at different depths. In the zones with the most light and warmth and least pressure, there is a greater diversity of living things.

Ocean Zones and Diverse Forms of Life

Imagine boarding a submarine and being submerged in the ocean. In the first zone that you travel through, the temperature is moderate, light is sufficient and the pressure can support the development of many living things. As you descend, the light begins to disappear, the water becomes colder, and the pressure increases. As you arrive at the bottom, you find strange forms of life that have adapted to living in this cold, dark zone.

In the ocean, there are two distinct depths: the **photic zone** and the **aphotic zone**. The luminosity, temperature and pressure are very different in these zones, so we find different forms of life.

Word Focus

Photosynthesis is the process by which plants and algae use carbon dioxide, water and the sun's rays to make their own food.

Ocean Zones

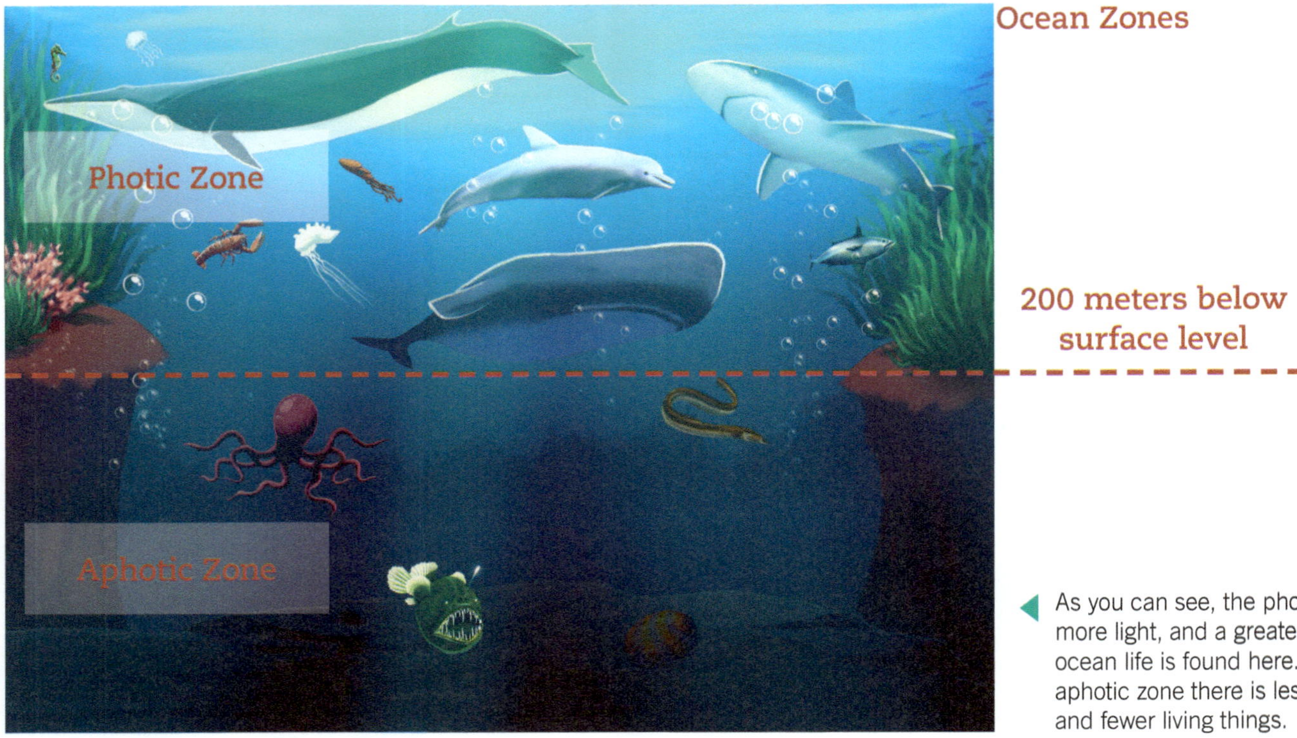

As you can see, the photic zone receives more light, and a greater diversity of ocean life is found here. In contrast, in the aphotic zone there is less diversity of life and fewer living things.

Photic Zone

This zone occupies the first 200 meters under the surface. It receives a large amount of sunlight, which allows various forms of life to develop. Through the process of **photosynthesis**, seaweed and other plants can use the sunlight to obtain energy for themselves and generate nutrients for marine animals. The majority of marine organisms **inhabit** the first 50 meters under the surface of the water.

seaweed: marine algae

Aphotic Zone

This zone starts at 200 meters under the surface of the ocean and ends at the ocean floor. It receives no sunlight, so there is no seaweed in this zone. As the water gets deeper, the pressure increases and the temperature decreases, so forms of life are less abundant. This zone is inhabited by animals such as the octopus and the squid, which are able to swim up closer to the surface to find food.

squid: a mollusk with ten arms

octopus: a mollusk with eight arms

Practicing

1. Describe the characteristics of each zone of the ocean. Mention the quantity and diversity of living beings, luminosity, temperature and pressure in each. Describe

	Photic Zone	Aphotic Zone
Quantity and Diversity of Living Beings		
Luminosity		
Temperature		
Pressure		

Summarizing

In the ocean, there is a great diversity of ______________. The quantity and variety of this depends on ______________, ______________ and ______________.

In the deepest parts of the ocean, there is ______________ sunlight, lower temperatures and more ______________.

The ocean can be divided into the ______________ zone, which receives sunlight, and the ______________ zone, which does not receive any sunlight.

Connecting

Lakes

Lakes are accumulations of water surrounded by land and not connected to the ocean. Although the majority of lakes have fresh water, some have salt water. Depending on their location and characteristics, we can find diverse forms of life in lakes.

There are many differences between lakes and oceans. A lake is much smaller, and the water is calmer and shallower. However, if a lake is deep enough, it can also have an aphotic zone.

A lake is divided into three zones: the **littoral** zone, the **limnetic** zone and the **profundal** zone.

Did You Know...?

The Dead Sea in Israel, despite its name, is actually a lake. It has such a large amount of salt that it supports very little life. Objects float much more easily in the Dead Sea than in other bodies of water because of the high salt levels.

Living Things in Lakes

In lakes, as in oceans, the temperature decreases with depth. This influences the living things that live there.

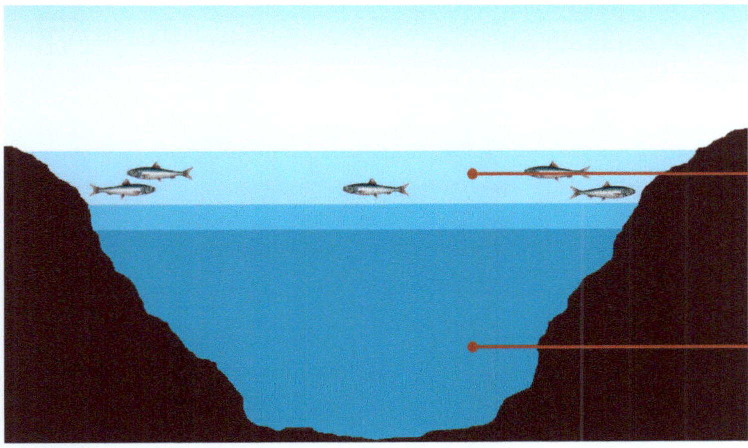

The distribution of the zones in a lake can change as the temperature in the environment changes. For example, in an area where the environmental temperature drops below zero during the winter, the upper layer of the lake freezes. However, under this layer of ice the water is still in a liquid state. Fish and other wildlife can continue to live beneath the frozen layer as they possess **adaptations** that help them survive these changes in temperature. During this time, the surface of the lake is the coldest zone.

beneath → under

Practicing

1. Complete the table with the characteristics of lakes compared with oceans.
Describe

Lakes vs. Oceans		
Type of Water	**Size**	**Depth**

Summarizing

Lakes are accumulations of water surrounded by ______________. The majority of lakes are fresh water, and they are smaller and shallower than ______________.

Connecting

Seas

Can the sea level change? Yes! Every day the level of the sea rises and falls. This **phenomenon** is called the **tide**. Tides can be seen at the beach because the coast grows wider or narrower according to the sea level. The sea level changes throughout the day.

Low Tide	High Tide

Water moves away from the beach, which becomes wider. The lowest point that the water reaches is called **low water** or **low tide**.	The sea begins to rise again, and the beach becomes narrower. The highest point that the water reaches is called **high water** or **high tide**.

The moon is primarily responsible for the tides. When the earth and moon are close, they attract each other. This causes the water in the ocean to move, creating one or more high and low tides every day.

Fun Fact!

There are two types of tides: Solar tides depend on the attraction between the earth and sun, and lunar tides depend on the attraction between the earth and moon. Both change the sea level and alternate between high and low tides.

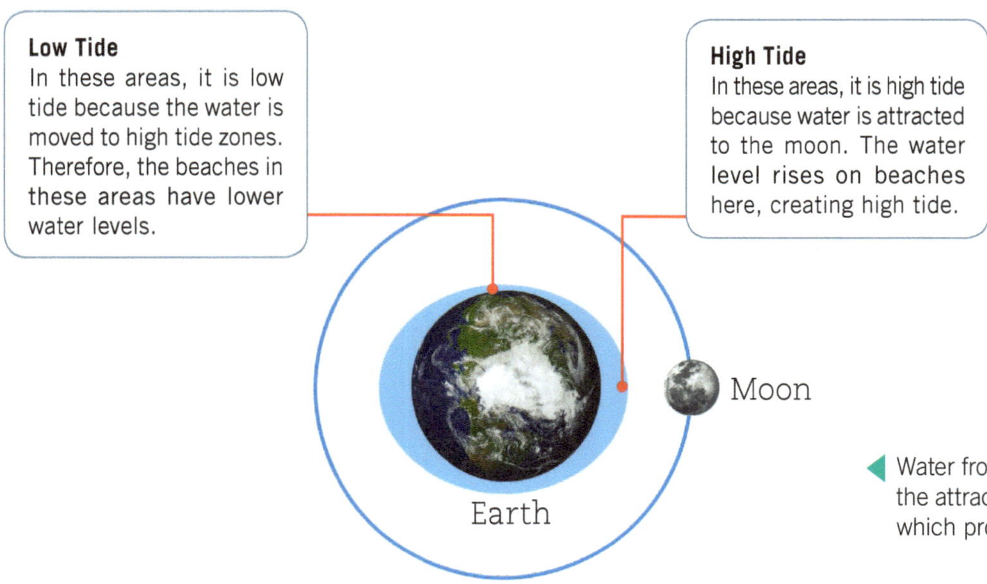

Water from the oceans is moved because of the attraction between the moon and earth, which produces tides.

Ocean Currents

Have you ever heard anyone talking about the El Niño current? What about the effects of the La Niña current? These names refer to different ways the water moves in the ocean. **Currents** are movements of large amounts of water in seas and oceans. They have different depths and directions. Currents are caused by differences in temperature, salt content and wind. Because of the way they move, currents are considered rivers under the ocean. They can be warm currents, like El Niño, or cold, like La Niña, depending on their sources. These currents alter regional weather patterns and cause floods and droughts in some areas in the world. They also affect the diversity of living things in a particular area.

patterns → systems

droughts → deficiency or absence of water

Word Focus

A swell: an upward and downward movement of water.
To swell: to grow larger or increase.

Waves

Waves can be smooth **swells** or giant waves like the ones you find in a storm. This phenomenon has to do with the movement of air on the surface of the ocean, although very large waves can also come from seismic activity like earthquakes.

Waves are produced in these steps:

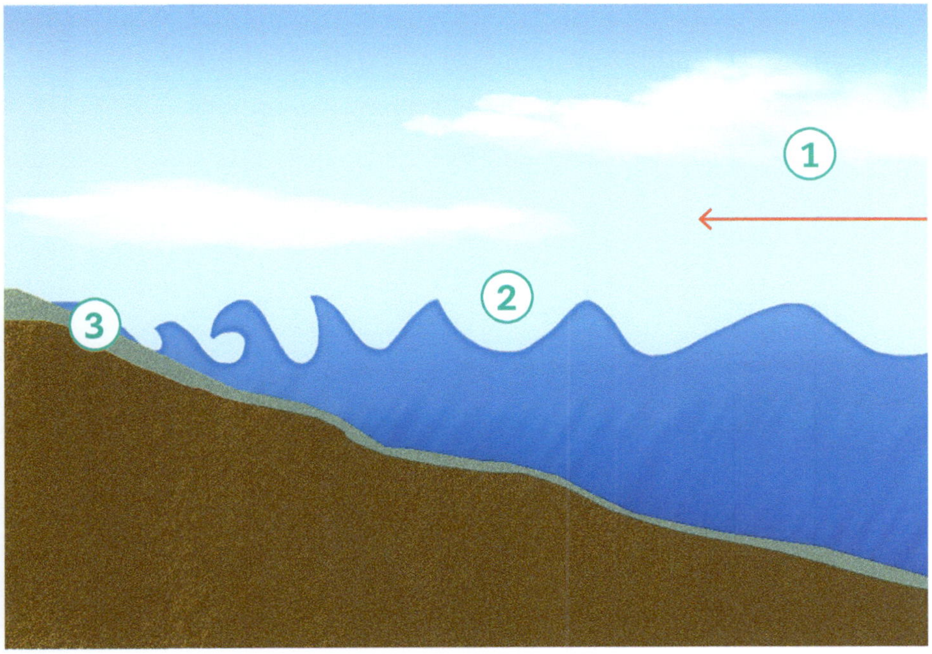

1. The wind blows toward the shore, pushing the water.
2. Close to the shore, waves begin to change shape.
3. Waves break on the shore.

Practicing

1. Find **Cutout 13** on **page 183**. Glue the images in the boxes. Then write the name of each type of water movement shown.

Water Movement		
______________	______________	______________
These are like rivers under the ocean that move in different directions and can be warm or cold.	These are changes in the level of the ocean, which can rise or fall. They can be seen primarily from the shore.	These are swells on the surface of the water that break on the shore.

Summarizing

Water Movement

- Tides — are — ______________
- Waves — are — ______________
- ______________ — are — the movement of water in the ocean.

Quiz Yourself

1. Label the photic and aphotic zones in the diagram. Complete the information about the luminosity, temperature, pressure and diversity of life in each zone.

Luminosity: ______________________

Temperature: ______________________

Pressure: ______________________

Diversity of living organisms: ______________________

____

Zone: ______________________

Zone: ______________________

Luminosity: ______________________

Temperature: ______________________

Pressure: ______________________

Diversity of living organisms: ______________________

____

2. Draw and describe each type of water movement.

Waves	Tides	Currents
______________________ ______________________ ______________________	______________________ ______________________ ______________________	______________________ ______________________ ______________________

Let's Check!

1. Mark the chart that correctly represents the distribution of salt water and fresh water on earth with a ✔. Explain.

points
/ 3

salt water   fresh water

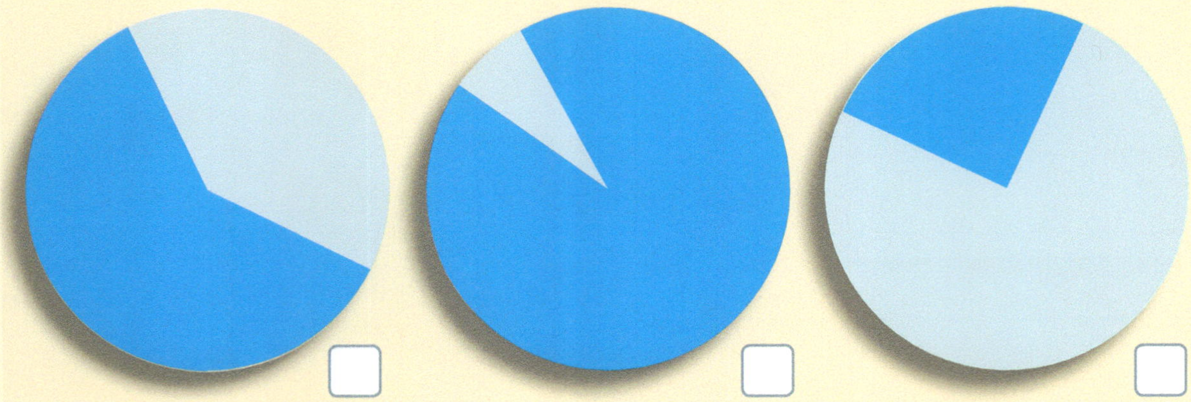

____

____

2. Go to **Cutout 14** on **page 183**. Match each description with an image.

points
/ 4

Solid freshwater reserves in the form of ice.	Large quantities of fresh water that flow over land.
Formed after water infiltrates into the earth's surface.	Large bodies of salt water that separate the continents.

3. Complete the chart with the characteristics of each zone.

points
/ 10

	Photic Zone	Aphotic Zone
Depth		
Luminosity		
Temperature		
Pressure		
Diversity of living things		

4. Look at the image of a lake. Label each zone.

points
/ 3

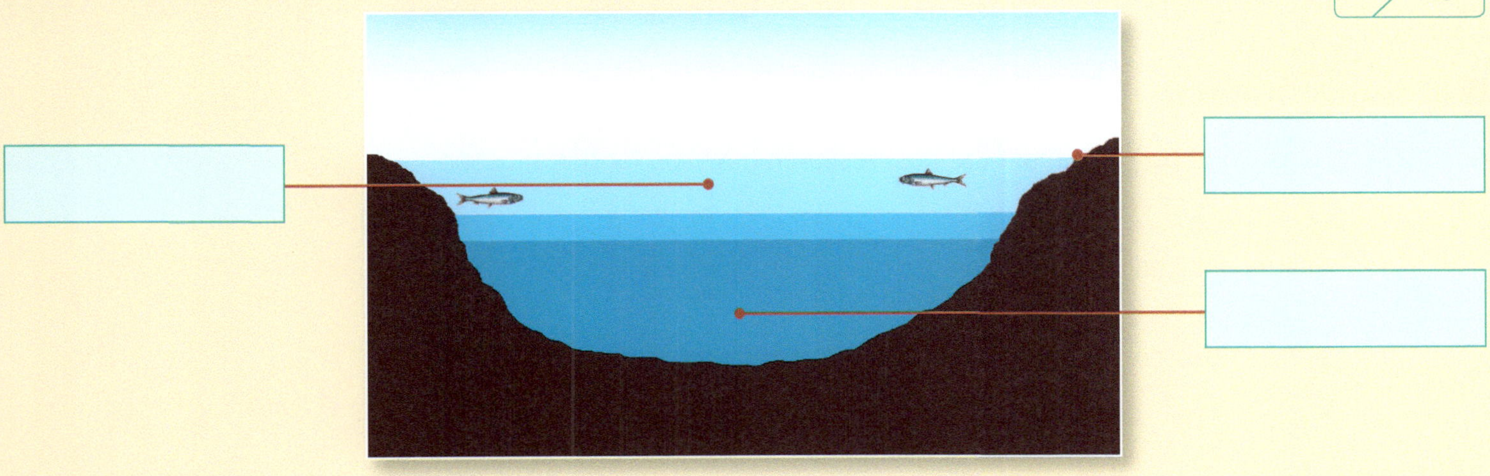

5. Write the characteristics of each type of water movement.

points
/ 3

Water Movement	Description
Tides	
Currents	
Waves	

Scientific Skill: Communicate and represent evidence

The Effects of Water Pollution on Living Things

Basic Framework

Water pollution affects the **environment** and the **living things** that live there. For example, the pollution in a river changes the properties of the water, severely affecting the organisms that use it as a home or a source of nutrition. In human beings, water pollution causes serious **health** problems.

Observation

deposits as waste

A group of students passing by a river observe that in the area near a factory (image 1) that dumps contaminants into the water, there is less wildlife than in other parts of the river (image 2).

What do you think is causing the difference in the number of living things in each part of the river?

____

____

____

Research Question

According to what you observed, mark the best research question for this situation.

- [ ] What effects does pollution have on the quality of water in the river?
- [ ] What effects does pollution have on the development of wildlife in the river?

Hypothesis

The presence of contaminants harms the development of wildlife inhabiting the river.

Predictions

Form two predictions about what is observed:

Prediction 1: ______________________________

Prediction 2: ______________________________

Experimental Procedure

1. What variable are you working with? In other words, what is the **independent variable** in this experiment?

   - [ ] The presence of pollution.
   - [ ] The effect of pollution on wildlife.

2. With four classmates, collect the following materials:

   - 2 ten centimeter pieces of the aquatic plant elodea
   - 2 glass jars of equal size
   - 1 marker
   - gravel → small stones
   - 1 lamp
   - 1 lightbulb
   - cooking oil
   - water
   - 1 plastic syringe
   - 1 ruler

3. Using the marker, label the jars 1 and 2.

4. Put the same amount of gravel in each jar. Then plant an elodea in each. Make sure the elodea is firmly planted in the gravel.

5. Fill the jars with equal amounts of water, covering the plants completely. Pour the water carefully so that the plant does not come out of the gravel.

6. Add oil to jar 2 with the syringe until a three-centimeter layer is formed. Be careful while you do this.

7. Place the lamp on a table. Place both jars close to it and at the same distance so that they receive the same amount of light.

8. Observe the experiment daily for one week and record any changes in the **Results** section.

What do you think will happen to the elodea plant in each jar?

How can you relate these answers to your predictions?

Results

1. In the table, record the changes you observed during the week.

Day	Jar 1	Jar 2
1		
2		
3		
4		
5		
6		
7		

Interpreting and Analyzing the Results

1. Did the same thing happen in both jars? Explain.

____

____

2. What does the oil represent in the experiment? Explain. Consider the **Basic Framework**.

____

____

3. What other factors could have affected the results of the experiment? Explain.

____

____

Conclusions

most important

In your conclusions, the core ideas derived from **interpreting** and **analyzing** your **data** should be contrasted with the **hypothesis** proposed at the beginning of the experiment. This way you will be able to accept or reject your hypothesis.

1. Is the hypothesis proposed at the beginning of the activity accepted or rejected? Explain.

2. What would happen if there were a large oil spill in a lake?

In addition to accepting or rejecting a hypothesis, the conclusion should also reflect the completed activity. The information acquired allows you to present new research questions for future experiments on the same or a related topic.

3. What effect does water contamination have on living organisms that use or live in water?

4. What importance do you think this type of experiment has for human beings?

When you have enough results to support your hypothesis, your knowledge should be shared. Generally, the information that comes from scientific experiments is not widely distributed to the public. It can only be found in specialized publications or at conventions where scientists display their work to be recognized by their **colleagues**. You too can **communicate and represent** your data in a report or scientific statement addressed to your school.

5. Write a scientific statement or report about the experiment you did in this lab. **Cutout 15** on **page 185** will help guide you.

What Did You Learn?

1. Franky represented the distribution of fresh water and salt water on earth with cups.

points ___ /10

cup 1

cup 2

Respond.

a. Which cup represents the amount of fresh water on earth? Which cup represents the amount of salt water? Explain.

Fresh water: ____

____

Salt water: ____

____

b. Using the same materials as Franky, how would you represent the distribution of water and land on our planet? Draw a diagram.

Water	Land

c. Name the different types of freshwater and saltwater reserves on earth.

Freshwater reserves: ____

____

Saltwater reserves: ____

____

2. Match the numbers with the types of water reserve.

points
/ 5

☐ Large saltwater reserve.

☐ Freshwater reserve in a solid state.

☐ Freshwater reserves that flow over the surface of the earth.

☐ Flow of water under the surface of the earth.

☐ Water in a gas state or in tiny drops.

3. Complete the table. Indicate which zone has more and less of each characteristic.

points
/ 10

Characteristic / Zone	Diversity of Life	Temperature	Light	Pressure
Photic				
Aphotic				

a. Why do you think there is a greater diversity of living things in the photic zone? Explain using the factors from the table.

____

____

4. Complete the table. Describe each zone in a lake.

points
/6

Littoral Zone	
Limnetic Zone	
Profundal Zone	

5. Complete the diagram.

points
/6

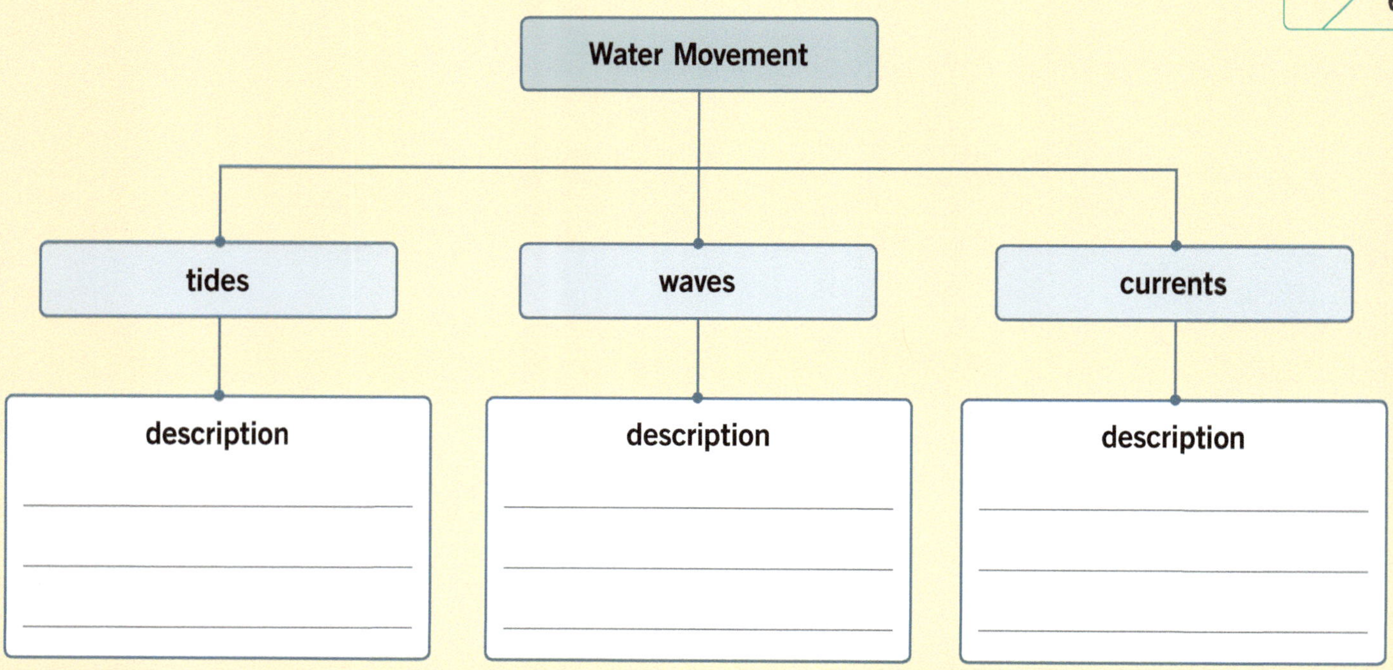

6. Which of the following processes corresponds to the change of water from a liquid to a gas that then rises into the atmosphere?

points ___ / 1

A. Condensation.
B. Precipitation.
C. Evaporation.
D. Surface runoff.

points ___ / 6

7. Complete the table.

Effects of Human Activity on Water Reserves	
Positive Effects	**Negative Effects**

Scientific Skill: Communicate and represent evidence

8. Go to **Activity Card 6**, which discusses living organisms as indicators of water quality. With this information, write a scientific report to present to another class. Follow the format shown in the **Science Lab**.

points ___ / 7

Title of Report:

Find Test 4 Study Page

Glossary

5.1 Key Words Unit 1

cell – *n*, the basic structural unit of all living things

function – *n*, what something or someone is meant to do; the purpose of something

system – *n*, a group of things that work or act together in a particular way as a whole

convert – *v*, to change into something different

circulate – *v*, to move around continuously through an area or a system

5.2 Key Words Unit 2

consume – *v*, to eat or drink; to use up or destroy

energy – *n*, the power to move or heat things or to do other kinds of work, provided by such things as the burning of fuel, the flow of electricity or the force of wind or moving water

diet – *n*, the food or drink that a person or animal usually eats; a restricted range of food and drink

risk – *n*, the possibility that something bad will happen

humid – *adj*, moist and damp, often warm

5.3 Key Words Unit 3

transform – *v*, to change something completely

efficient – *adj*, able to do things well and on time

predict – *v*, to guess what is going to happen ahead of time

device – *n*, a machine or tool designed for a particular purpose

safety – *n*, freedom from danger, harm or risk

5.4 Key Words Unit 4

salt water – *n*, water with a high salt content, such as from the ocean

fresh water – *n*, water with little salt in it, such as from lakes and rivers

shallow – *adj*, not far from the top; not deep

deep – *adj*, far below the surface

reserve – *n*, an area of land set aside for a specific purpose

A

absorb – *v*, to slowly take something in

absorption – *n,* the process by which one thing is absorbed by another

abundant – *adj,* possessing a large amount or quantity of something

accumulate – *v,* to gather or acquire

adapt – *v*, to make suitable for a different situation—something changed in this way is an adaptation

adaptor – *n*, a device that joins two pieces of machinery of different types or sizes

adequate – *adj*, as it should be; suitable; enough

amber – *n*, a hardened resin from long-dead trees used to make jewelry and other ornaments

antibiotic – *n*, a medical drug that can help cure illnesses caused by germs

B

backward – *adv*, toward the rear; moving in reverse

biological – *adj*, related to the study of living organisms

beat – *v*, to pulsate rhythmically

burn – *v*, to set fire to something; to damage or destroy by heating

C

capacity – *n*, the ability to do something; the amount that can be held by a container

checkup – *n*, a medical inspection

clog – *v*, to block or become blocked with

cluster – *n*, a group of things positioned closely together

colleague – *n*, a person who works with you

complex – *adj*, consisting of many different parts, complicated

condensation – *n,* the process by which a gas cools and becomes a liquid

condense – *v*, to change or be changed into a liquid from a gas or vapor

conditions – *n*, the situation in which something exists

contaminant – *n*, a substance that spoils the purity of something

contaminate – *v*, to make something dangerous or dirty by adding something harmful

continent – *n*, one of the great divisions of land, such as South America or Australia

contract – *v*, to make shorter or smaller

crucial – *adj*, of great importance; having a major effect

D

daily – *adj*, happening every day

decompose – *v*, to rot, decay, break down

depth – *adj*, a distance below a surface

desalination – *n*, the process of removing salt from seawater

descend – *v*, to go downward

deteriorate – *v*, to become gradually worse; to break down

dispose – *v*, to throw away or get rid of

diverse – *adj*, showing a lot of variety

diversity – *n*, the state of having a lot of differences

E

electrocute – *v*, to injure or kill by electric shock

enough – *adj/adv*, as many or as much as necessary

essential – *adj*, necessary or important

evaporate – *v*, to turn from a liquid to a gas

evaporation – *n*, the process by which a liquid heats up and becomes a gas

excess – *n*, an amount of something that is more than necessary *adj*, more than the necessary amount

F

facilitate – *v*, to make easier; help

fresh water – *n*, water that is not salty and can be purified for human consumption

freshwater – *adj*, of or living in fresh water

fundamental – *adj*, serving as a foundation or a base

G

guide – *v*, to instruct or direct *n*, an indication, a recommendation or a standard

H

handle – *n*, the part of something that you touch v, to manage or deal with

heal – *v*, to get better and become healthy again

healthy – *adj*, having or showing good health

heartbeat – *n*, the action or sound of the heart as it pumps blood

household – *n*, a place where people live; all the people who live together in a house

hydroelectric – *adj*, relating to electricity generated by the force of fast moving water, such as a river or a waterfall

hydrologic cycle – *n*, another name for the water cycle

hydrosphere – *n*, all the water on earth

hygiene – *n*, the cleanliness necessary to preserve good health and prevent disease

I

iceberg – *n*, a very large mass of ice that has broken off from polar cap and is floating in the ocean

imply – *v*, to express in an indirect way; to involve something as a natural part

infiltrate – *v*, to enter or permeate by filtration

inflammation – *n*, an area that has become red, swollen and painful

inhabit – *v*, to live on or in

interview – *n*, a meeting, usually held face to face, in which people have a discussion

L

lagoon – *n*, a body of seawater partly or fully separated from the sea by a sandbar, rocks or a coral reef

limit – *n*, a line, point or level where something must end; a boundary

luminosity – *n*, the quality of emitting light

luminous – *adj*, producing light; shining or glowing

M

mineral – *n*, a natural substance that is not of plant or animal origin

moderate – *adj*, not in excess, average, not extreme

multicellular – *adj*, of an organism that consists of many cells

N

naked eye – *n*, unassisted vision, with no optical aids like glasses or a microscope

O

obesity – *n*, the condition of being extremely overweight

origin – *n*, the beginning or cause of something

P

penicillin – *n*, an antibiotic used to treat infections caused by bacteria

phenomenon – *n*, an occurrence or event that can be seen to exist; an unusual or rare event

photosynthesis – *n*, the process by which plants make food from sunlight, water and carbon dioxide

physical – *adj*, having to do with the body

plant – *n*, any living thing that makes its food from nonliving substances, has cell walls and does not have the power to move from one place to another on its own

platform – *n*, a raised, flat area

polar – *adj*, having to do with the North Pole or South Pole

polar ice cap – *n*, a region near the North or South Pole covered in ice

portion – *n*, a serving of food

precipitation – *n*, water that falls from the atmosphere as rain, hail or snow

procedure – *n*, an established way of doing something that often involves steps

process – *n*, a series of actions carried out to achieve a particular result

prohibited – *adj*, not allowed

property – *n*, a quality or characteristic of something

prove – *v*, to demonstrate as true

proximity – *n*, closeness

pulse – *n*, the rhythmic movement of blood through the arteries that can be felt on the wrist or neck

Q

quality – *n*, a feature of someone or something

R

radiant – *adj*, emitting heat or energy in the form of waves

raw material – *n*, the basic material used to make something

reach – *v*, to arrive, to touch, to make contact with

recommend – *v*, to speak in favor of; to praise; to give support; to suggest as a good idea

regularly – *adv*, often

reliable – *adj*, trustworthy

reservoir – *n*, a storage area for liquids, such as a dam to collect river water

rich – *adj*, having a large amount of something; abundant

rise – *v*, to go in an upward direction

rub – *v*, to move against with pressure

runoff – *n*, water that flows over land to the oceans

S

salt water – *n*, water that contains a high level of salt; seawater

saltwater – *adj*, relating to salt water

scarce – *adj*, difficult to find or obtain

secrete – *v*, to produce and give off a liquid

secretion – *n*, a substance produced by a cell, a gland or an organ for a particular function

seismic – *adj*, relating to earthquakes

smoke – *n*, the visible gas and other particles given off as something burns

sterile – *adj*, clean, germ free

structure – *n*, something that is built or constructed; an arrangement of parts

suggestion – *n*, an idea or plan for consideration

supply – *v*, to provide with or stock

surface runoff – *n*, the water that flows over land and back to bodies of water

swallow – *v*, to push food down the throat

symbology – *n*, the study or use of symbols

T

torrential – *adj*, coming in a large, fast stream

transpiration – *n*, water that evaporates from plants

transport – *v*, to move; to go from one place to another

U

unicellular – *adj*, of an organism consisting of a single cell

V

verify – *v*, to prove or check

vibrate – *v*, to move from side to side with short, quick movements

vital – *adj*, having to do with life; necessary or important

vitamin – *n*, a substance that is needed for the body for growth and nutrition

volt – *n*, a unit that measures the force of an electric current

W

warn – *v*, to tell of possible danger or problems; to give advice in order to avoid possible problems

withstand – *v*, to bear or put up with; to hold out against or resist

wound – *n*, a cut or an injury

Cutout 1
Use on page 9 (**Unit 1**).

heart

lungs

stomach

Cutout 2
Use on page 26 (**Unit 1**).

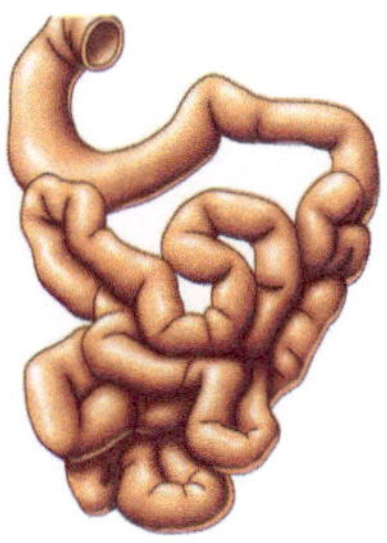

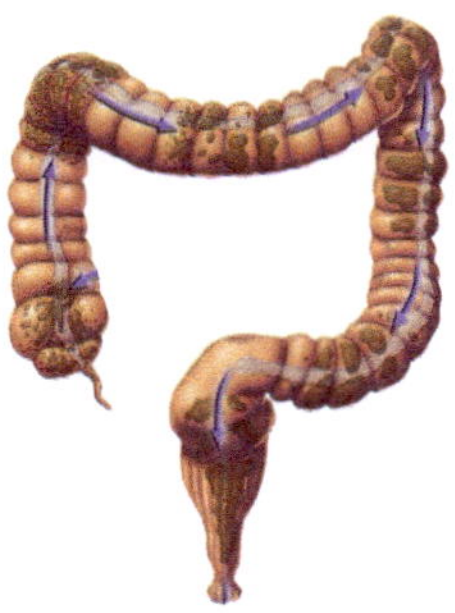

Cutout 3

Use on page 32 (**Unit 1**).

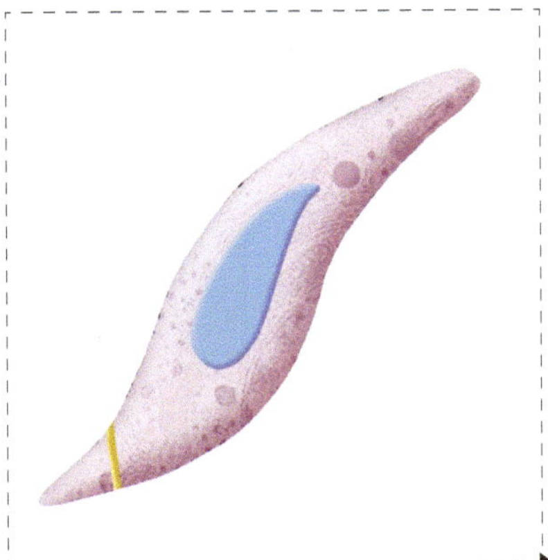

Cutout 4

Use on page 42 (**Unit 1**).

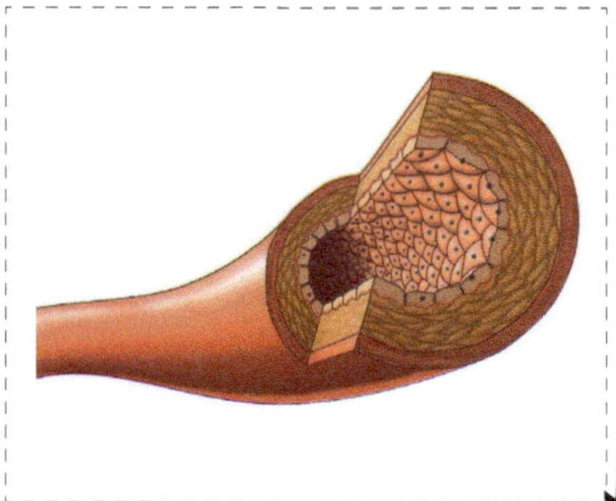

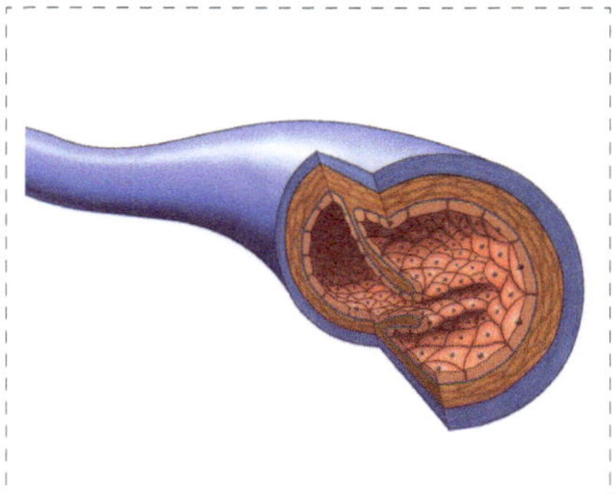

Cutout 5

Use on page 51 (**Unit 1**).

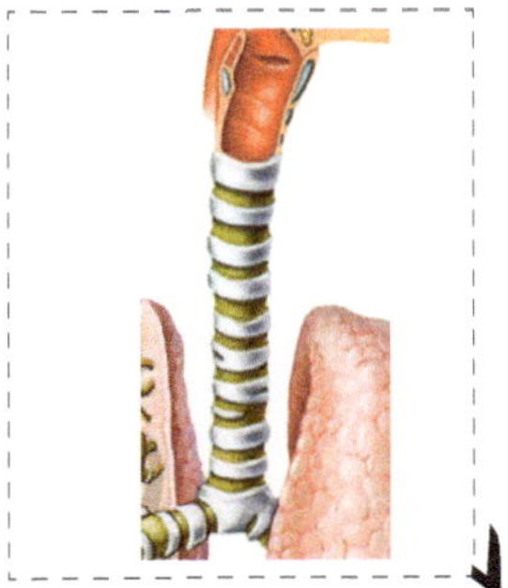

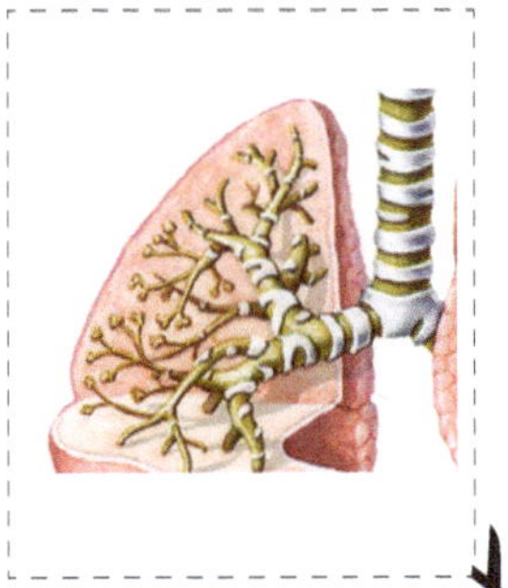

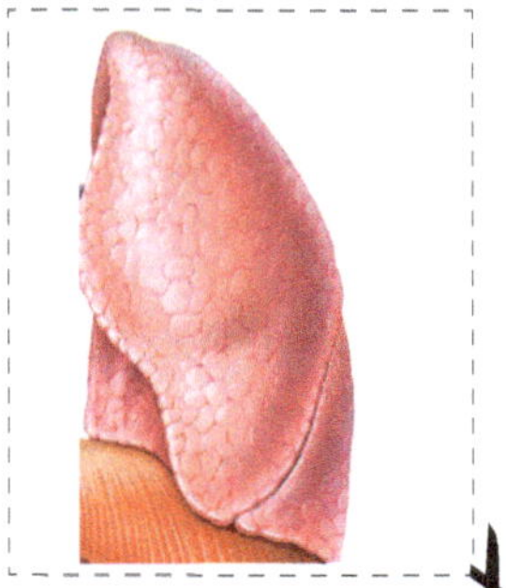

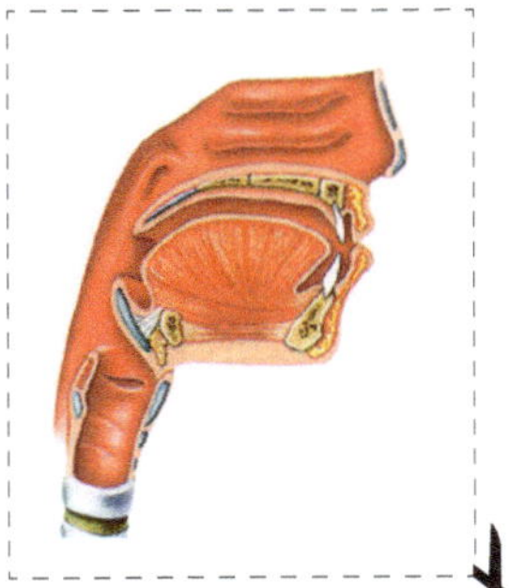

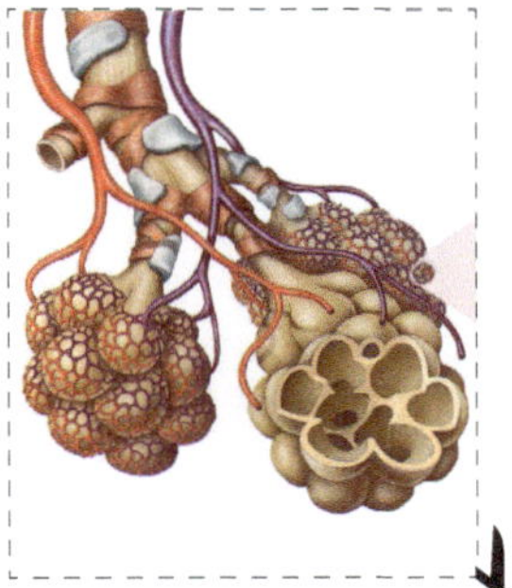

Cutouts

Cutout 6

Use on page 68 (**Unit 2**).

Cutout 7

Use on page 69 (**Unit 2**).

oil

cake

butter

eggs

peaches

meat and nuts

rice

cheese

grapes

milk

pineapple

bread

pasta

lettuce

broccoli

bell pepper
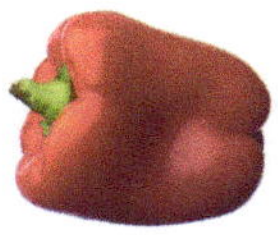

Cutout 8

Use on page 69 (**Unit 2**).

Cutout 9
Use on page 79 (**Unit 2**).

Name an illness caused by a virus. Make sure it is not one that has already been said!	Which type of microorganism is yeast?	Name an illness caused by bacteria. Make sure it is not one that has already been said!
Name a beneficial use of bacteria. Make sure it is not one that has already been said!	Which microorganism causes mycosis?	What positive effect do viruses have on humans?
Name microorganisms that have negative effects on humans.	Which type of microorganism causes tuberculosis?	Name a beneficial effect of fungi. Make sure it is not one that has already been said!
Name microorganisms that have positive effects on humans.	Mushrooms are fungi that we can eat. What effect do they have on humans?	Which type of microorganism is used to make antibiotics?

Cutout 10
Use on page 85 (**Unit 2**).

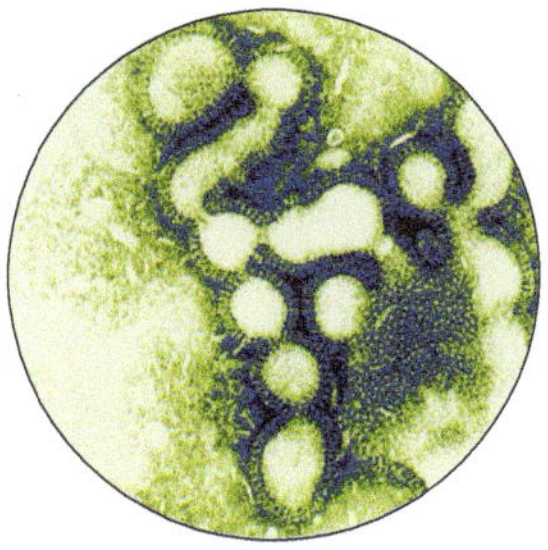
viruses

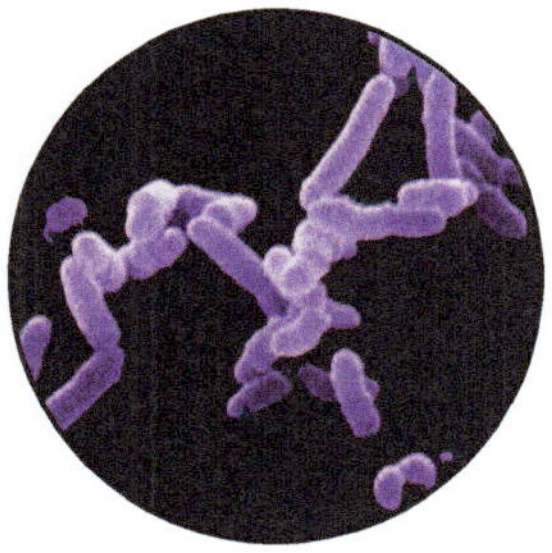
bacteria

fungi

Cutouts

Cutout 11

Use on page 102 (**Unit 3**).

plug

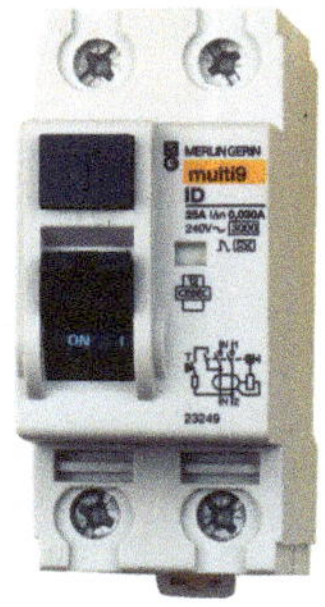

circuit breaker

electricity meter

switch

outlet box

electric cables

Cutouts

Cutout 12
Use on page 118 (**Unit 3**).

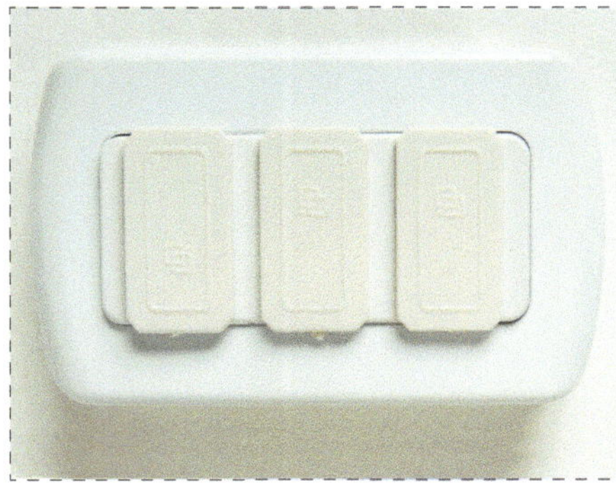

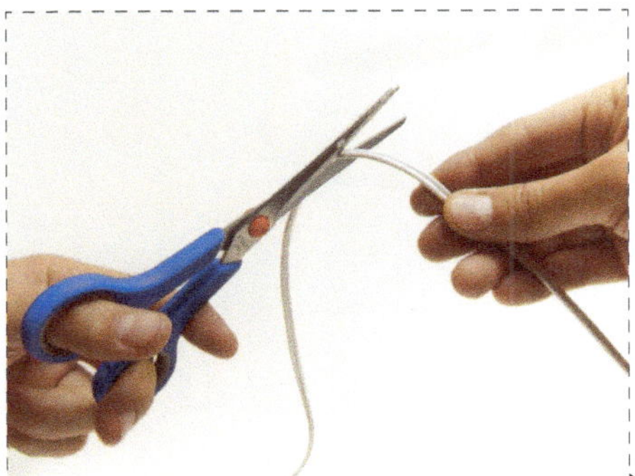

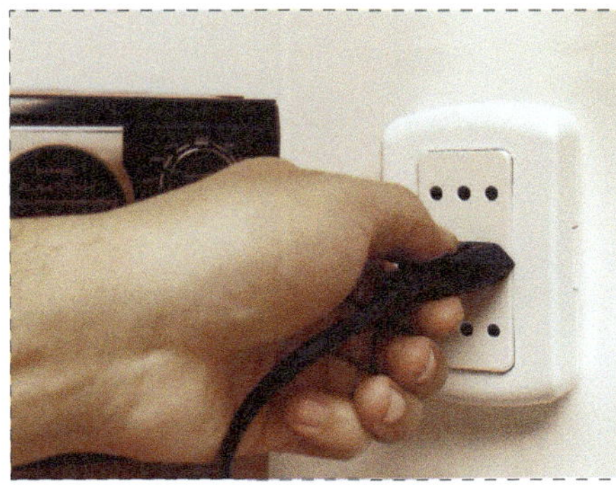

Cutout 13
Use on page 146 (**Unit 4**).

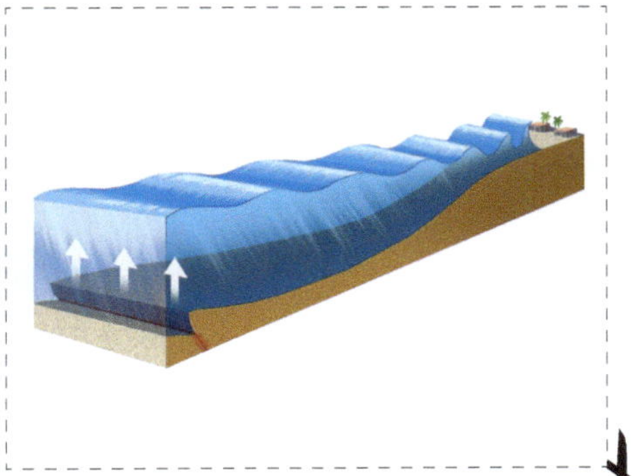

Cutout 14
Use on page 148 (**Unit 4**).

Cutout 15

Use on page 153 (**Unit 4**).

Writing a Scientific Report

Activity Title:

Scientist's Name:

Research Question:

____

Basic Framework:

____

____

____

____

(glue an image from the experiment here)

Results:

Analyzing the Data and Conclusions:

____

____

____

____

Air Pathways in the Respiratory System

Number the pictures in the respiratory system in order according to the path air takes from when it enters the nasal passage to when it arrives in the lungs.

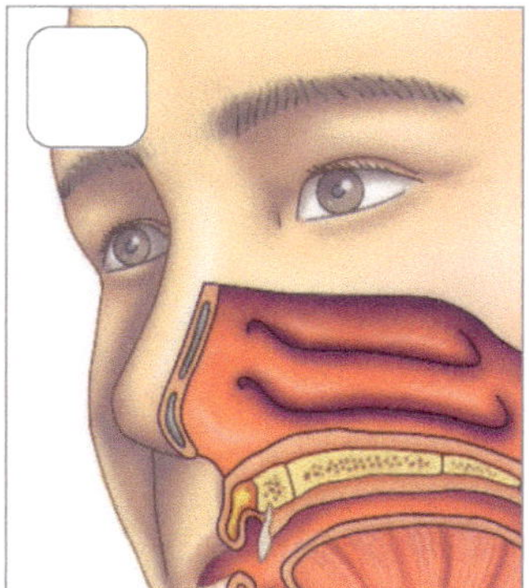

nasal passageways

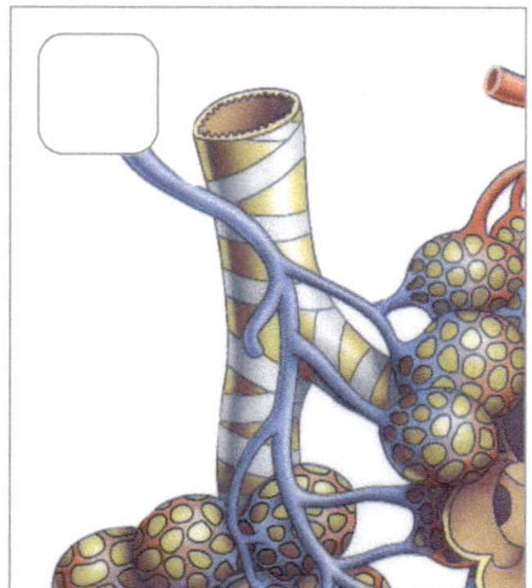

bronchial tubes

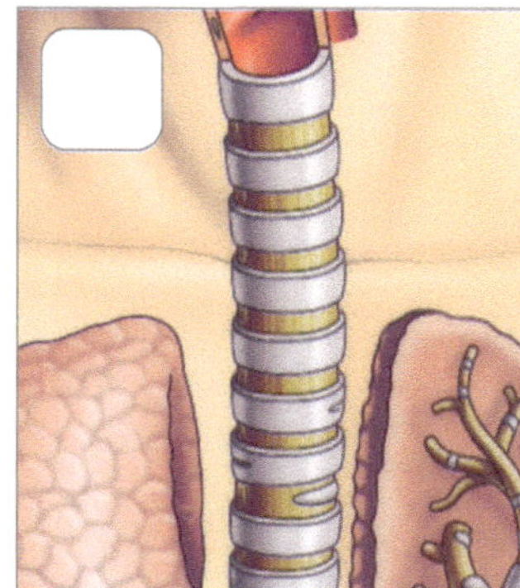

trachea

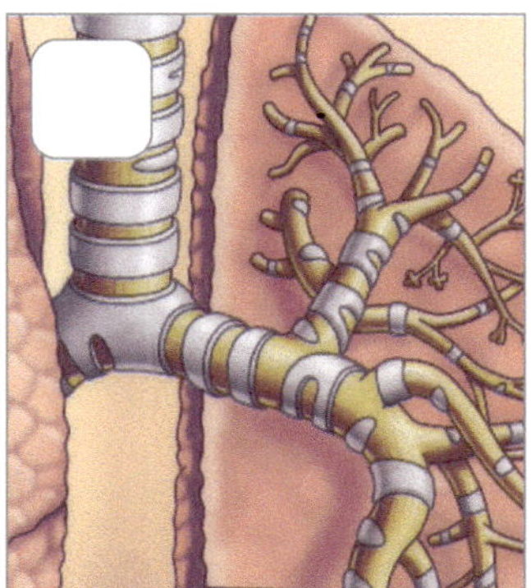

bronchi

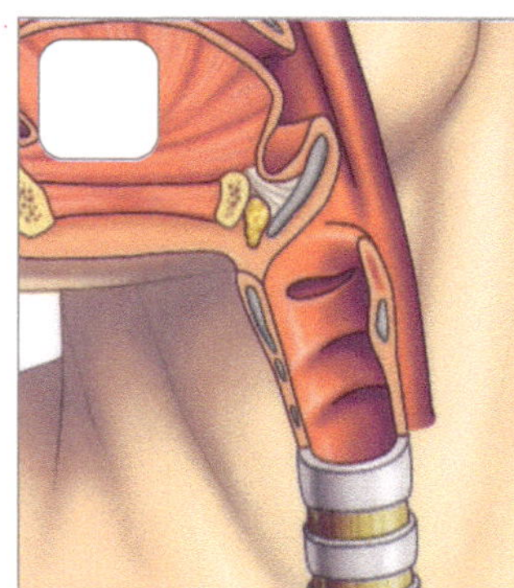

larynx

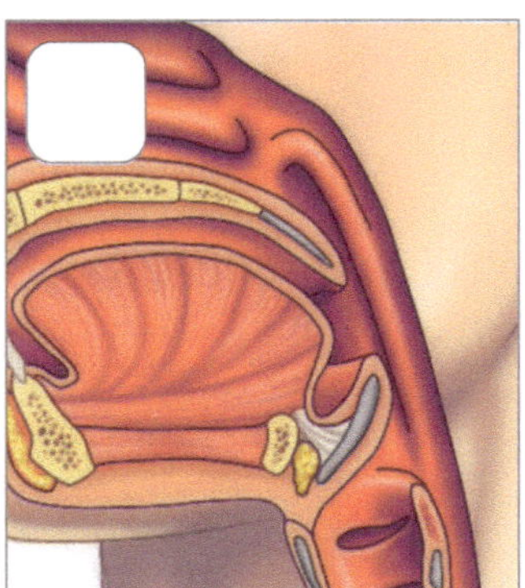

pharynx

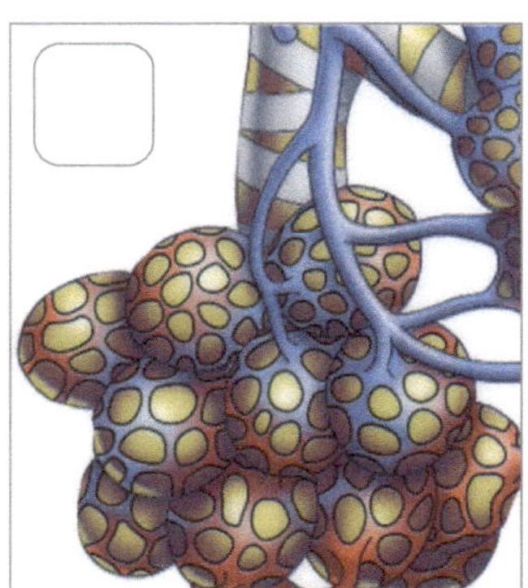

alveoli

Activity Card 2

Food Pyramid

Complete each level of the pyramid with foods from **Cutout 7**.

Good and Bad Effects of Microorganisms

Game rules: To play, all you need is your creativity. For each correct answer, move forward two spaces. For each incorrect answer, go back a space. The first to reach the finish wins!
Look for the question cards from **Cutout 9**.

Activity Card 4

The Water Cycle

Cut out the pictures on this page and the texts on **Activity Card 5**. With a partner, match each stage of the water cycle with its description.

Activity Card 5

Water from oceans, rivers and lakes changes from a liquid state to a gas and rises into the atmosphere.	Movement of water over the surface of the earth, in the form of rivers.
Water vapor, very high up in the atmosphere, changes from a gaseous state to a liquid, forming very small droplets.	Part of the water on the surface of the earth is absorbed into the ground.
Clouds accumulate a large amount of water that falls to the ground in the form of rain, snow and hail.	Water loss from the bodies of living things, especially plants, in the form of vapor.

Activity Card 6

Read the following text.

Bioindicators: A Method of Evaluating the Quality of Water

A useful tool for determining the quality of water is the use of known organisms as bioindicators.

This technique consists of studying the number of organisms found in water with respect to the conditions of temperature and salinity, among others. If the characteristics of the water change, the organisms will no longer be able to develop, which affects the quantity of these organisms. For example, if a bioindicator organism inhabits a river into which pollutants have been dumped, the pollution changes the characteristics of the water and as a result, the number of organisms decreases.

Aquatic organisms used as bioindicators include bacteria, fish, algae and invertebrates (mostly insects), among others.

There are several advantages to using organisms as indicators of water quality:

Bacteria are abundant and easy to maintain, and they demonstrate rapid growth, which allows the development of a large quantity of bacteria in a short period of time. They are very useful organisms for studying water that has been polluted by domestic and industrial waste.

Aquatic invertebrates are the most useful group in this type of study as they are found in all oceans, rivers and lakes, have a long life span and are easily identifiable. Also, because the organisms tend to stay in the same place, it makes it easier to perform an analysis of their environment.

Although the information found by using bioindicators is not intended to replace laboratory studies that check the quality of water, these organisms are an alternative tool that can reduce the cost of these studies in an easy and environmentally friendly manner.

Name: ______________________________ Grade: __________

Level 4: System

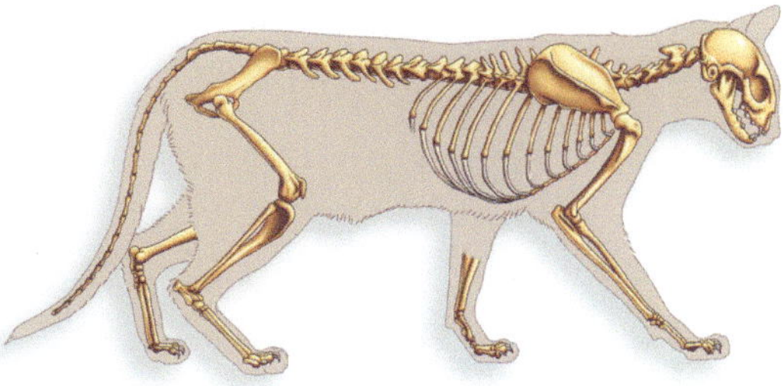

A group of organs that work together.

Level 5: Organism

A group of systems that work together.

stances to all parts of
latory system are:

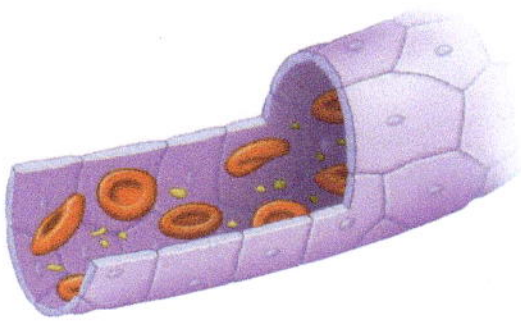

oumps blood to
the body.

els ▶
els are
circulate
parts of

Respiratory System: allows oxygen to enter the body and eliminates carbon dioxide.

Air enters through the **nasal passages (1)** and passes through the **pharynx (2)** and **trachea (3)**. Then it enters the **bronchi (4)** and goes to the **lungs (5)** and **bronchial tubes (6)**. Finally, gas exchange occurs in the **alveoli (7)**, where oxygen is exchanged with carbon dioxide.

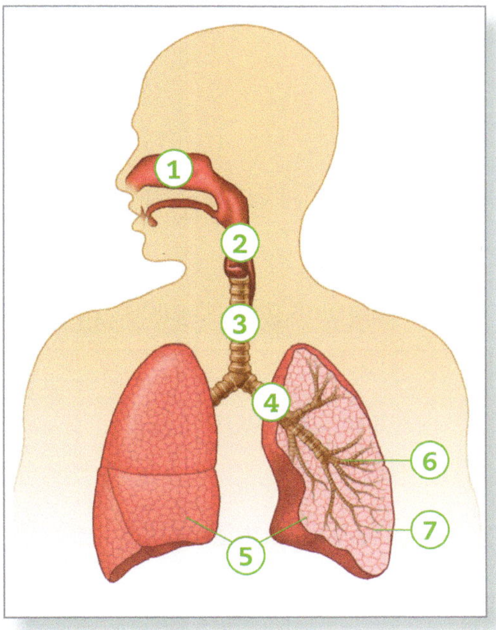

Test 1 Study Page • Review

Remove, answer, and glue in your notebook.

Section 1

1. Read the definitions and think of the correct word. Then find the words in the word search.

a. A group of cells that work together.

b. The most complex level of biological organization.

c. A group of organs that work together.

d. A group of tissues that work together.

e. All living things consist of these.

A	C	E	L	L	S	S	O
F	P	W	Q	Z	V	C	R
G	O	E	P	L	L	D	G
J	T	I	S	S	U	E	A
K	L	A	O	Y	T	H	N
N	F	M	I	S	K	Y	I
O	B	H	U	T	P	U	S
V	R	N	Y	E	O	I	M
D	C	G	I	M	L	J	H
N	X	C	A	R	K	D	S
R	G	S	T	N	F	Q	A
U	P	Z	K	E	W	G	S

Section 2

2. In the following diagram, match each description with the correct organ.

Where digestion starts. ◯

Secretes gastric juices and helps with digestion. ◯

Eliminates waste. ◯

Absorbs nutrients. ◯

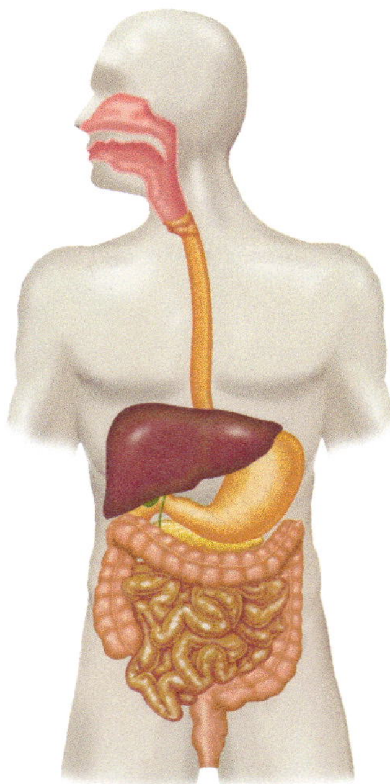

Name: ______________________________ Grade: ____________

In the ocean, masses of water experience three types of movement:

Tides: changes in the level of the sea.

Waves: swells of water usually caused by the wind.

Currents: movements of water similar to a river, under the ocean and in different directions.

Water is an important resource for human beings: it regulates the global temperature, irrigates crops and helps us maintain good personal hygiene, among other functions.

Water has been polluted by many human activities, such as livestock farming, agriculture, domestic activities and industrial activities. For this reason, it has been necessary to establish natural reserves to protect this resource.

Everyone can help save and protect water with simple actions such as turning off the tap when brushing your teeth and taking quick showers.

Test 4 Study Page • Review

Remove, answer, and glue in your notebook.

Section 1

1. Answer the questions as if 10 glasses of water represent the total amount of water on the earth.

a. Approximately how many glasses of water represent the total amount of fresh water on the planet? Explain.

____

____

b. About how many glasses represent the amount of salt water on earth? Explain.

____

____

Section 2

2. Complete the table.

	Ocean	Lake
Type of Water		
Size		
Depth		

Name: ______________________________ Grade: __________

In the ocean, masses of water experience three types of movement:

Tides: changes in the level of the sea.

Waves: swells of water usually caused by the wind.

Currents: movements of water similar to a river, under the ocean and in different directions.

Water is an important resource for human beings: it regulates the global temperature, irrigates crops and helps us maintain good personal hygiene, among other functions.

Water has been polluted by many human activities, such as livestock farming, agriculture, domestic activities and industrial activities. For this reason, it has been necessary to establish natural reserves to protect this resource.

Everyone can help save and protect water with simple actions such as turning off the tap when brushing your teeth and taking quick showers.

Test 4 Study Page • Review

Remove, answer, and glue in your notebook.

Section 1

1. Answer the questions as if 10 glasses of water represent the total amount of water on the earth.

a. Approximately how many glasses of water represent the total amount of fresh water on the planet? Explain.

____

____

b. About how many glasses represent the amount of salt water on earth? Explain.

____

____

Section 2

2. Complete the table.

	Ocean	Lake
Type of Water		
Size		
Depth		

Name: ______________________________ Grade: __________

Microorganisms, like bacteria, fungi and viruses, can have positive and negative effects on our bodies. Although it is debatable whether they are living beings, viruses are part of this group because they cause diseases.

Negative Effects: bacteria, fungi and viruses cause illnesses like cholera, typhoid fever, tuberculosis, chicken pox and AIDS.

Positive Effects: bacteria form part of our human microbiome and produce vitamin K. Fungi and bacteria are used to make antibiotics and insulin. They are also important ingredients in foods like cheese, yogurt and bread.

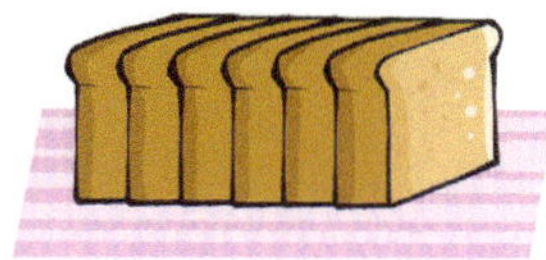

One way to avoid illnesses is to have healthy habits, like good hygiene.

Microorganism	Structure	Diseases
bacteria	unicellular	typhoid, cholera
fungi	unicellular or multicellular	ringworm, such as athlete's foot
viruses	no complete cell	the flu, AIDS

Test 2 Study Page • Review

Remove, answer, and glue in your notebook.

Section 1

1. Look at the images.

A

B

a. Which meal shows part of a balanced diet? Explain.

____

____

b. Which meal shows part of an **unhealthy** diet? Explain.

____

____

c. Complete the table with the principal nutrient of each meal and its function.

Meal	Principal Nutrient	Function
A		
B		

Section 2

2. Match the types of illnesses with the descriptions.

a. Degenerative diseases	are caused by parasites that live inside or outside our bodies and have negative effects.
b. Deficiency diseases	are caused by microorganisms. They act fast and are very contagious.
c. Infectious diseases	are caused by the deterioration or aging of an organ.
d. Parasitic diseases	are caused by the lack of or deficiency of necessary nutrients.

3. Complete the diagram.

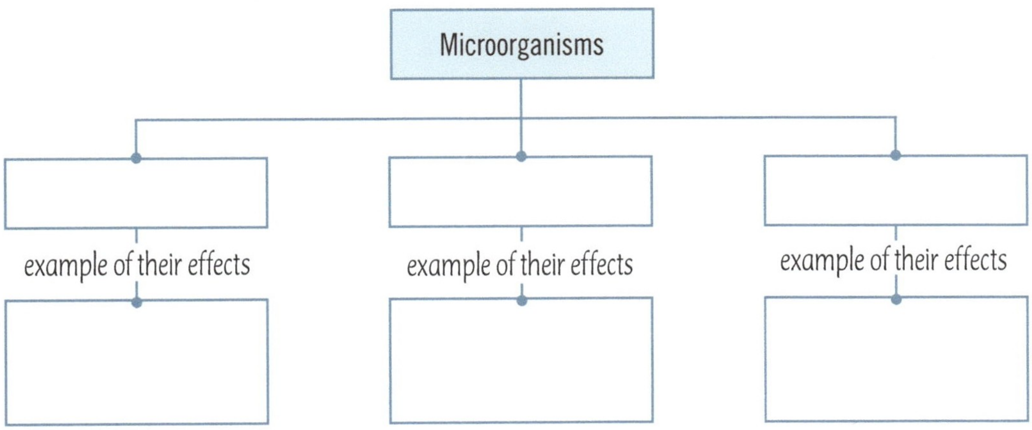

glue here

glue here

glue here

glue here

Test 2 Study Page • Summary

Foods contains different nutrients that are necessary for the body to function. They include:

Proteins: build and repair body structures like bones and muscles. Milk and fish are rich in protein.

Lipids: provide the energy that is stored in tissue as body fat. Butter, oil, mayonnaise and peanuts have a high quantity of lipids.

Vitamins and Minerals: regulate different processes in the body. Fruits and vegetables are rich in vitamins and minerals.

Carbohydrates: provide immediate energy for the body. Pasta, bread and potatoes are rich in carbohydrates.

A **balanced diet** means eating foods with the right nutrients and portions for your body.

Vitamin or Mineral	Function	Food Sources
Vitamin B	Contributes to the functions of the nervous, digestive and muscular systems—for example, it maintains the structure of nervous system cells	red meat, legumes
Vitamin D	Helps the body absorb calcium, which strengthens bones and teeth	fish, milk, cheese, yogurt
Iron	Forms part of the red blood cells and has an important role in oxygen transportation	green vegetables, eggs, red meat
Calcium	Helps bones and teeth grow and helps blood clot	dairy products, almonds

Name: ______________________________ Grade: __________

Materials can be classified as **conductors** or **insulators**, depending on their capacity to transport a current.

Conductors are generally metals: copper, aluminum, iron, silver and gold.

Insulators include plastic, wood, rubber, cloth, air and glass, among others.

The characteristics of conductors and insulators make them useful when making many things we use every day, like pliers, voltage testers and plugs/outlets.

Electricity is very important to humans. However, it can also be dangerous if people do not follow the correct **safety precautions**.

Conductors	Insulators
	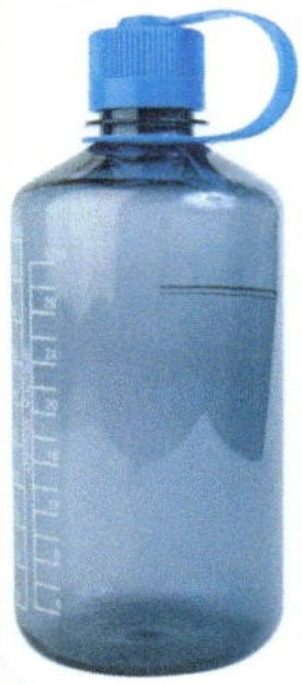 

Electric energy is important to everyday life.

Most energy is used in electricity generation and transportation.

Lighting, refrigeration, heating and cooling consume most of the energy in households. We should try and save energy when using devices for these purposes.

Electricity should be used efficiently, without wasting it.

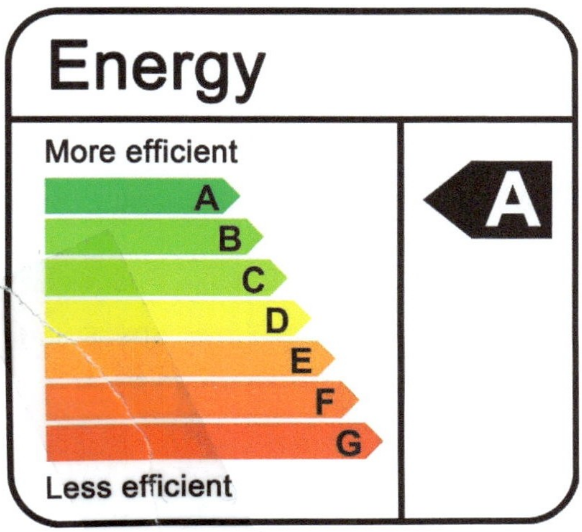

Test 3 Study Page • Review

Remove, answer, and glue in your notebook.

Section 1

1. Look at the image. Write the type of energy the lamp needs to function in box **A** and the type of energy it creates in box **B**.

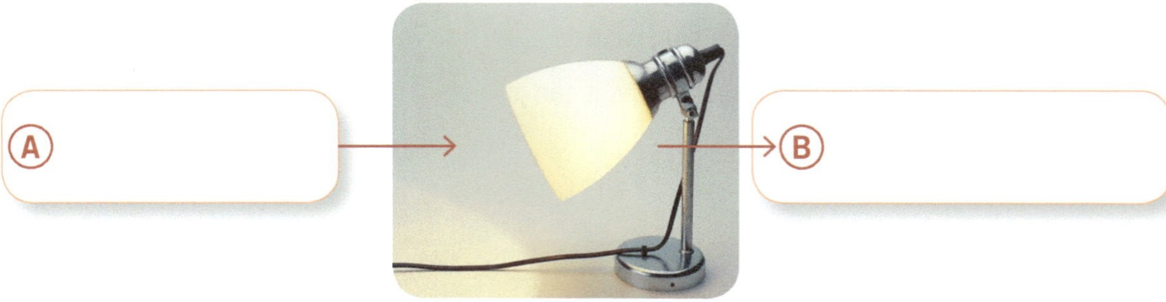

Section 2

2. Complete the sentences using the words below.

electric current | generator | receptor

electric cables | switch

The movement of negative electric charges inside a material is called ________________________________.

A ______________________ is the source of energy in an electric circuit.

Wires that conduct the electric current are called ______________________________________.

A ______________ opens and closes, preventing or allowing electric current to pass.

A __________ receives and transforms electric energy into another form of energy.

Section 3

3. Write the characteristics of conductors and insulators. Then give three examples of each.

Conductors	Insulators
Examples	**Examples**

4. Look at the following images. Mark those that show a safe way to work with electricity.

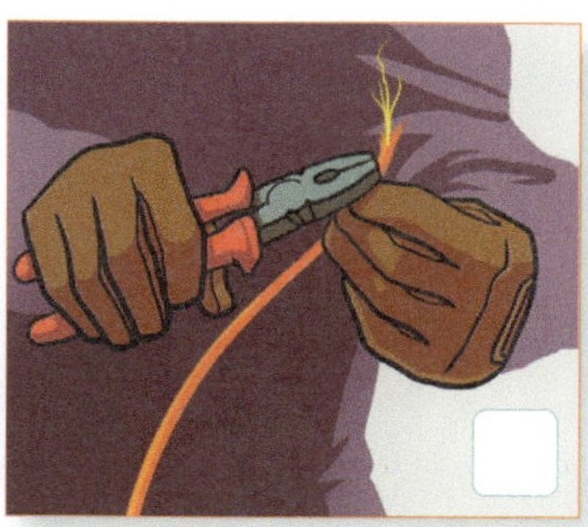

glue here

glue here

glue here

glue here

Test 3 Study Page • Summary

Energy is everywhere. It can be defined as the capacity to produce changes in the properties of objects.

Electric energy can be generated from renewable resources in hydroelectric dams, wind farms, and geothermic or solar energy plants.

Electric energy is **transformed** into other types of energy by electric devices.

Thales of Miletus, William Gilbert and Benjamin Franklin, among others, all made important contributions to the study of electric energy.

An **electric current** is the movement of negative electric charges. There are two types of currents: direct and alternating.

An **electric circuit** is a system through which a current circulates. It allows electric energy to be transformed into other types of energy. The basic parts of a circuit are:

Electric cables/wires: conduct the electric current.

Generator: source of electric energy.

Switch: a device that has two positions (opened and closed), allowing current to pass through the circuit.

Receptor: receives and transforms the electric energy into a new type of energy.

There are two basic types of circuits: series and parallel.

3. Match each type of water movement with its description.

waves	Changes in sea level near the coast.
currents	Swells of water usually caused by wind.
tides	Movements of water in the ocean in a specific direction.

4. Mark the activities that pollute with an ✗ and the activities that help with a ✓.

5. What actions would you propose to care for the planet's water reserves?

____

____

____

glue here

glue here

glue here

glue here

Test 4 Study Page • Summary

Water covers three-fourths of the surface of the planet. The majority of this water is salt water, and a smaller part is fresh water. Salt water, unlike fresh water, has a large quantity of dissolved minerals and salt that gives it its taste.

Water is found in many forms: glaciers, polar ice caps, oceans, rivers, lakes, groundwater and as clouds or vapor in the atmosphere.

In the hydrologic cycle, or water cycle, water circulates continuously between these different forms.

Oceans and **lakes** are important saltwater and freshwater reserves. In both cases, the difference in luminosity temperature and pressure in the water affect the diversity of life forms.

Section 3

3. Patrick uses the following model to represent the circulatory system.

What does each of the materials represent? Explain.

a. The bottle represents ______________________________

____

b. The straw represents ______________________________

____

c. The liquid represents ______________________________

____

Section 4

4. Number the body parts in the order air passes through them during inhalation. Then circle the part of the body where gas exchange occurs.

☐ alveoli ☐ pharynx ☐ nasal passage

☐ bronchus ☐ trachea

glue here

glue here

glue here

glue here

Test 1 Study Page • Summary

The levels of biological organization are:

Level 1: Cells

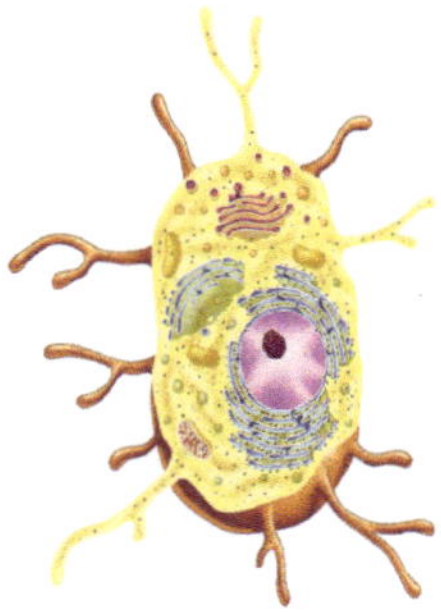

A basic unit of living things.

Level 2: Tissue

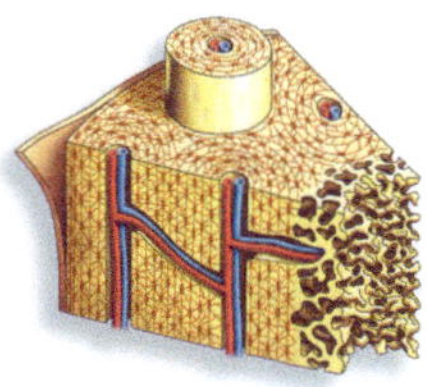

A group of cells that work together.

Level 3: Organs

A group of tissues that work together.

Digestive System: converts food into nutrients and eliminates waste. This process occurs in four stages:

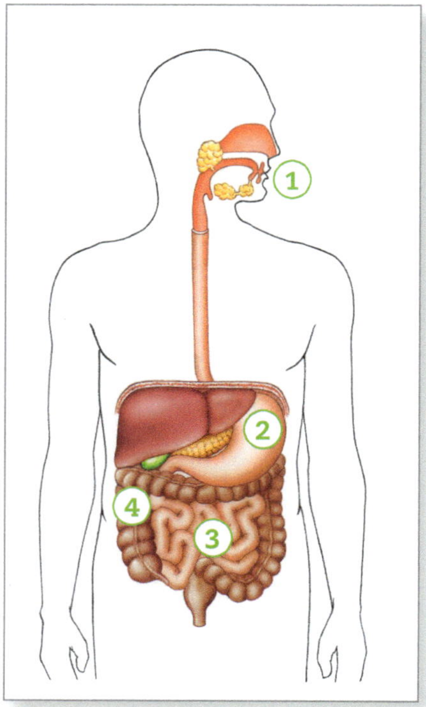

Ingestion occurs when food enters the **mouth (1)**. **Digestion** starts with the help of teeth and saliva. When the food reaches the **stomach (2)**, it mixes with gastric juices. Then, in the **small intestine (3)**, the nutrients are absorbed. Finally, waste is eliminated through the **large intestine (4)** in a process called **egestion**.

Circulatory System: transports su
the body. The components of the circ

Blood

Blood circulates inside the blood vessels. It transports nutrients and oxygen.

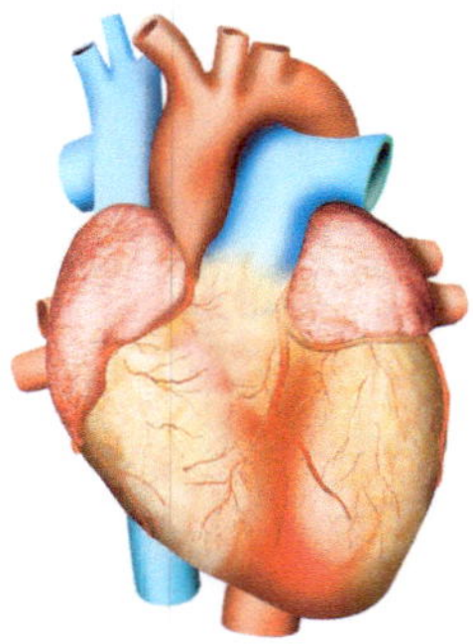

The Heart
The heart
all parts c

Blood Ves
Blood ves
tubes tha
blood to a
the body.